SCARECROW AREA BIBLIOGRAPHIES
Edited by Jon Woronoff

Area Bibliography of Japan

Ria Koopmans-de Bruijn

Scarecrow Area Bibliographies, No. 14

The Scarecrow Press, Inc.
Lanham, Md., & London
1998

SCARECROW PRESS, INC.

Published in the United States of America
by Scarecrow Press, Inc.
4720 Boston Way
Lanham, Maryland 20706

British Library Cataloguing in Publication Information Available

Library of Congress Cataloging-in-Publication Data

Koopmans-de Bruijn, Ria
Area bibliography of Japan / Ria Koopmans-de Bruijn
p.   cm. — (Scarecrow area bibliographies; no. 14)
Includes index.
ISBN: 0-8108-8108-3374-3 (cloth: alk. paper)
1. Japan—Bibliography. I. Title. II. Series: Scarecrow area bibliographies;
no. 14
Z3306.K86   1998
[DS806]
016.952—dc21   97-37522
                                                                      CIP

ISBN 0-8108-3374-3 (cloth : alk. paper)

⊖™ The paper used in this publication meets the minimum requirements of
American National Standard for Information Sciences—Permanence of
Paper for Printed Library Materials, ANSI Z39.48–1984.
Manufactured in the United States of America.

To the memory of my sister Agnes de Bruijn

CONTENTS

EDITOR'S FOREWORD

Anyone browsing through a bookstore in New York, London, Paris, or Berlin would immediately be impressed by the number of books on Japan in the section on foreign countries. On few other places would there be as many, not only in English but also in French, German, and other languages. This first impression would be sustained when moving to the section on religion and noting the number of books on Zen, or on Japanese martial arts, literature, or flower arrangement in their respective sections, to say nothing of those on Japanese management among the business books. And yet these are only a smattering of the more popular and more recent works. The quantity of books that can be found in a good specialized library is simply overwhelming. So overwhelming, indeed, that any bibliography that can provide a survey of the field should be most welcome.

That is the purpose of this *Area Bibliography of Japan*. By listing titles under carefully selected headings and subheadings, these arranged in alphabetical order, it is much easier to locate works on specific subjects or, alternatively, by specific authors through the Author Index. This facilitates the task of both readers and librarians. Both can find books on a vast range of topics, from abortion to zen, with larger sections on areas of particular interest, including art, economics, history, literature, politics, and religion. Naturally, given the enormous outpouring of books on Japan, not all could be included, but the choice remains ample. Two thousand six hundred and seventy-six works are mainly in English but in other European languages as well, among them numerous books by Japanese authors.

This bibliography was compiled by Ria Koopmans-de Bruijn, who was fortunately able to approach the task from two directions. She has a degree in Japanese studies and is personally familiar with many aspects of the field. She also has a degree in Library Science and has worked as the East Asian Studies Librarian at the C. V. Starr East Asian Library of Columbia University since 1993. So she knows what readers are looking for and has considerable experience in helping them find it. Usually, this was done in specific cases. This bibliography is a worthwhile extension to the more general case of the many readers who want to know more about an intriguing and sometimes confusing country.

Jon Woronoff
Series Editor

PREFACE

Until just a few short decades ago, a Japan scholar could, with some effort, keep up with all scholarship going on in the field, even knowing in broad outline what went on in the other East Asian areas. These scholars were true generalists, with perhaps a *preference* for a specific aspect of the field, but command of its full range. These days, the amount of scholarship conducted, and (consequently) professional literature produced, forces scholars to become specialists in ever more detailed subjects, while trying to keep up with the broad outline of the field. For the general public with an interest in the subject of Japan, but no professional background in the field, this dilemma is even more daunting.

The amount of literature related to Japan published today is as overwhelming as the degree to which the field has become specialized. And although a reasonable amount of bibliographies have been published, most of these are either geared toward a certain specialization (history, literature, etc.), or are highly selective.

Contrary to these approaches, this bibliography provides a general overview of literature relating to Japan, in as broad a range of subjects as possible. The main focus is on recent literature. The aim is to aid a variety of readers in accessing literature on Japan. As with any bibliography, no pretense is made of exhaustive coverage of every letter written on the subject. That would be neither feasible nor desirable. What is included and excluded is determined by a number of considerations, which will be explained in the introduction.

Compiling this bibliography has been a long, and on occasion frustrating, undertaking. I found myself spending long evening and weekend hours well beyond my everyday professional responsibilities, and in the process had to deal with my share of hardware and software problems, too. It is due to the continued moral support and encouragement of family, friends, and colleagues that I managed to persevere and get the job done. I have drawn much inspiration from the faculty, students, and other library users who through their reference queries provided me with much added insight into the information needs and search habits of the prospective users of a bibliography such as this one. I hope the publication will prove useful to them. Much appreciation is due to Amy Vladeck Heinrich, who not only actively encouraged me in my work on this publication, but as my supervisor, helped me obtain a brief leave of absence at a time when the project was at a low ebb and badly in need of some undivided attention. The Italian, Spanish, and Portuguese titles included here were kindly translated by my colleague Gladys Markoff-Sotomayor. Most particular appreciation and gratitude is due to my husband Matthijs Koopmans, who, on an almost daily basis, acted as my sounding board; uncomplainingly took over responsibility for our household when I was too tired or simply too preoccupied to think of it; and who in the course of this project found out more about compiling bibliographies than he had ever thought (or hoped) to learn.

INTRODUCTION

In the process of a research project the researcher, be that an advanced academic specialist or a member of the general public with a curiosity about a certain topic, will need to gather information about that subject before being able to form an educated opinion about it. Such information is, even in this so-called electronic age, largely to be found in the printed literature by earlier researchers on the subject. Although there are more ways than one to find such literature, unless one knows exactly which book or other information source one wants, the best starting point is to consult a reference source, such as the present bibliography, to find an initial selection of readings that will help one to focus on the subject at hand. It forms a more structured, and consequently often better, or simply faster introduction than, for instance, a browse through a library catalog, since it has already narrowed down the options.

Bibliographies come in different forms, addressing different needs. They can range from very general to highly specialized. This bibliography falls in the middle of such a range. It is specialized in that it deals only with Japan, yet is general since it covers a broad range of subjects within that context. Sometimes a bibliography includes annotations, which can be very useful, but tend to limit the number of entries, and therefore the number of options to choose from. Annotations are most useful in the more specialized bibliographies.

Since the average reader is most interested in recent literature, currency is an issue. By their very nature, bibliographies cannot ever be entirely up-to-date because of the time that elapses between the preparation of the manuscript and the actual publication. Therefore new compilations are constantly needed. This bibliography aims to fill that need by bringing together information about publications on the broadest possible range of subjects related to Japan, published since 1980. It also aims to serve the broadest possible range of readers. For advanced scholars and graduate students it can serve as a quick reference to secondary literature, as well as a guide to subjects outside his/her immediate specialization. For undergraduate students, and the general public it can serve as a starting point that can help focus a newly developing interest. The emphasis here must be on starting point, as, like every other bibliography, this one, too, has its limitations. What is and is not included in the present bibliography is explained below.

Content

Included in this bibliography are books on Japan and on Japanese culture published from 1980 to the present. In addition a number of so-called classics are included as well. Some of these classics have never gone out of print and are still actively in use as college textbooks, others are no longer available in bookstores but are accessible in libraries. It is encouraging to find that several publishers have, in recent years, become active in reprinting such classics, making them readily available again for those who prefer to own, rather than borrow, their literature.

In terms of the subject matter included, a broad approach is taken, although certain limitations apply. Certain subjects are less generously represented than others. For instance, Japan is very active in the fields of science and technology, but most of the publications in those fields apply to the subject matter itself, and relatively little literature deals with science and technology as it applies specifically to Japan. As a result, relatively few entries occur under these subject headings. The same is true for subjects that are no longer very popular among the writers on Japan or, conversely, subjects that are too new to have generated much literature at this stage. Whereas such subjects as history, religion, philosophy, and art have generally received due attention, subjects such as women studies and ethnic issues are relative newcomers, while even within the established subjects there is a distinct shift noticeable to different aspects of the subject than were studied before.

Apart from such concerns as imprint date and subject matter, an important additional consideration for inclusion is accessibility of the material. Since the time frame covered in this bibliography is current, a reasonable amount of the included titles will still be available through the better bookstores. However, publications from some of the more obscure sources, as well as materials from foreign publishers are not always as easy to come by, while at the same time the trend among publishers in general seems to be to take titles out of print ever sooner. Therefore, a better measure of accessibility is whether a title is available in a library. It is for this reason that I have relied heavily on online library databases for the collection of the entries in this bibliography.

Only materials related to the geographical area of Japan, and to Japanese culture within that area, are included. Books about cross-cultural subjects, e.g., East Asia (or even larger areas), are excluded. Works comparing Japan with other cultures are likewise excluded, as are works dealing with the experience of Japanese abroad, or with people of Japanese descent in other countries, such as Japanese Americans. Cultural elements of Japanese origin as practiced by non-Japanese, outside Japan, such as martial arts, flower arrangement, and the like are also excluded. Japanese literature in translation is excluded, with the exception of those annotated translations that form part of works in literary criticism. Short of the small number of classics mentioned, retrospective literature and pre-1980 literature is excluded. Information sources on the former are mentioned below, and other sources, such as Frank Joseph Shulman's *Japan* (entry 492) provide information on the latter.

As far as reasonable, only English-language materials are listed. Other Western European languages are included only if very little English material exists on the given subject, or if the foreign title is of particular importance. For example, a considerable amount of important work is being done in Austria, on issues concerning the elderly in Japan; most of this work is published in German. Therefore the section on the elderly in this bibliography includes multiple German language titles.

The focus is further on book-length publications. Journal articles and individual essays are not included, nor are dissertations. In principle, only "substantial" works, here defined as works of at least a hundred pages, are cited. Exceptions are made for some shorter works, when their content is considered important. This applies most notably to volumes in the *About Japan* series, which are very slim volumes, produced by the Japanese government, and which provide excellent, concise introductions to important aspects of Japanese culture.

Method

As a starting point for the data collection, I searched the holdings of the Columbia University libraries, as these collections are most readily physically accessible to me. As a next step I performed a series of searches in the RLIN (Research Libraries Information Network) database of the Research Libraries Group (RLG). This database contains information on the holdings of a large number of research libraries both in North America and abroad (at the time of writing, 155 members are listed on RLG's home-page). It is thus an invaluable source for this type of data collection. A useful aid in the initial catalog searches was the publication *LC Subject Headings Related to Japan: Topical Headings* (entry 1725). Many of the bibliographies listed throughout this bibliography were cross-checked, to ensure that no crucial titles were overlooked. As a librarian I found it reassuring to see, however, that the on-line catalogs essentially provide complete coverage of the publications included in the assorted bibliographies consulted.

Arrangement and Structure

The bibliography is organized as a running alphabet of subject headings, under which relevant titles are cited. Each entry was assigned a unique entry number. Whereas generic subject headings suffice in some areas, others are so extensively covered in recent literature that a single subject heading would yield an unmanageably long list of titles. In these cases the headings have been divided into subheadings, and when necessary even sub-subheadings. General titles appear under the generic heading, all other, more specialized titles appear under the subsequent subheadings and sub-subheadings. As a rule, no heading runs on for more than two pages. Through this system of subheadings and sub-subheadings, related subjects are, as much as feasible, placed closely together. To achieve this, some subject headings occur as inverted phrases, e.g., "History—Legal." The most obvious diversion from the practice of grouping related subjects occurs for the subject "Diplomatic Relations." All general titles on this subject are listed under this subject heading and its subheadings, but titles dealing with relations between Japan and specific other countries or regions are arranged under the name of that particular country or region, e.g., "United States—Relations with"; "South and Southeast Asia—Relations with." Bibliographies, when of a general character, are listed under the generic subject heading "Bibliographies." However, if a bibliography refers to a specific subject, it is listed under the corresponding subject heading, with the subheading "Bibliographies." As this bibliography is about Japan alone, the word "Japanese" is, apart from one exception, not used in subject headings.

In determining the subject arrangement of the bibliography, as well as the choice of words in the subject headings, I was initially inclined to use Library of Congress subject headings (LCSH). However, I know from experience at the reference desk that those terms often do not make much sense to non-librarians, and that consequently it is not the best system for a bibliography that is meant to serve beginners as well as the more advanced researcher. I have, therefore, instead allowed my reference experience and intuition to be my guide, and used the way library users refer to the subjects of their interest as an important source.

See and *See also* references are used as little as possible. They are mainly used in one of three situations. When ambiguity might exist about a subject term, synonyms are included accompanied by a *See* reference to the term actually used. Secondly, when distinct, but overlapping subjects occur, *See also* references point from one to the other in order to alert the reader to more potentially useful titles. Thirdly, when an entry covers more than one subject, it is cited under the primary subject, while a *See also* reference under the secondary subject points the reader to the exact entry number where an additional title of interest is cited.

Throughout the bibliography *The Chicago Manual of Style* (13th ed. Chicago, I.L.: University of Chicago Press, 1982) rules are followed. All foreign-language titles are accompanied by translations in square brackets. Names of authors, editors, and compilers are quoted as they occur on the item in question, with no adjustment to spelling and/or diacritics. In the author index, on the other hand, the most complete form of a name is listed. Since certain author names occur in several different variations, author names are quoted for each individual entry, even if several entries by the same author are cited consecutively. Where personal names are mentioned in the subject headings, birth and, if applicable, death dates are quoted where available. In subject headings, personal names are always given in the most authoritative form.

Useful Other Sources

What follows is a brief overview of some of the most important bibliographic sources available at this time. Three types of literature in particular are highlighted here. They are the main types of literature not considered for inclusion in this bibliography: retrospective literature, periodical literature, and dissertations. Information on modern literature is well covered in the bibliographies cited in the body of the present bibliography. These will not be repeated here. The reader is instead encouraged to consult the subject headings of their interest, as well as the general subject heading "Bibliographies" to find full citation of these sources. I do, however, want to call the reader's particular attention to entry 489 (*Japan and the Japanese: A Bibliographic Guide to Reference Sources*). This is the most up-to-date overview of reference sources on a very broad range of subjects related to Japanese Studies. It covers (virtually) only English-language titles, and is aimed particularly at an academic public. It includes annotated citations of no less than 532 titles. Entry 484 (*Japan Access: A Bibliography of Bibliographies*) is a comparable source, citing 588 entries, but is geared more toward a general public.

Retrospective bibliographic sources are a largely European affair. They include: *Bibliography of the Japanese Empire: Being a Classified List of All Books, Essays and Maps in European Languages Relating to Dai Nihon [Great Japan] Published in Europe, America and in the East from 1859-93 A.D.* by Friedrich Von Wenckstern (v. 1, Leiden, Netherlands: Brill, 1895; v.2, Tokyo: Maruzen, 1907); followed by *Bibliography of the Japanese Empire 1906-1926: Being a classified List of the Literature Issued in European Languages Since the Publication of Fr. Von Wenckstern's "Bibliography of the Japanese Empire" up to the Year 1926.* by Oskar Nachod (2 vols. London: Edward Goldston, 1928). This second title also appeared under the German title *Bibliographie von Japan, 1906-1926.* Four works followed under essentially that same title, for the periods 1927-1929, 1930-1932, 1933-1935, and 1936-1937. The first of these was likewise compiled by Oskar Nachod; the next by Hans Praesent; and the latter two jointly by Wolf Haenisch and Hans Praesent.

For periodical literature, the best source by far, despite its currency problem (at the time of this writing the most recent volume available is for 1990), is the *Bibliography of Asian Studies*, published since 1970 as an annual publication, by the Association for Asian Studies. This is a print index providing citations to articles from a vast amount of journals, including a large number of quite esoteric titles, as well as a limited amount of information on monographs and individual essays in compiled works. The annual was preceded by the 5-volume *Bulletin of Far Eastern Bibliography, 1936-1940*, compiled by Earl H. Pritchard (Washington, D.C.: American Council of Learned Societies, 1936-1940), followed by the *Cumulative Bibliography of Asian Studies 1941-1965*, which was divided in a *Subject Bibliography* and an *Author Bibliography*, both four volumes long. A six-volume update was published, covering the years 1966-1970, by the Association for Asian Studies (Boston, M.A.: G. K. Hall, 1972-73). A cumulative CD-ROM version of the index, to be updated on a regular basis, is currently under construction. 1991 is expected to be the last year to be covered in a print edition. More up-to-date information on journal literature is available only to a limited degree through some of the more general periodical indexes, which are now generally available in easy-to-search electronic format. However, these databases tend to cover only the most commonly read journals in the field, and no satisfactory indexing is available on the more obscure publications.

Other important sources of information, particularly for the academic researcher, are dissertations. These have been very ably and exhaustively indexed, for many years now, by Frank Joseph Shulman, first under the title *Japan and Korea: An Annotated Bibliography of Doctoral Dissertations in Western Languages, 1877-1969*. (Chicago, I.L.: American Library Association, 1970). This was followed by *Doctoral Dissertations on Japan and Korea 1969-1979: An Annotated Bibliography of Studies in Western Languages*. (Seattle, W.A.: University of Washington Press, 1982). After that Japan-related dissertations were integrated into the serial publication *Doctoral Dissertations on Asia: An Annotated Bibliographical Journal of Current International Research*. Ann Arbor, M.I.: Association for Asian Studies, 1975-).

Ria Koopmans-de Bruijn
New York, January 1997

JAPAN BIBLIOGRAPHY

Abortion

1. LaFleur, William R. *Liquid Life: Abortion and Buddhism in Japan.* Princeton, NJ: Princeton University Press, 1992.

2. Miura, Domyo. *The Forgotten Child.* Translated by Jim Cuthbert. Nuffield, U.K.: Aidan Ellis, 1983.

Academic Freedom

3. Horio, Teruhisa. *Educational Thought and Ideology in Modern Japan: State Authority and Intellectual Freedom.* Edited and translated by Steven Platzer. Tokyo: University of Tokyo Press, 1988.

4. Marshall, Byron K. *Academic Freedom and the Japanese Imperial University, 1868-1939.* Berkeley, CA: University of California Press, 1992.

Accounting

5. Arai, Kiyomitsu. *Accounting in Japan.* IRBA Series, no. 25. Tokyo: Institute for Research in Business Administration, Waseda University, 1994.

6. Business Accounting Deliberation Council, Ministry of Finance, Japan. *Financial Accounting Standard on Consolidated Financial Statements.* Tokyo: Japan Institute of Certified Public Accountants, 1987.

7. Choi, Frederick D. S., and Kazuo Hiramatsu, eds. *Accounting and Financial Reporting in Japan: Current Issues and Future Prospects in a World Economy.* Wokingham, U.K.: Van Nostrand Reinhold, 1987.

8. Cooke, T.E., and M. Kikuya. *Financial Reporting in Japan: Regulation, Practice, and Environment.* Oxford, U.K.: Cambridge, MA: Blackwell, 1992.

9. *Corporate Disclosure in Japan: Accounting*. Tokyo: Japanese Institute of Certified Public Accountants, 1987.

10. *CPA Profession in Japan*. 5th ed. Tokyo: Japanese Institute of Certified Public Accountants, 1987.

11. Fujita, Yukio. *An Analysis of the Development and Nature of Accounting Principles in Japan*. New Works in Accounting History. New York: Garland, 1991.

12. McKinnon, Jill. *The Historical Development and Operational Form of Corporate Reporting Regulation in Japan*. Accounting Thought and Practice Through the Years. New York: Garland, 1986.

13. Monden, Yasuhiro, and Michiharu Sakurai, eds. *Japanese Management Accounting: A World Class Approach to Profit Management*. Cambridge, MA: Productivity Press, 1989.

14. Nobes, Christopher. *Accounting and Financial Reporting in Japan*. 2d ed. London: Lafferty, 1991.

15. Someya, Kyōjirō. *Japanese Accounting: A Historical Approach*. Oxford, U.K.; New York: Oxford University Press, 1996.

Adult Education *See*: Education—Adults

Aesthetics

16. Hume, Nancy G., ed. *Japanese Aesthetics and Culture: A Reader*. SUNY Series in Asian Studies Development. Albany, NY: State University of New York Press, 1995.

17. Itoh, Teiji, Ikko Tanaka, and Tsune Sesoko, eds. *Wabi, Sabi, Suki: The Essence of Japanese Beauty*. Hiroshima, Japan: Mazda Motor Co., 1993.

18. Izutsu, Toshihiko, and Toyo Izutsu. *The Theory of Beauty in the Classical Aesthetics of Japan*. The Hague, Netherlands; Boston, MA: Martinus Nijhoff, 1981.

19. Koren, Leonard. *Wabi-Sabi for Artists, Designers, Poets & Philosophers*. Berkeley, CA: Stone Bridge Press, 1994.

20. Takamura, Hideya, ed. *Japanese Aesthetics in the Commercial Environment*. Process Architecture, no. 53. Tokyo: Process Architecture, 1984.

21. Ueda, Makoto. *Literary and Art Theories in Japan*. Cleveland, OH: Press of Western Reserve University, 1967. Reprint: Michigan Classics in Japanese Studies, no. 6. Ann Arbor, MI: Center for Japanese Studies, University of Michigan, 1991.

22. Yoshida, Mitsukuni, Ikko Tanaka, and Tsune Sesoko, eds. *The Compact Culture: The Ethos of Japanese Life*. Hiroshima, Japan: Toyo Kogyo, 1982.

23. Yoshida, Mitsukuni, Ikko Tanaka, and Tsune Sesoko, eds. *Tsu Ku Ru: Aesthetics at Work*. Hiroshima, Japan: Mazda Motor Co., 1990.

Africa—Relations with

24. Owoeye, Jide. *Japan's Policy in Africa*. Lewiston, NY: E. Mellen Press, 1993.

25. Sono, Themba. *Japan and Africa: The Evolution and Nature of Political, Economic and Human Bonds, 1543-1993*. Pretoria: HSRC, 1993.

26. Takahashi, Motoki. *The Quest for Effectiveness: A Changing Southern Africa and Japanese Economic Cooperation*. IDCJ Working Paper Series, no. 50. Tokyo: International Development Center of Japan, 1995.

Agriculture

27. *Agricultural Policy Reform and Adjustment in Japan*. Paris: Organization for Economic Co-operation and Development, 1995.

28. Hayami, Yūjirō, and Saburo Yamada. *The Agricultural Development of Japan: A Century's Perspective*. Tokyo: University of Tokyo Press, 1991.

29. Hayami, Yūjirō. *Japanese Agriculture Under Siege: The Political Economy of Agricultural Policies*. Studies in the Modern Japanese Economy. London: Macmillan, 1988.

30. Hillman, Jimmye S., and Robert A. Rothenberg. *Agricultural Trade and Protection in Japan*. Thames Essay, 0306-6991, no. 52. Aldershot, U.K.; Brookfield, VT: Gower, 1988.

31. *Japanese Agricultural Policies: A Time of Change*. Policy Monograph, no. 3. Canberra: Australian Government Publishing Service, 1988.

32. Kanai, Michio, ed. *Some Aspects of Japanese Agriculture: Collected Research Papers, 1987-91*. Tokyo: National Research Institute of Agricultural Economics, Ministry of Agriculture, Forestry, and Fisheries, 1991.

33. Masuda, Toshiaki. *Agricultural Development in Post-war Japan*. Tokyo: Japan FAO Association, 1990.

34. Meer, C.L.J. van der, and Saburo Yamada. *Japanese Agriculture: A Comparative Economic Analysis*. London; New York: Routledge, 1990.

35. *National Policies and Agricultural Trade: Country Study, Japan*. Paris: Organisation for Economic Co-operation and Development, 1987.

36. Ogura, Takekazu B. *Can Japanese Agriculture Survive? A Historical and Comparative Approach*. 3d ed. Tokyo: Agricultural Policy Research Center, 1982.

37. Ogura, Takekazu B., ed. *Japanese Agricultural Policy Reconsidered*. Report of Study Group on International Issues (SGII), no. 14. Tokyo: Food and Agriculture Policy Research Center (FAPRC), 1993.

38. Ogura, Takekazu B. *Toward Structural Reform of Japanese Agriculture*. 2d ed. Tokyo: Food and Agriculture Policy Research Center, 1983.

39. Ogura, Takekazu B. *A Treatise on Cooperation in Japanese Agriculture*. Report of Study Group on International Issues (SGII), no. 4. Tokyo: Food and Agriculture Policy Research Center, 1990.

40. *Recent Agricultural Technology in Japan*. Tokyo: Japan FAO Association, 1983.

41. Takahashi, Man'emon. *The History and Future of Rice Cultivation in Hokkaido*. HSDP-JE Series, 0379-5780. Tokyo: United Nations University, 1980.

42. Yoshioka, Yutaka. *Food and Agriculture in Japan*. 3d ed. "About Japan" Series, 18. Tokyo: Foreign Press Center, Japan, 1996.

Agriculture—History

43. Francks, Penelope. *Technology and Agricultural Development in Pre-war Japan*. New Haven, CT: Yale University Press, 1984.

44. Latz, Gil. *Agricultural Development in Japan: The Land Improvement District in Concept and Practice*. Geography Research Paper, no. 225. Chicago, IL: University of Chicago, 1989.

45. Madane, Madhav Vishvanath. *Agricultural Cooperatives in Japan: The Dynamics of their Development*. 2d ed. New Delhi: International Co-operative Alliance, Regional Office for Asia and the Pacific, 1992.

46. Nishimura, Hiroyuki. *Rural Urban Balance Study, Japan*. CIRDAP Study Series, no. 7. Comilla, Bangladesh: Center on Integrated Rural Development of Asia and the Pacific, 1982.

47. Smethurst, Richard J. *Agricultural Development and Tenancy Disputes in Japan, 1870-1940*. Princeton, NJ: Princeton University Press, 1986.

Ainu *See*: Minorities—Ainu

Anthropology *See*: Ethnology

Archaeology

48. Barnes, Gina L., and Masaaki Okita. *The Miwa Project: Survey, Coring and Excavation at the Miwa Site, Nara, Japan*. BAR International Series, 582. Oxford, U.K.: Tempus Reparatum, 1993.

49. Barnes, Gina Lee. *Protohistoric Yamato: Archaeology of the First Japanese State*. Anthropological Papers / Museum of Anthropology, University of Michigan, no. 78. Michigan Papers in Japanese Studies, no. 17. Ann Arbor, MI: Published jointly by the University of Michigan, Center for Japanese Studies and the Museum of Anthropology, University of Michigan, 1988.

50. Suzuki, Hisashi, and Kazuro Hanihara, eds. *The Minatogawa Man: The Upper Pleistocene Man from the Island of Okinawa.* Bulletin (Tokyo Daigaku, Sogo Kenkyu Shiryokan), no. 19. Tokyo: University of Tokyo Press, 1982.

51. Tsuboi, Kiyotari, ed. *Recent Archaeological Discoveries in Japan.* Translated by Gina L. Barnes. Paris: UNESCO; Tokyo: Centre for East Asian Cultural Studies, 1987.

Architects

52. *Invisible Language: Tokyo 1990s: A Dialogue with Five Japanese Architects.* London: Architectural Association, c1993.

53. Kestenbaum, Jackie, ed. *Emerging Japanese Architects of the 1990s.* Columbia Studies on Art, no. 3. New York: Columbia University Press, 1991.

54. Meyhöfer, Dirk, ed. *Contemporary Japanese Architects.* Cologne, Germany: Benedikt Taschen, 1993.

Architects—Aida, Takefumi, 1937-

55. Aida, Takefumi. *Takefumi Aida: Buildings and Projects.* New York: Princeton Architectural Press, 1990.

Architects—Andō, Tadao, 1941-

56. Andō, Tadao. *Sketches.* Basel, Switzerland; Boston, MA: Birkhauser, 1990.

57. Andō, Tadao. *Tadao Ando: Complete Works.* London: Phaidon, 1995.

58. Andō, Tadao. *Tadao Ando: Details.* Edited by Yukio Futagawa. Tokyo: A. D. A. Edita, 1991.

59. Andō, Tadao. *Tadao Andō: The Yale Studio & Current Works.* New York: Rizzoli, 1989.

60. Frampton, Kenneth, ed. *Tadao Ando: Buildings, Projects, Writings.* New York: Rizzoli, 1984.

61. Furuyama, Masao. *Tadao Andō.* 2d ed. Basel, Switzerland; Boston, MA: Birkhauser, 1995.

Architects—Ashihara, Yoshinobu, 1918-

62. *An Architect Looks Back.* Translated by Lynne E. Riggs. Tokyo: Shinkenchiku-sha, 1985.

Architects—Hara, Hiroshi, 1911-

63. Hara, Hiroshi. *Hiroshi Hara.* Edited by Yukio Futagawa. GA Architect, 13. Tokyo: A. D. A. Edita, 1993.

Architects—Hasegawa, Itsuko,

64. Hasegawa, Itsuko. *Itsuko Hasegawa: Architecture as Another Nature.* Miniseries, 5. New York: Columbia University Graduate School of Architecture, Planning and Preservation, 1991.

65. *Itsuko Hasegawa.* Architectural Monographs, no. 31. London: Academy Editions; Berlin, Germany: Ernst & Sohn, 1993.

Architects—Isozaki, Arata, 1931-

66. Drew, Philip. *The Architecture of Arata Isozaki.* London; New York: Granada, 1982.

67. Isozaki, Arata. *Arata Isozaki.* Edited by Yukio Futagawa. GA Architect, 6. Tokyo: A. D. A. Edita, 1991.

Architects—Itō, Toyō, 1941-

68. Roulet, Sophie, and Sophie Soulié. *Toyo Ito, Architecture of the Ephemeral.* Paris: Moniteur, 1991.

69. *Toyo Ito.* Architectural Monographs, no. 41. London: Academy, 1995.

Architects—Kuramata, Shiro, 1934-

70. *The Works of Shiro Kuramata, 1967-1981.* Tokyo: PARCO, 1981.

Architects—Kurokawa, Kishō, 1934-

71. Kurokawa, Kishō. *Kisho Kurokawa.* Monographie d'Architecture. Paris: Moniteur, 1995.

72. Kurokawa, Kishō. *Kisho Kurokawa: From Metabolism to Symbiosis.* London: Academy Editions; New York: St. Martin's Press, 1992.

73. Kurokawa, Kishō. *Kisho Kurokawa: The Architecture of Symbiosis.* New York: Rizzoli, 1988.

Architects—Maki, Fumihiko, 1928-

74. Salat, Serge, and Françoise Labbé. *Fumihiko Maki: An Aesthetic of Fragmentation.* New York: Rizzoli, 1988.

Architects—Mozuna, Kiko, 1941-

75. Kiko, Mozuna. *The Architecture of Memory: The Works of Monta Mozuna Kikoo.* Tokyo: Parco, 1985.

Architects—Murano, Tōgo, 1891-

76. Bognar, Botond. *Togo Murano: Master Architect of Japan.* New York: Rizzoli, 1996.

Architects—Shinohara, Kazuo, 1925-

77. Shinohara, Kazuo. *Kazuo Shinohara.* Berlin, Germany: Ernst & Sohn, 1994.

Architects—Suzuki, Edward, 1947-

78. *Edward Suzuki: Buildings and Projects.* Stuttgart, Germany: Axel Menges, 1996.

Architects—Takamatsu, Shin, 1948-

79. Takamatsu, Shin. *Shin Takamatsu.* San Francisco, CA: San Francisco Museum of Modern Art, 1993.

80. Takamatsu, Shin. *Shin Takamatsu.* Edited by Yukio Futagawa. GA Architect, 9. Tokyo: A. D. A. Edita, 1990.

81. Takamatsu, Shin, et al. *Shin Takamatsu.* Rome: Carte Segrete, 1989.

Architects—Takeyama, Minoru, 1934

82. Takeyama, Minoru. *Minoru Takeyama.* Edited by Botond Bognar. Architectural Monographs, 42. London: Academy Editions, 1995.

Architecture

83. Coaldrake, William Howard. *Architecture and Authority in Japan.* The Nissan Institute / Routledge Japanese Studies Series. London; New York: Routledge, 1996.

84. Egenter, Nold. *Semantic and Symbolic Architecture: An Architectural-Ethnological Survey into Hundred Villages of Central Japan.* Architectural Anthropology. Lausanne, Switzerland: Structura Mundi, 1994.

85. Finn, Dallas. *Meiji Revisited: The Sites of Victorian Japan.* New York: Weatherhill, 1995.

86. Harada, Jirō. *The Lesson of Japanese Architecture: 165 Photographs.* Edited by C. G. Holme. New York: Dover, 1985.

87. Hibi, Sadao. *Japanese Detail Architecture: Traditional Architecture, Gardens, Interiors.* London: Thames and Hudson, 1989.

88. The Japan Architect, ed. *A Guide to Japanese Architecture: A Photographic Guide to the Notable Modern Buildings and the Famous Architectural Classics in Japan.* Tokyo: Shinkenchiku-sha, 1984.

89. Kurokawa, Kishō. *The Philosophy of Symbiosis.* London: Academy Editions, 1994.

90. Murai, Osamu. *The Works of Takenaka: Light and Forms: Photographs.* Tokyo: Kyuryudo, 1989.

91. Nishi, Kazuo, and Kazuo Hozumi. *What is Japanese Architecture?* Translated by H. Mack Horton. Tokyo; New York: Kodansha International, 1984.

92. Nitschke, Günther. *From Shinto to Ando: Studies in Architectural Anthropology in Japan.* London: Academy Editions; Berlin, Germany: Ernst & Sohn, 1993.

93. Rosemann, H. J., C. H. T. van Slagmaat, and H. D. Stolte, eds. *Architectuur, Stedebouw en Landschap in Japan* [Architecture, City Planning, and Landscape in Japan]. Bussum: Thoth, 1995.

94. Watanabe, Hiroshi. *Amazing Architecture from Japan.* New York: Weatherhill, 1991.

Architecture—Castles

95. Hinago, Motoo. *Japanese Castles*. Translated by William H. Coaldrake. Japanese Arts Library, 14. Tokyo; New York: Kodansha International and Shibundo, 1986.

Architecture—Domestic

96. Engel, Heino. *Measure and Construction of the Japanese House*. Rutland, VT: Tuttle, 1985.

97. Fawcett, Chris. *The New Japanese House: Ritual and Anti-Ritual Patterns of Dwelling*. New York: Harper & Row, 1980.

98. Hayakawa, Kunihiko. *Housing Developments: New Concepts in Architecture & Design*. Tokyo: Meisei, 1994.

Architecture—Drawing and Illustration

99. *Architectural Illustrations: Bird's-Eye View*. 3 vols. BSS Illustration series. Tokyo: Bijutsu Shuppansha, 1992.

100. *Architectural Rendering*. Tokyo: Graphic-sha, 1993.

101. *Architectural Rendering Illustrated: A Best Collection of Modern Exterior Renderings*. 2 vols. Tokyo: Meisei, 1992.

102. Azuchi, Minoru. *Architectural Marker Techniques*. Step by Step. Tokyo: Graphic-sha, 1991.

103. *Drawings by Japanese Contemporary Architects*. Tokyo: Graphic-sha, 1982.

104. *Exterior Rendering: Shop & Restaurant: A Practical Introduction to Architectural Illustrations*. Tokyo: Graphic-sha, 1989.

105. *Exteriors: Perspectives in Architectural Design*. Tokyo: Graphic-sha, 1987.

106. *Interior Rendering: Shop & Restaurant: A Practical Introduction to Architectural Illustrations*. Tokyo: Graphic-sha, 1990.

107. *Interiors: Perspectives in Architectural Design*. Includes an actual CG (Computer Graphics) perspective. Tokyo: Graphic-sha, 1987.

108. *Waterfronts*. Architectural Rendering, 3. Tokyo: Graphic-sha, 1991.

Architecture—Interior Design

109. Japan Interior Designers' Association, ed. *Feeling the Aesthetic: Interior Design in Japan*. Tokyo: Rikuyo-sha, 1984.

110. *Residential Style: Superb Selection of Contemporary Home Interiors*. Tokyo: Sigma Union, 1990.

111. Slesin, Suzanne, Stafford Cliff, and Daniel Rozensztroch. *Japanese Style*. New York: Potter, 1987.

112. Tsuzuki, Kyoichi. *Tokyo Style*. Translated by Alfred Birnbaum. Kyoto, Japan: Kyoto Shoin, 1993.

113. Ueda, Atsushi. *The Inner Harmony of the Japanese House*. Tokyo; New York: Kodansha International, 1990.

Architecture—Landscape

114. Bring, Mitchell, and Josse Wayembergh. *Japanese Gardens: Design and Meaning*. McGraw-Hill Series in Landscape and Landscape Architecture. New York: McGraw-Hill, 1981.

115. Davidson, A. K. *The Art of Zen Gardens: A Guide to their Creation and Enjoyment*. Los Angeles, CA: J. P. Tarcher, 1983.

116. *Element & Total Concept of Urban Landscape Design*. Tokyo: Graphic-sha, 1988.

117. Hibi, Sadao. *A Celebration of Japanese Gardens*. Translated by Scott Brause. Tokyo: Graphic-sha, 1994.

118. Itō, Teiji. *The Gardens of Japan*. Tokyo; New York: Kodansha International, 1984.

119. Kuck, Loraine E. *The World of the Japanese Garden: From Chinese Origins to Modern Landscape Art*. New York: Weatherhill, 1980.

120. Kuitert, Wybe. *Themes, Scenes and Taste in the History of Japanese Garden Art*. Japonica Neerlandica, v. 3. Amsterdam, Netherlands: J. C. Gieben, 1988.

121. Nitschke, Günther. *Japanese Gardens: Right Angle and Natural Form*. Translated by Karen Williams. Cologne, Germany: Benedikt Taschen, 1993.

122. Ōhashi, Haruzō. *Japanese Courtyard Gardens: Photographs.* Tokyo: Graphic-sha, 1988.

123. Ōhashi, Haruzō. *The Japanese Garden: Island of Serenity.* Tokyo: Graphic-sha; New York: Kodansha International, 1986.

124. Shigemori, Kanto. *The Japanese Courtyard Garden: Landscapes for Small Spaces.* New York: Weatherhill, 1981.

125. Slawson, David A. *Secret Teachings in the Art of the Japanese Gardens: Design Principles, Aesthetic Values.* Tokyo; New York: Kodansha International, 1987.

126. Treib, Marc, and Ron Herman. *A Guide to the Gardens of Kyoto.* Tokyo: Shufunotomo, 1980.

127. Yamashita, Michael S., and Elizabeth Bibb. *In the Japanese Garden.* Washington, DC: Starwood, 1991.

Architecture—Landscape—National Parks

128. Sutherland, Mary, and Dorothy Britton. *National Parks of Japan.* Tokyo; New York: Kodansha International, 1980.

Architecture—Landscape—Ornamentation

129. *Aquascapes II: Water in Japanese Landscape Architecture.* Tokyo: Process Architecture Co., 1994.

130. Covello, Vincent T., and Yuji Yoshimura. *The Japanese Art of Stone Appreciation: Suiseki and its use with Bonsai.* Rutland, VT: Tuttle, 1984.

131. Newsom, Samuel. *Japanese Garden Construction.* Poughkeepsie, NY: Apollo, 1988.

132. Rambach, Pierre, and Susanne Rambach. *Gardens of Longevity in China and Japan: The Art of the Stone Raisers.* Translated by Andre Marling. Geneva, Switzerland: Skira; New York: Rizzoli, 1987.

133. Yoshikawa, Isao. *Japanese Stone Gardens.* Translated by Jay W. Thomas. Tokyo: Graphic-sha, 1992.

134. Yoshikawa, Isao. *Stone Basins: The Accents of Japanese Garden.* Tokyo: Graphic-sha, 1989.

Architecture—Modern

135. Ashihara, Yoshinobu. *The Hidden Order: Tokyo through the Twentieth Century.* Translated by Lynne E. Riggs. Tokyo; New York: Kodansha International, 1989.

136. Bognar, Botond. *Contemporary Japanese Architecture, its Development and Challenge.* New York: Van Nostrand Reinhold, 1985.

137. Bognar, Botond. *The Japan Guide.* New York: Princeton Architectural Press, 1995.

138. Bognar, Botond. *The New Japanese Architecture.* New York: Rizzoli, 1990.

139. Frampton, Kenneth, and Kunio Kudo, eds. *Nikken Sekkei: Building Modern Japan, 1900-1990.* New York: Princeton Architectural Press, 1990.

140. Kroll, Lucien, Manfred Speidel, and Patrice Goulet. *Team Zoo: Buildings and Projects 1971-1990.* Edited by Manfred Speidel. Translated by Michael Robinson. New York: Rizzoli, 1991.

141. Kurokawa, Kishō. *Intercultural Architecture: The Philosophy of Symbiosis.* London: Academy Editions, 1991.

142. Kurokawa, Kishō. *New Wave Japanese Architecture.* London: Academy Editions, 1993.

143. Stewart, David B. *The Making of a Modern Japanese Architecture: 1868 to the Present.* Tokyo; New York: Kodansha International, 1987.

144. Suzuki, Hiroyuki, and Reyner Banham, eds. *Contemporary Architecture of Japan 1958-1984.* New York: Rizzoli, 1985.

145. Tajima, Noriyuki. *Tokyo: A Guide to Recent Architecture.* London: Ellipsis London, 1995.

Architecture—Non-domestic

146. *Commercial Building Facades.* Tokyo: Shotenkenchiku-sha, 1993.

147. *Educational Facilities: New Concepts in Architecture & Design.* Tokyo: Meisei, 1994.

148. Hartkopf, Volker, et al. *Designing the Office of the Future: The Japanese Approach to Tomorrow's Workplace.* New York: Wiley, 1993.

149. *Medical Facilities: New Concepts in Architecture & Design.* Tokyo: Meisei, 1994.

150. *Office Buildings.* New Concepts in Architecture & Design. Tokyo: Meisei, 1995.

151. *Shop Designing.* Tokyo: Graphic-sha, 1989.

152. *Theaters & Halls.* New Concepts in Design and Architecture. Tokyo: Meisei, 1995.

Architecture—Space

153. Carver, Norman F. *Form & Space in Japanese Architecture.* 2d ed. Kalamazoo, MI: Documan, 1993.

154. Greenbie, Barry B. *Space and Spirit in Modern Japan.* New Haven, CT: Yale University Press, 1988.

155. Higuchi, Tadahiko. *The Visual and Spatial Structure of Landscape.* Translated by Charles S. Terry. Cambridge, MA: MIT Press, 1983.

156. Inoue, Mitsuo. *Space in Japanese Architecture.* Translated by Hiroshi Watanabe. New York: Weatherhill, 1985.

157. *Japan, Climate, Space and Concept.* Process Architecture, no. 25. Tokyo: Process Architecture, 1981.

158. Jinnai, Hidenobu. *Tokyo, A Spatial Anthropology.* Translated by Kimiko Nishimura. Berkeley, CA: University of California Press, 1995.

159. Kato, Akinori. *Japanese Open Space as an Amenity: Plaza, Square, and Pedestrian Space.* Tokyo: Process Architecture, 1993.

160. Kurokawa, Kishō. *Rediscovering Japanese Space.* New York: Weatherhill, 1988.

161. Thompson, Fred S., Sheri Blake, and Yasumasa Someya. *Ritual and Space.* Waterloo, Ont.: University of Waterloo Press, 1988.

Architecture—Temples and Shrines

162. Blaser, Werner. *Tempel und Teehaus in Japan / The Temple and Teahouse in Japan.* 2d ed. English version by D. Q. Stephenson. Basel, Switzerland; Boston, MA: Birkhauser, 1988.

163. Brown, S. Azby. *The Genius of Japanese Carpentry: An Account of a Temple's Construction.* Tokyo: New York: Kodansha International, 1989.

164. Buisson, Dominique. *L'Architecture Sacrée au Japon* [Sacred Architecture in Japan]. Courbevoie, Paris: ACR, 1989.

165. Buisson, Dominique. *Temples et Sanctuaires au Japon* [Temples and Shrines in Japan]. Paris: Moniteur, 1981.

166. Parent, Mary Neighbour. *The Roof in Japanese Buddhist Architecture.* New York; Tokyo: Weatherhill, 1983.

167. Parmenter, Ross. *A House for Buddha: A Memoir with Drawings.* New York: Woodstock Press, 1994.

168. Popham, Peter. *Wooden Temples of Japan.* Travel to Landmarks. London: Tauris Parke Books, 1990.

169. Richie, Donald. *The Temples of Kyoto.* Rutland, VT: Tuttle, 1995.

170. Seckel, Dietrich. *Buddhistische Tempelnamen in Japan* [Buddhist Temple Names in Japan]. Münchener Ostasiatische Studien, Bd. 37. Stuttgart, Germany: F. Steiner, 1985.

171. Suzuki, Kakichi. *Early Buddhist Architecture in Japan.* Translated by Mary Neighbour Parent and Nancy Shatzman Steinhardt. Japanese Arts Library. Tokyo; New York: Kodansha International, 1980.

Architecture—Traditional

172. Carver, Norman F. *Japanese Folkhouses.* Kalamazoo, MI: Documan Press, 1984.

173. Fieve, Nicolas. *L'Architecture et la Ville du Japon Ancien: Espace Architectural de la Ville de Kyoto et des Résidences Shogunal aux XIVe et XVe Siècles: Suivi de la Traduction du Livre des Ornementations de Soami* [Architecture and City of Old Japan: Architectural Space of the City of Kyoto and the Shogunal Residences of the 14th and 15th Centuries: Followed by a Translation of the Soami Book of Decoration]. Bibliothèque de L'Institut des Hautes Études Japonaises. Paris: Maisonneuve & Larose with CNRS, 1996.

174. Fujioka, Michio. *Japanese Residences and Gardens: A Tradition of Integration.* Translated by H. Mack Horton. Great Japanese Art series. Tokyo; New York: Kodansha International, 1982.

175. Fujioka, Michio. *Kyoto Country Retreats: The Shugakuin and Katsura Palaces.* Translated by Bruce A. Coats. Great Japanese Art Series. Tokyo; New York: Kodansha International, 1983.

176. Hashimoto, Fumio, ed. *Architecture in the Shoin Style: Japanese Feudal Residences.* Translated by H. Mack Horton. Japanese Arts Library; 10. Tokyo; New York: Kodansha International, 1981.

177. Isozaki, Arata. *Katsura Villa: Space and Form.* New York: Rizzoli, 1987.

178. Itoh, Teiji. *Kura, Design and Tradition of the Japanese Storehouse.* Abridged ed. Adapted by Charles S. Terry. Seattle, WA: Madrona Publishers, 1980.

179. Itoh, Teiji. *Traditional Japanese Houses.* Edited by Yukio Futagawa. Translated by Richard L. Gage. New York: Rizzoli, 1983.

180. Katoh, Amy Sylvester. *Japan Country Living: Spirit, Tradition, Style.* Rutland, VT: Tuttle, 1993.

181. Kawashima, Chūji. *Minka: Traditional Houses of Rural Japan.* Translated by Lynne F. Riggs. Tokyo; New York: Kodansha International, 1986.

182. Muntschick, Wolfgang. *Das traditionelle japanische Bauernhaus: eine kulturhistorische Studie* [The Tradidional Japanese Farmhouse: A Cultural-Historical Study]. Mitteilungen der Deutschen Gesellschaft für Natur- und Völkerkunde Ostasiens, Bd. 99. Hamburg, Germany: Deutschen Gesellschaft für Natur- und Völkerkunde, 1985.

183. Smith, Henry DeWitt. *Taizansō: Matsuura Takeshiro no Ichijojiki no Sekai / Taizansō and the One-Mat Room*. Tokyo: Kokusai Kirisutokyo Daigaku Hakubutsukan Yuasa Hachiro Kinnenkan, 1993.

184. Wada, Kunihei. *Katsura, Imperial Villa*. 8th ed. Translated by Don Kenney. Osaka, Japan: Hoikusha, 1980.

185. Yamagata, Saburō. *The Japanese Home Stylebook: Traditional Details and Motifs*. Edited by Peter Goodman. Berkeley, CA: Stone Bridge Press, 1992.

Architecture—Traditional—Bibliography

186. Stark, Ulrike, ed. *Holzhauser in Japan* [Wooden Houses in Japan]. IRB-Literaturauslese, Nr. 2090. Stuttgart, Germany: IRB-Verlag, 1988.

Armed Forces *See*: Military

Arms and Armor

187. Fuller, Richard, and Ron Gregory. *Military Swords of Japan, 1868-1945*. London; New York: Arms & Armour Press, 1986.

188. Harris, Victor, and Nobuo Ogasawara. *Swords of the Samurai*. London: British Museum Publications, 1990.

189. Kapp, Leon, Hiroko Kapp, and Yoshindo Yoshihara. *The Craft of the Japanese Sword*. Tokyo; New York: Kodansha International, 1987.

190. Ogasawara, Nobuo. *Japanese Swords*. 9th ed. Hoikusha Color Books, v. 22. Osaka, Japan: Hoikusha, 1984.

191. Ogawa, Morihiro. *Japanese Master Swordsmiths: The Gassun Tradition*. Boston, MA: Museum of Fine Arts, Boston, 1988.

192. Ogawa, Morihiro. *Japanese Swords & Sword Furniture in the Museum of Fine Arts, Boston*. Boston, MA: Museum of Fine Arts, 1987.

193. Pepper, David. *Flower of the Chisel: Soul of the Samurai*. Windsor, U.K.: Art Gallery of Windsor, 1985.

194. Robinson, B. W. *Japanese Sword-Fittings and Associated Metalwork*. Baur Collection Catalogue, v. 7. Cahier des Collections Baur, no. 1. Geneva, Switzerland: Collection Baur, 1988.

195. Satō, Kanzan. *The Japanese Sword*. Translated by Joe Earle. Japanese Arts Library, 12. Tokyo; New York: Kodansha International, 1983.

196. *Spectacular Helmets of Japan, 16th-19th Century*. New York: Japan Society, 1985.

197. Trotter, George. *Japanese Swords and Fittings in the Western Australian Museum*. Perth, Australia: Western Australian Museum, 1989.

198. Yumoto, John M. *The Samurai Sword: A Handbook*. Rutland, VT: Tuttle, 1988.

Art

199. Addiss, Stephen. *How to Look at Japanese Art*. New York: Abrams, 1996.

200. Cunningham, Louisa. *The Spirit of Place: Japanese Paintings and Prints of the Sixteenth through Nineteenth Centuries*. New Haven, CT: Yale University Art Gallery, 1984.

201. Cunningham, Michael R. *The Triumph of Japanese Style: 16th-Century Art in Japan*. Cleveland, OH: Cleveland Museum of Art in cooperation with the Indiana University Press, 1991.

202. Dresser, Christopher. *Japan: Its Architecture Art and Art Manufactures*. London: Longmans, Green & Co., 1882. Reprinted as: *Traditional Arts and Crafts of Japan*. New York: Dover, c1994.

203. Elisseeff, Danielle, and Vadim Elisseeff. *Art of Japan*. New York: Abrams, 1985.

204. Guth, Christine. *Art of Edo Japan: The Artist and the City 1615-1868*. Perspectives. New York: Abrams, 1996.

205. Guth, Christine. *Japanese Art of the Edo Period*. Everyman Art Library. London: Weidenfeld and Nicholson, 1996.

206. *The Heibonsha Survey of Japanese Art*. 31 volumes. New York: Weatherhill / Heibonsha, 1971-1980.

207. Hempel, Rose. *The Golden Age of Japan, 794-1192.* Translated by Katherine Watson. New York: Rizzoli, 1983.

208. Ishizawa, Masao, et al. *The Heritage of Japanese Art.* Tokyo; New York: Kodansha International, 1982.

209. Paine, Robert Treat, and Alexander Soper. *The Art and Architecture of Japan.* 3d rev. ed. The Pelican History of Art. New Haven, CT: Yale University Press, 1981.

210. Screech, Timon. *The Western Scientific Gaze and Popular Imagery in Late Edo Japan: The Lens Within the Heart.* Cambridge Studies in New Art History and Criticism. Cambridge, U.K.; New York: Cambridge University Press, 1996.

211. Tadashi, Inumaru, and Mitsukuni Yoshida, eds. *The Traditional Crafts of Japan.* 8 vols. Tokyo: Diamond, 1992.

212. Yamasaki, Shigehisa, ed. *Chronological Table of Japanese Art.* Tokyo: Geishinsha, 1981.

Art—Artists

213. Blakemore, Frances. *Who's Who in Modern Japanese Prints.* New York: Weatherhill, 1975.

214. Havens, Thomas R. H. *Artist and Patron in Postwar Japan: Dance, Music, Theater, and the Visual Arts, 1955-1980.* Princeton, NJ: Princeton University Press, 1982.

215. Roberts, Laurance P. *A Dictionary of Japanese Artists: Painting, Sculpture, Ceramics, Prints, Lacquer.* Tokyo; New York: Weatherhill, 1976.

216. Tazawa, Yutaka, ed. *Biographical Dictionary of Japanese Art.* Tokyo; New York: Kodansha International in collaboration with the International Society for Educational Information, 1981.

217. Weidner, Marsha. *Flowering in the Shadows: Women in the History of Chinese and Japanese Painting.* Honolulu, HI: University of Hawaii Press, 1990.

Art—Artists—Andō, Hiroshige, 1797-1858

218. Adams, Marie, et al. *Tokkaido, Adventures on the Road in Old Japan*. Edited by Stephen Addiss. Lawrence, KA: University of Kansas, Spencer Museum of Art, 1980.

219. Ando, Hiroshige, Henry D. Smith II, and Amy G. Poster. *One Hundred Famous Views of Edo*. New York: Braziller, 1986.

220. Bicknell, Julian. *Hiroshige in Tokyo: The Floating World of Edo*. Rohnert Park, CA: Pomegranate Artbooks, 1994.

221. Impey, O. R. *Hiroshige's Views of Tokyo: A Selection from the Woodblock Print series "One Hundred Views of Famous Places in Edo" by Ando Hiroshige 1797-1858*. Oxford, UK: Ashmolean Museum, 1993.

222. Oka, Isaburō. *Hiroshige: Japan's Great Landscape Artist*. Translated by Stanleigh H. Jones. Great Japanese Art Series. Tokyo; New York: Kodansha International, 1992.

223. Rappard-Boon, Charlotte van. *Hiroshige and the Utagawa School: Japanese Prints, c. 1810-1860*. Edited by J. P. Filedt Kok. Catalogue of the collection of Japanese Prints, pt. 4. Amsterdam: Rijksprentenkabinet, Rijksmuseum, 1984.

Art—Artists—Enkū, 1632-1695

224. Tanahashi, Kazuaki. *Enku, Sculptor of a Hundred Thousand Buddhas*. Edited by Becky Jennison. Boulder, CO: Shambhala, 1982.

Art—Artists—Gosōtei, Hirosada, fl. 1847-1861

225. Keyes, Roger S. *Hirosada, Ōsaka Printmaker: An Exhibition*. Edited by Jane K. Bledsoe. Long Beach, CA: The Museum, 1984.

Art—Artists—Ike, Taiga, 1723-1776

226. Takeuchi, Melinda. *Taiga's True Views: The Language of Landscape Painting in Eighteenth-Century Japan*. Stanford, CA: Stanford University Press, 1992.

Art—Artists—Inoue, Kozo, 1937-

227. Inoue, Kozo. *Kozo: The Work of Kozo*. Tokyo: ABE, 1989.

Art—Artists—Itō, Jakuchū, 1716-1800

228. Itō, Jakuchū, and Daiten. *On a Riverboat Journey: A Handscroll.* Translation by Hiroshi Ōnishi. New York: Braziller, 1989.

Art—Artists—Katsushika, Hokusai, 1760-1849

229. Forrer, Matthi, and Edmond de Goncourt. *Hokusai.* New York: Rizzoli, 1988.

230. Forrer, Matthi, Willem R. van Gulik, and Heinz M. Kaempfer, comps. *Hokusai and his School: Paintings, Drawings and Illustrated Books.* Haarlem, Netherlands: Frans Halsmuseum, 1982.

231. Hillier, Jack Ronald. *The Art of Hokusai in Book Illustration.* London: Sotheby Parke Bernet; Berkeley, CA: University of California Press, 1980.

232. Katsushika, Hokusai, and Henry D. Smith II. *Hokusai: One Hundred Views of Mt. Fuji.* New York: Braziller, 1988.

233. Morse, Peter. *Hokusai, One Hundred Poets.* New York: Braziller, 1989.

Art—Artists—Kimura, Chūta, 1917-

234. *Kimura: Paintings and Works on Paper 1968-1984.* Washington, DC: Phillips Collection, 1985.

Art—Artists—Kitagawa, Utamaro, 1753-1806

235. Kitagawa, Utamaro. *Utamaro: Songs of the Garden.* Translated by Yasuko Betchaku and Joan B. Mirviss. New York: Metropolitan Museum of Art; London: Secker & Warburg, 1984.

236. Kobayashi, Tadashi. *Utamaro: Portraits from the Floating World.* Translated by Mark A. Harbison. London: Sawers, 1982. Reprint: Tokyo; New York: Kodansha International, 1993.

237. Meech-Pekarik, Julia. *Utamaro: A Chorus of Birds.* Note on kyoka and translations by James T. Kenney. New York: The Metropolitan Museum of Art; Viking, 1981.

Art—Artists—Kobayashi, Kiyochika, 1847-1915

238. Smith, Henry DeWitt. *Kiyochika, Artist of Meiji Japan.* Santa Barbara, CA: Santa Barbara Museum of Art, 1988.

Art—Artists—Kuroda, Seiki, 1866-1924

239. *Seiki, Kuroda.* Tsu, Japan: Mie Prefectural Art Museum, 1986.

Art—Artists—Munakata, Shiko, 1903-1975

240. Yanagi, Sori, ed. *The Woodblock Print and the Artist: The Life and Work of Shiko Munakata.* Tokyo; New York: Kodansha International, 1991.

Art—Artists—Nagare, Masayuki, 1923-

241. Nagare, Masayuki. *Masayuki Nagare: The Life of a Samurai Artist.* New York: Weatherhill, 1994.

Art—Artists—Sakaki, Hyakusen, 1697-1752

242. Cahill, James. *Sakaki Hyakusen and Early Nanga Painting.* Japan Research Monograph, 3. Berkeley, CA: Institute of East Asian Studies, University of California, Berkeley, Center for Japanese Studies, 1983.

Art—Artists—Tsukioka, Yoshitoshi, 1839-1892

243. Stevenson, John. *Yoshitoshi's Thirty-Six Ghosts.* New York: Weatherhill / Blue Tiger, 1983.

244. Stevenson, John. *Yoshitoshi's Women: The Woodblock Print Series "Fuzoku Sanjuniso."* Boulder, CO: Avery Press, 1986.

Art—Artists—Utagawa, Kunisada, 1786-1864

245. Izzard, Sebastian, J. Thomas Rimer, and John T. Carpenter. *Kunisada's World.* New York: Japan Society, in collaboration with Ukiyo-e Society of America, 1993.

Art—Basketry

246. Cort, Louise Allison, and Kenji Nakamura. *A Basketmaker in Rural Japan*. New York: Weatherhill; Washington, DC: Arthur M. Sackler Gallery, Smithsonian Institution, 1994.

247. McCallum, Toshiko M., and Jung-Yu S. Lien. *Containing Beauty: Japanese Bamboo Flower Baskets*. Los Angeles, CA: UCLA Museum of Cultural History, 1988.

248. Oster, Maggie, Yi-an Chou. *Bamboo Baskets: Japanese Art and Culture Interwoven with the Beauty of Ikebana*. New York: Viking, 1995.

Art—Book Illustration

249. *Animal Illustrations*. BSS Illustration series. Tokyo: Bijutsu Shuppan-sha, 1992.

250. Anno, Mitsumasa, et al., eds. *Illustration in Japan*. 2 vols. Tokyo: Kodansha International, 1981-1982.

251. Brown, Yu-Ying. *Japanese Book Illustration*. London; Wolfboro, NH: British Library, 1988.

252. Hillier, Jack Ronald. *The Art of the Japanese Book*. 2 vols. London: Philip Wilson Publishers for Sotheby's Publications, 1987.

253. Hillier, Jack Ronald. *The Japanese Picture Book: A Selection from the Ravicz Collection*. New York:. Abrams, 1991.

254. Ikegami, Kōjirō. *Japanese Bookbinding: Instructions from a Master Craftsman*. New York: Weatherhill, 1986.

255. *Japanese Woodcut Book Illustrations*. vols. New York: Abaris, 1979-1982.

256. Roach, Philip Henry, Jr., and Roger Start Keyes. *Pilot Study of Kuchi-e in the Murakami Collection of Meiji Books*. Berkeley, CA: East Asiatic Library, University of California, 1992.

257. Yoshida, Kogorō, and Ryūshin Matsumōto. *Tanrokubon, Rare Books of Seventeenth Century Japan*. Translated by Mark A. Harbison. Tokyo; New York: Kodansha International, 1984.

Art—Buddhist

258. Addis, Stephen. *The Art of Zen: Paintings and Calligraphy by Japanese Monks, 1600-1925.* New York: Abrams, 1989.

259. Brinker, Helmut, and Hiroshi Kanazawa. *Zen: Masters of Meditation in Images and Writings.* Translated by Andreas Leisinger. Artibus Asiae, Supplementum, 40. Zurich, Switzerland: Artibus Asiae, 1996.

260. Ishida, Hisatoyo. *Esoteric Buddhist Painting.* Tokyo; New York: Kodansha International, 1987.

261. Little, Stephen, comp. *Visions of the Dharma: Japanese Buddhist Paintings and Prints in the Honolulu Academy of Arts.* Honolulu, HI: Honolulu Academy of Arts, 1991.

262. McCallum, Donald F. *Zenkoji and its Icon: A Study in Medieval Japanese Religious Art.* Princeton, NJ: Princeton University Press, 1994.

263. Morse, Anne Nishimura, and Samuel Crowell Morse. *Object as Insight: Japanese Buddhist Art & Ritual: Katonah Museum of Art.* Katonah, NY: Katonah Museum of Art, 1995.

264. *Nara, Trésors Bouddhiques du Japon Ancien: Le Temple du Kōfukuji* [Nara, Buddhist Treasures of Ancient Japan: The Kofukuji Temple]. Paris: Réunion des Musées Nationaux, 1996.

265. *Sengai, the Zen Master: Paintings from the Idemitsu Museum of Arts, Tokyo.* Sydney, Australia: Trustees of the Art Gallery of New South Wales, 1985.

266. Shimano, Eidō, and Kōgetsu Tani. *Zen Word, Zen Calligraphy.* Boston, MA: Shambhala, 1992.

267. Tanabe, Willa J. *Paintings of the Lotus Sutra.* New York: Weatherhill, 1988.

Art—Calligraphy

268. Ōmori, Sōgen, and Katsujō Terayama. *Zen and the Art of Calligraphy: The Essence of Sho.* Translated by John Stevens. London; Boston, MA: Routledge & Kegan Paul, 1983. Reprinted: London: Arkana, 1990.

269. Reed, William. *Shodo: The Art of Coordinating Mind, Body and Brush.* Tokyo; New York: Japan Publications, 1989.

270. Tanahashi, Kazuaki. *Brush Mind: Text, Art, and Design.* Berkeley, CA: Parallax Press, 1990.

Art—Ceramics

271. Andacht, Sandra. *Treasury of Satsuma.* Des Moines, IA: Wallace-Homestead, 1981.

272. Arts, P. L. W. *Japanese Porcelain, A Collector's Guide to General Aspects and Decoratif Motifs.* Lochem, Netherlands: Tijdstroom, 1983.

273. Ayers, John. *The Baur Collection, Geneva, Japanese Ceramics.* Geneva, Switzerland: Collection Baur, 1982.

274. Baekeland, Frederick, and Robert Moses. *Modern Japanese Ceramics in American Collections.* New York: Japan Society, 1993.

275. Becker, Johanna O. S. B. *Karatsu Ware: A Tradition of Diversity.* Tokyo; New York: Kodansha International, 1986.

276. Cort, Louise Allison. *Seto and Mino Ceramics.* Japanese Collections in the Freer Gallery of Art. Washington, DC: Freer Gallery of Art, Smithsonian Institution, 1992.

277. *Famous Ceramics of Japan.* vols. Tokyo; New York: Kodansha International, 1981-1984.

278. Kenrick, Douglas M. *Jomon of Japan: The World's Oldest Pottery.* London; New York: Kegan Paul International, 1994.

279. Klein, Adalbert. *A Connoisseur's Guide to Japanese Ceramics.* Translated by Katherine Watson. London: Alpine Fine Arts Collection, 1987.

280. Lawrence, Louis. *Satsuma: Masterpieces from the World's Important Collections.* London: Dauphin, 1991.

281. Moeran, Brian. *Lost Innocence: Folk Craft Potters of Onta, Japan.* Berkeley, CA: University of California Press, 1984.

282. Murobushi, Tetsuro. *Togei Jiten / Encyclopedia of Ceramics.* Tokyo: Nihon Bijutsu Shuppan, 1991.

283.   Philip, Leila. *The Road Through Miyama*. New York: Random House, c1989.

284.   Rhodes, Daniel. *Tamba Pottery: The Timeless Art of a Japanese Village*. Tokyo; New York: Kodansha International, 1982.

285.   *The Rise of a Great Tradition: Japanese Archaeological Ceramics from the Jomon through Heian Periods (10,500 B.C. - A.D. 1185)*. New York: Agency for Cultural Affairs, Government of Japan, Japan Society, 1990.

286.   Sanders, Herbert H., and Kenkichi Tomimoto. *The World of Japanese Ceramics*. Tokyo; New York: Kodansha International, 1982.

287.   Sugihara, Sōsuke. *The Cemetery by Secondary Burials of Yayoi Age at Izuruhara, Tochigi Pref., Japan*. Report of the Research by the Faculty of Literature, Meiji University. Archaeology, 8. Tokyo: Rinsen, 1984.

288.   Wood, Donald Alan, Teruhisa Tanaka, and Frank Chance. *Echizen: Eight Hundred Years of Japanese Stoneware*. Birmingham, AL: Birmingham Museum of Art, 1994.

Art—Cloisonné

289.   Coben, Lawrence A., and Dorothy C. Ferster. *Japanese Cloisonne: History, Technique, and Appreciation*. New York: Weatherhill, 1982.

Art Collections

290.   Earle, Joe, ed. *The Toshiba Gallery: Japanese Art and Design*. Photography Ian Thomas. London: Victoria and Albert Museum, 1986.

291.   Guth, Christine. *Art, Tea, and Industry: Masuda Takashi and the Mitsui Circle*. Princeton, NJ: Princeton University Press, 1993.

292.   Kakudo, Yoshiko. *The Art of Japan: Masterworks in the Asian Art Museum of San Francisco*. San Francisco, CA: Asian Art Museum: Chronicle Books, 1991.

293.   MOA Bijutsukan. *The Quintessence of Japanese Beauty: An Introduction to Selected Works in the MOA Museum of Art*. Atami, Japan: MOA, 1991.

294. *Seikado Art Treasures.* 2 vols. Tokyo: The Seikado Foundation, 1992.

Art—Costumes

295. Hibi, Sadao. *Japanese Detail: Traditional Costume and Fashion.* London: Thames & Hudson, 1989.

296. Koren, Leonard. *New Fashion Japan.* Tokyo; New York: Kodansha International, 1984.

297. Kyoto National Museum of Modern Art. *Evolution of Fashion 1835-1895: Clothing that Captured the Imagination of Japan, the Impact of Romantic Clothing.* Kyoto, Japan: Kyoto Costume Institute, 1980.

298. Minnich, Helen Benton, and Shojiro Nomura. *Japanese Costume and the Makers of its Elegant Tradition.* Rutland, VT: Tuttle, 1963.

299. Sichel, Marion. *Japan.* National Costume Reference. London: B. T. Batsford, 1987.

300. Wada, Emi. *My Costumes.* Tokyo: Kyuryudo, 1989.

Art—Costumes—Kimono

301. Dalby, Liza Crihfield. *Kimono: Fashioning Culture.* New Haven, CT: Yale University Press, 1993.

302. *Five Centuries of Japanese Kimono: On this Sleeve of Fondest Dreams.* Museum Studies, v. 18, no. 1. Chicago, IL: The Art Institute of Chicago, 1992.

303. Gluckman, Dale Carolyn, and Sharon Sadako Takeda. *When Art Became Fashion: Kosode in Edo-Period Japan.* Los Angeles, CA: Los Angeles County Museum of Art; New York: Weatherhill, 1992.

304. Ishimura, Hayao, and Nobuhiko Maruyama. *Robes of Elegance: Japanese Kimonos of the 16th-20th Centuries.* Translated by Haruko Ward. Raleigh, NC: North Carolina Museum of Art, 1988.

305. Kennedy, Alan. *Japanese Costume: History and Tradition.* Paris: Adam Biro, 1990.

306. Liddell, Jill. *The Story of the Kimono.* New York: Dutton, 1989.

307. Peebles, Merrily. *Dressed in Splendor: Japanese Costume from 1700 to 1926.* Santa Barbara, CA: Santa Barbara Museum of Art, 1987.

308. Stinchecum, Amanda Mayer. *Kosode, 16th-19th Century Textiles from the Nomura Collection.* Edited by Naomi Noble Richard and Margot Paul. New York: Japan Society: Kodansha International, 1984.

309. Yamanaka, Norio. *The Book of Kimono.* Tokyo; New York: Kodansha International, 1982.

Art—Costumes—Theater

310. Kirihata, Ken. *Kyogen Costumes: Suo (Jackets) and Kataginu (Shoulder-Wings): With 102 Colour Illustrations.* London: Thames & Hudson, 1980.

311. Nagasaki, Iwao, and Monica Bethe. *Patterns and Poetry: No Robes from the Lucy Truman Aldrich Collection at the Museum of Art, Rhode Island School of Design.* Providence, RI: Museum of Art, Rhode Island School of Design, 1992.

312. *The Reproduction of Noh Costumes.* Japan: Yamaguchi Noh Costume Research Center: Traditional Cultures Exchange Forum, 1984.

313. Shaver, Ruth M. *Kabuki Costume.* Rutland, VT: Tuttle, 1990.

Art—Decorative

314. *The Dawns of Tradition.* Yokohama, Japan: Nissan Motor Co., 1983.

315. Faulkner, Rupert. *Japanese Studio Crafts: Tradition and the Avant-garde.* Philadelphia, PA: University of Pennsylvania Press, 1995.

316. Florence, Gene. *The Collector's Encyclopedia of Occupied Japan Collectibles.* Fourth series. Paducah, KY: Collector Books, 1990.

317. Impey, Oliver R., and Malcolm Fairley. *The Dragon King of the Sea: Japanese Decorative Art of the Meiji Period from the John R. Young Collection.* Oxford, U.K.: Ashmolean Museum, 1991.

318. *Japan's Traditional Crafts: Spirit and Technique.* Tokyo: Asahi Shimbun, 1990.

319. Levy, Dana, and Lea Sneider. *Kamban, Shop Signs of Japan*. New York: Weatherhill, 1983.

320. *Living National Treasures of Japan*. Tokyo: Committee of the Exhibition of Living National Treasures of Japan, 1982.

321. Lowe, John. *Japanese Crafts*. London: J. Murray, 1983.

322. *The Shogun Age Exhibition from the Tokugawa Art Museum, Japan*. 2nd ed. Tokyo: Shogun Age Exhibition Executive Committee, 1983.

323. Tadashi, Inumaru, and Mitsukuni Yoshida, eds. *The Traditional Crafts of Japan*. 8 vols. Tokyo: Diamond, 1992.

324. Tadashi, Inumaru. *Writing Utensils and Household Buddhist Altars*. Traditional Crafts of Japan. Japan: Diamond, 1992.

325. Yanagi, Munayoshi. *The Unknown Craftsman: A Japanese Insight Into Beauty*. Rev. ed. New York: Kodansha International, 1989.

326. Yoshida, Mitsukuni. *Harmony with Nature: A Heritage of Craftsmanship*. Translated by Lynne E. Riggs and Takechi Manabu. Hiroshima: Mazda Motor Corp., 1986.

Art—Design

327. Hiesinger, Kathryn B., and Felice Fischer. *Japanese Design: A Survey Since 1950*. Philadelphia, PA: Philadelphia Museum of Art in association with H. N. Abrams, New York, 1995.

328. Lee, Sherman E. *The Genius of Japanese Design*. Tokyo; New York: Kodansha International, 1981.

329. Sparke, Penny. *Japanese Design*. London: Michael Joseph, 1987.

Art—Dolls

330. Baten, Lea. *Japanese Dolls: The Image and the Motif*. Tokyo: Shufunotomo, 1988.

331. *Ningyo: The Art of the Human Figurine: Traditional Japanese Display Dolls from the Ayervais Collection: With Additional Pieces from the Peabody Essex Museum, Salem, Massachusetts, the Newark Museum, and the Museum of the City of New York*. New York: Japan Society, 1995.

332. Tadashi, Inumaru, ed. *Paper and Dolls*. Traditional Crafts of Japan. Japan: Diamond, 1992.

333. Takeuchi, Chizuko, and Roberta Stephens. *An Invitation to Kokeshi Dolls*. Hirosaki-shi, Japan: Tsugaru Shobo, 1982.

Art—Drawing

334. *The Drawings of Kaii Higashiyama*. Sandy Hook, CT: Shorewood Fine Art Books; Tokyo: Asia Press, 1992.

335. Forrer, Matthi. *Drawings by Utagawa Kuniyoshi from the Collection of the National Museum of Ethnology, Leiden*. Leiden, Netherlands: Rijksmuseum voor Volkenkunde, 1988.

336. Hillier, Jack Ronald. *Japanese Drawings of the 18th and 19th Centuries*. Washington, DC: International Exhibitions Foundation, 1980.

337. *Japan in Transition: Drawings of the Meiji Period*. London: Henderson, Milne, Gallery, 1983.

338. *Yasuo Kuniyoshi: Drawings of the 1920s*. New York: Zabriskie Gallery, 1986.

Art—Embroidery

339. Berger, Patricia, and Richard L. Mellot. *Asian Embroideries*. San Francisco, CA: Asian Art Museum, 1988.

340. Hays, Mary V., and Ralph E. Hays. *Fukusa: The Shojiro Nomura Fukusa Collection*. Oakland, CA: Mills College Art Gallery, 1983.

341. Milgram, Lynne. *Narratives in Cloth: Embroidered Textile from Aomori, Japan: From the Collection of the Keiko Kan Museum Foundation*. Toronto, Ont.: Museum for Textiles, 1993.

342. Takemura, Akihiko. *Fukusa: Japanese Gift Covers*. Translated by Keiko Kobayashi. Edited by Mary V. Hays and Ralph E. Hays. Tokyo: Iwasaki Bijutsu-sha, 1991.

343. Tosk, Eugene, and Susan Tosk. *Silk, Gold and the World's most Elegant Return Receipt*. New York: Orientations Oriental Antiques, 1990.

Art—Fans

344. Hutt, Julia, and Hélène Alexander. *Ogi: A History of the Japanese Fan*. London: Dauphin, 1992.

345. Irons, Neville John. *Fans of Imperial Japan*. Kaiserreich Kunst Oriental Art Series. Hong Kong: Kaiserreich Kunst, 1982.

Art—Folk

346. Addis, Stephen, ed. *Japanese Ghosts & Demons: Art of the Supernatural*. New York: Braziller, 1985.

347. *Mingei: Masterpieces of Japanese Folkcraft*. Japan Folk Craft Museum. Tokyo; New York: Kodansha International, 1991.

348. Moes, Robert. *Japanese Folk Art: A Triumph of Simplicity*. Exhibition organized by the Japan Society. New York: Japan Society, 1992.

349. Moes, Robert. *Mingei: Japanese Folk Art from the Montgomery Collection*. Alexandria, VA: Art Services International, 1995.

Art—Furniture and Carpentry

350. Clarke, Rosy. *Japanese Antique Furniture: A Guide to Evaluating and Restoring*. New York: Weatherhill, 1983.

351. Coaldrake, William Howard. *The Way of the Carpenter: Tools and Japanese Architecture*. New York: Weatherhill, 1990.

352. Heineken, Ty, and Kiyoko Heineken. *Tansu, Traditional Japanese Cabinetry*. New York: Weatherhill, 1981.

353. Keil, Dorothee. *Kijiya: Geschichte und materielle Kultur* [Kijiya: History and Material Culture]. Bonner Zeitschrift für Japanologie, Bd. 7. Bonn, Germany: Förderverein "Bonner Zeitschrift für Japanologie," 1985.

354. Koizumi, Kazuko. *Traditional Japanese Furniture*. Tokyo; New York: Kodansha International, 1986.

Art—Graphic

355. Burer, Catherine, ed. *Kirei: Posters from Japan, 1978-1993.* London: Thames and Hudson, 1994.

356. *Business Card Graphics.* Rockport, MA: Rockport Publishers, 1992.

357. Fraser, James, Steven Heller, and Seymour Chwast. *Japanese Modern: Graphic Design between the Wars.* San Francisco, CA: Chronicle Books, 1996.

Art—Lacquer

358. Collections Baur. *Laques du Japon / Japanese Lacquer.* Geneva, Switzerland: Collection Baur, 1988.

359. Kesel, W. G. de. *Japanese Export Lacquers (16th-17th century) from the Castle of Beloeil.* Drongen, Belgium: Rectavit, 1994.

360. National Museum of Modern Art, Tokyo, ed. *Japanese Lacquer Art: Modern Masterpieces.* Translated by Richard L. Gage. New York: Weatherhill; Kyoto, Japan: Tankosha, 1982.

361. Piert-Borgers, Barbara. *Restaurieren mit Urushi: japanischer Lack als Restaurierunsmittel* [Restoring with Urushi: Japanese Lacquer as Restoration Tool]. Kleine Monographien, 6. Cologne, Germany: Museum für Ostasiatische Kunst, 1987.

362. Pinto, Maria Helena Mendes. *Namban Lacquerware in Portugal: The Portuguese Presence in Japan (1543-1639).* Collection History of Art. Lisbon: Edicoes INAPA, 1990.

Art—Leather

363. Scholten, Frits, ed. *Goudleer Kinkarakawa: de Geschiedenis van het Nederlands Goudleer en zijn invloed in Japan* [Gilded Leather Kinkarakawa: The History of Dutch Gilded Leather and its Influence in Japan]. Zwolle, Netherlands: Waanders, 1989.

Art—Modern

364. *A Cabinet of Signs: Contemporary Art from Post-Modern Japan.* Liverpool, U.K.: Tate Gallery, 1991.

365. *Japon des Avant Gardes, 1910-1970: Exposition* [Avant-Garde Japan, 1910-1970: An Exhibition. Paris: Centre Pompidou, 1986.

366. Linhartova, Vera, comp. *Dada et Surréalisme au Japon* [Dada and Surrealism in Japan]. Arts du Japon. Paris: Publications Orientalistes de France, 1987.

367. Munroe, Alexandra. *Japanese Art after 1945: Scream Against the Sky.* New York: Abrams, 1994.

Art—Motifs and Themes

368. D'Adetta, Joseph. *Traditional Japanese Design Motifs.* Dover Pictorial Archive series. New York: Dover, 1984.

369. *Asobi: Play in the Arts of Japan.* Katonah, NY: Katonah Museum of Art, 1992.

370. Britton, Dorothy Guyver, and Tsuneo Hayashida. *The Japanese Crane: Bird of Happiness.* Rev. ed. Tokyo; New York: Kodansha International, 1993.

371. *The Feminine Image: Women of Japan.* Honolulu, HI: Honolulu Academy of Arts, 1985.

372. Lillehoj, Elizabeth. *Woman in the Eyes of Man: Images of Women in Japanese Art from the Field Museum.* Chicago, IL: Field Museum, 1995.

373. Meech-Pekarik, Julia. *Rain and Snow: The Umbrella in Japanese Art.* New York: Japan Society, 1993.

Art—Netsuke and Inro

374. Ehrich, Kurt S. *Shichifukujin: die sieben Glücksgötter Japans: ein Versuch über Genesis und Bedeutung volkstümlicher ostasiatischer Gottheiten* [Shichifukujin: The Seven Lucky Gods of Japan: An Attempt at Genesis and Meaning of East Asian Folk Gods]. Recklinghausen, Germany: A. Bongers, 1991.

375. Kinsey, Robert O. *Ojime: Magical Jewels of Japan.* New York: Abrams, 1991.

376. Lawrence, Louis, and Shep Brozman. *Japanese Inro: From the Brozman Collection.* Edited by Clare Lawrence. London: Genlux Holdings, 1993.

377. Lazarnick, George. *Netsuke & Inro Artists; and how to read their Signatures.* 2 vols. Honolulu, HI: Reed, 1982.

378. Masatoshi, and Raymond Bushell. *The Art of Netsuke Carving.* Tokyo; New York: Kodansha International, 1981.

Art—Painting

379. Adams, Celeste. *Heart, Mountains, and Human Ways: Japanese Landscape and Figure Painting: A Loan Exhibition from the University of Michigan Museum of Art.* Houston, TX: Museum of Fine Arts, 1983.

380. Conant, Ellen P., Steven D. Owyoung, and J. Thomas Rimer. *Nihonga: Transcending the Past: Japanese-Style Painting, 1868-1968.* St. Louis, MO: St. Louis Art Museum, 1995.

381. *Exhibition of Japanese Paintings from the Collection of Museum of Fine Arts, Boston.* Tokyo: Tokyo National Museum, 1983.

382. Gittert, Kurt A., and Pat Fister. *Japanese Fan Paintings from Western Collections.* New Orleans, LA: New Orleans Museum of Art, 1985.

383. *Ōkyo and the Maruyama-Shijō School of Japanese Painting: The Saint Louis Art Museum, Seattle Art Museum.* St. Louis, MO: Saint Louis Art Museum, 1980.

Art—Painting—Haiga

384. Addis, Stephen. *Haiga: Takebe Socho and the Haiku-Painting Tradition.* Honolulu, HI: Marsh Art Gallery, University of Richmond in association with University of Hawaii Press, 1995.

385. Zolbrod, Leon M. *Haiku Painting.* Great Japanese Art. Tokyo; New York: Kodansha International, 1982.

Art—Painting—Ink

386. Barnet, Sylvan, and William Burton. *Zen Ink Painting.* Great Japanese Art. Tokyo; New York: Kodansha International, 1982.

387. Nakamura, Nihei. *Die Tuschmalerei des Shubun und das Problem der unbemalten weissen Flächen* [Shubun's Ink Paintings and the Problem of the Unpainted White Surfaces]. Persönlichkeit und Werk, Bd. 6. Konstanz, Germany: L. Leonhardt, 1981.

388. Satō, Shōzō, and Thomas A. Heenan. *The Art of Sumi-e: Appreciation, Techniques, and Application.* Tokyo; New York: Kodansha International, 1984.

Art—Painting—Mural

389. Dower, John W., and John Junkerman, eds. *The Hiroshima Murals: The Art of Iri Maruki and Toshi Maruki.* Tokyo; New York: Kodansha International, 1985.

Art—Painting—Nanga

390. *Nanga: Idealist Painting of Japan.* Victoria, Canada: Art Gallery of Greater Victoria, 1980.

391. Till, Barry, and Paula Swart. *Japanese Paintings in Canadian Collections.* Victoria, B.C.: Art Gallery of Greater Victoria, 1983.

Art—Painting—Narrative

392. Murase, Miyeko. *Emaki, Narrative Scrolls from Japan.* New York: Asia Society, 1983.

393. Murase, Miyeko. *Iconography of the Tale of Genji: Genji Monogatari Ekotoba.* New York: Weatherhill, 1983.

394. Murase, Miyeko. *Tales of Japan: Scrolls and Prints from the New York Public Library.* Oxford, U.K.; New York: Oxford University Press, 1986.

395. Ushioda, Yoshiko. *Tales of Japan: Three Centuries of Japanese Painting from the Chester Beatty Library, Dublin.* Alexandria, VA: Art Services International, 1992.

Art—Painting—Portrait

396. Lubarsky, Jared. *Noble Heritage: Five Centuries of Portraits from the Hosokawa Family.* Washington, DC: Smithsonian Institution Press for the National Portrait Gallery, 1992.

Art—Painting—Screen

397. Jacobsen, Robert D. *The Art of Japanese Screen Painting: Selections from the Minneapolis Institute of Arts.* Minneapolis, MN: The Minneapolis Institute of Arts, 1984.

398. Kuroda, Taizō, Melinda Takeuchi, and Yuzo Yamane. *Worlds Seen and Imagined: Japanese Screens from the Idemitsu Museum of Arts.* New York: Asia Society Galleries, 1995.

399. Murase, Miyeko. *Masterpieces of Japanese Screen Painting: The American Collections.* New York: Braziller, 1990.

400. *Quiet Elegance: Japanese Painted Screens of the Edo Period, 1615-1868.* Coral Gables, FL: Miami University, Lowe Art Museum, 1983.

Art—Paper

401. Buisson, Dominique. *The Art of Japanese Paper: Masks, Lanterns, Kites, Dolls, Origami.* Paris: Terrail, 1992.

402. Herring, Ann King. *The World of Chiyogami: Hand Printed Patterned Papers of Japan.* Tokyo; New York: Kodansha International, 1987.

403. Miura, Einen. *Fascinating Marble Paper.* Tokyo: Atelier Miura, 1988.

404. Schmoller, Hans. *Mr. Gladstone's Washi: A Survey of Reports on the Manufacture of Paper in Japan: "The Parkes Report of 1871."* Newtown, PA: Bird & Bull Press, 1984.

Art—Prints

405. Earle, Joe. *An Introduction to Japanese Prints.* V & A Introductions to the Decorative Arts. London: H.M.S.O., 1982.

406. Hajek, Lubor. *Japanese Graphic Art.* Translated by Helena Krejcova. Secaucus, NJ: Chartwell Books, 1989.

407. Hillier, Jack Ronald. *Japanese Colour Prints.* 4th ed. Phaidon Colour Library. Oxford, UK: Phaidon, 1981.

408. Illing, Richard. *The Art of Japanese Prints.* New York: Gallery Books, 1983.

409. Meech-Pekarik, Julia. *The World of the Meiji Print: Impressions of a New Civilization.* New York: Weatherhill, 1986.

410. Michener, James A., and Howard A. Link. *The Floating World.* Honolulu, HI: University of Hawaii Press, 1983.

411. Mosheim, K. R. *The Techniques of Japanese Wood-Block Printing.* Auckland, New Zealand: Winby, 1984.

412. Munsterberg, Hugo. *The Japanese Print: A Historical Guide.* New York: Weatherhill, 1982.

413. Narazaki, Muneshige, and C. H. Mitchell. *The Japanese Print: Its Evolution and Essence.* Tokyo; Palo Alto, CA, Kodansha International, 1966. Reprint: Tokyo; New York: Kodansha International, 1982.

414. Pins, Jacob. *The Japanese Pillar Print, Hashira-e.* London: R. G. Sawers, 1982.

Art—Prints—Bibliography

415. Abrams, Leslie E. *The History and Practice of Japanese Printmaking: A Selectively Annotated Bibliography of English Language Materials.* Art Reference Collection, no. 5. Westport, CT: Greenwood, 1984.

Art—Prints—Erotica

416. Evans, Tom, and Mary Anne Evans. *Shunga: The Art of Love in Japan.* New York: Paddington Press, 1975. Reprint: 1979.

417. Fowkes, Charles, ed. *The Pillow Book.* London: Hamlyn, 1988.

418. Marhenke, Dorit, and Ekkehard May. *Shunga: Erotic Art in Japan: Erotische Holzschnitte des 16. bis 19. Jahrhunderts* [Shunga: Erotic Art in Japan: Erotic Woodblock Prints of the 16th to 19th centuries]. Heidelberg, Germany: Edition Braus, 1995.

Art—Prints—Exhibition Catalogs

419. Avitabile, Gunhild. *Early Masters: Ukiyo-e Prints and Paintings from 1680 to 1750.* New York: Japan Society Gallery, 1991.

420. Clark, Timothy T., Osamu Ueda, and Donald Jenkins. *The Actor's Image: Print Makers of the Katsukawa School*. Edited by Naomi Noble Richard. Chicago, IL: Art Institute of Chicago in association with Princeton University Press, 1994.

421. Kalinsky, Nicola, ed. *50 Impressions: Japanese Colour Woodblock Prints in the College Art Collections, University College London*. London: University College London, 1993.

422. Keyes, Roger S., et al. *Japanese Woodblock Prints: Catalogue of the Mary A. Ainsworth Collection*. Oberlin, OH: Allen Memorial Art Museum, Oberlin College, 1984.

423. Keyes, Roger S. *The Male Journey in Japanese Prints*. Berkeley, CA: University of California Press, 1989.

424. Keyes, Roger S. *Surimono: Privately Published Japanese Prints in the Spencer Museum of Art*. New York: Kodansha International for the Spencer Museum of Art, 1984.

425. Link, Howard A., Juzo Suzuki, and Roger S. Keyes. *Primitive Ukiyo-e from the James A. Michener Collection in the Honolulu Academy of Arts*. Honolulu, HI: University Press of Hawaii for the Honolulu Academy of Arts, 1980.

426. Mirviss, Joan B., and John T. Carpenter. *The Frank Lloyd Wright Collection of Surimono*. New York: Weatherhill; Phoenix, AZ: Phoenix Art Museum, 1995.

427. Smith, Lawrence. *The Japanese Print: Bold Dreams and New Visions*. New York: Harper & Row, 1983.

428. Staatliche Kunstsammlungen Dresden. Kupferstich-Kabinett. *Gems of the Floating World: Ukiyo-e Prints from the Dresden Kupferstich-Kabinett*. New York: Japan Society; Dresden, Germany: Kupferstich-Kabinett, Staatliche Kunstsammlungen, 1995.

429. Swinton, Elizabeth de Sabato. *The Women of the Pleasure Quarter: Japanese Paintings and Prints of the Floating World*. New York: Hudson Hills Press, 1995.

430. Thompson, Sarah E., and H. D. Harootunian. *Undercurrents in the Floating World: Censorship and Japanese Prints*. New York: Asian Society Galleries, 1991.

431. Yonemura, Ann. *Yokohama: Prints from Nineteenth-Century Japan*. Washington, DC: Arthur M. Sackler Gallery: Smithsonian Institution Press, 1990.

Art—Prints—Modern

432. Brown, Kendall H., and Hollis Goodall-Cristante. *Shin-Hanga: New Prints in Modern Japan*. Los Angeles, CA: Los Angeles County Museum of Art; Seattle, WA: University of Washington Press, 1996.

433. Merritt, Helen. *Modern Japanese Woodblock Prints: The Early Years*. Honolulu, HI: University of Hawaii Press, 1990.

434. Pinckard, W. H. Jr. *Post-Meiji Japanese Woodblock Prints, 1912-1962*. Catalogue, three. Oakland, CA: W. H. Pinckard, Jr., 1983.

435. Uhlenbeck, Chris, and François Daulte. *La Nouvelle Vague: L'Estampe Japonaise de 1868 a 1939 dans la Collection Robert O. Muller* [The New Wave: Prints from 1868 to 1939 in the Robert O. Muller Collection]. Lausanne, Switzerland: Bibliothèque des Arts, 1994.

Art—Reference

436. Gobbi, Pietro. *Hon: Firme, Sigilli, Stemmi, Filologia dell'Ukiyo-e / Signatures, Seals, Crests, Philology of the Ukiyo-e Prints*. Turin, Italy: L'Angolo Manzoni, 1989.

437. Self, James, and Nobuko Hirose. *Japanese Art Signatures: A Handbook and Practical Guide*. London: Bamboo Publishers; Rutland, VT: Tuttle, 1987.

Art—Sculpture

438. *Bunka-viewing: Sculptors and their Drawings from Japan: Toshikatsu Endo et al.* Los Angeles, CA: Herbert Palmer Gallery, 1990.

439. Fox, Howard N. *A Primal Spirit: Ten Contemporary Japanese Sculptors*. Los Angeles, CA: Los Angeles County Museum of Art, 1990.

440. Frank, Bernard. *Le Panthéon Bouddhique au Japon: Collections d'Emile Guimet* [The Buddhist Pantheon in Japan: The Emile Guimet Collections]. Paris: Editions de la Réunion des Musées Nationaux, 1991.

441. Goepper, Roger. *Aizen-Myōō: The Esoteric King of Lust: An Iconological Study*. Artibus Asiae, Supplementum, 39. Zurich, Switzerland: Artibus Asiae: Museum Rietberg, 1993.

442. Goepper, Roger. *Die Seele des Jizō: Weihegaben im Inneren einer Buddhistischen Statue* [Jizō's Soul: Consecrated Gifts Inside a Buddhist Statue]. Kleine Monographien, 3. Cologne, Germany: Museum für Ostasiatische Kunst, 1984.

443. Guth, Christine. *Shinzō: Hachiman Imagery and its Development*. Harvard East Asian Monographs, 119. Cambridge, MA: Council on East Asian Studies, Harvard University, 1985.

444. Harris, Victor, and Ken Matsushima. *Kamakura: The Renaissance of Japanese Sculpture, 1185-1333*. London: British Museum Press for the Trustees of the British Museum, 1991.

445. Koplos, Janet. *Contemporary Japanese Sculpture*. Abbeville Modern Art Movement. New York: Abbeville Press, 1991.

446. Nishikawa, Kyotaro, and Emily J. Sano. *The Great Age of Japanese Buddhist Sculpture, AD 600-1300*. Fort Worth, TX: Kimbell Art Museum, 1982.

447. Sugiyama, Jirō. *Classic Buddhist Sculpture: The Tempyō Period*. Translated by Samuel Crowell Morse. Japanese Arts Library, 11. Tokyo; New York: Kodansha International, 1982.

Art—Textiles

448. Brandon, Reiko Mochinaga. *Country Textiles of Japan: The Art of Tsutsugaki*. New York: Weatherhill, 1986.

449. Itō, Toshiko. *Tsujigahana, the Flower of Japanese Textile Art*. Translated by Monica Bethe. Tokyo; New York: Kodansha International, 1985.

450. Nakano, Eiko, and Barbara B. Stephan. *Japanese Stencil Dyeing: Paste-Resist Techniques*. New York: Weatherhill, 1982.

451. Nihon Sen'i Isho Senta. *Textile Designs of Japan*. 3 vols. Osaka: Japan Textile Color Design Center, 1959-61.

452. Tomita, Jun, and Noriko Tomita. *Japanese Ikat Weaving: The Techniques of Kasuri*. London; Boston, MA: Routledge & Kegan Paul, 1982.

453. Wada, Yoshiko, Mary Kellogg Rice, and Jane Barton. *Shibori: The Inventive Art of Japanese Shaped Resist Dyeing: Tradition, Techniques, Innovation*. Tokyo; New York: Kodansha International, 1983.

Artificial Intelligence

454. Rubinger, Bruce. *Applied Artificial Intelligence in Japan: Current Status, Key Research and Development Performers, Strategic Focus*. New York: Hemisphere, 1988.

455. Unger, J. Marshall. *The Fifth Generation Fallacy: Why Japan is Betting its Future on Artificial Intelligence*. New York: Oxford University Press, 1987.

Atlases *See*: Maps

Asia—Relations with

456. Armour, Andrew J. L. *Asia and Japan: The Search for Modernization and Identity*. London; Dover, NH: Athlone Press; Tokyo: Keio University, 1985.

457. Funabashi, Yōichi. *Asia Pacific Fusion: Japan's Role in APEC*. Washington, DC: Institute for International Economics, 1995.

458. Latham, A. J. H., and Heita Kawakatsu, eds. *Japanese Industrialization and the Asian Economy*. London; New York: Routledge, 1994.

459. Lim, Hua Sing. *Japan's Role in Asia: Issues and Prospects*. 2d ed. Singapore: Times Academic Press, 1995.

460. Mendl, Wolf. *Japan's Asia Policy: Regional Security and Global Interests*. London; New York: Routledge, 1995.

42 AREA BIBLIOGRAPHY OF JAPAN

461. Tokunaga, Shojiro. *Japan's Foreign Investment and Asian Economic Interdependence: Production, Trade, and Financial Systems.* Tokyo: University of Tokyo Press, 1992.

462. Yasutomo, Dennis T. *Japan and the Asian Development Bank.* Studies of the East Asian Institute. New York: Praeger, 1983.

Australia—Relations with

463. Drysdale, Peter, et al. *The Australia-Japan Relationship: Towards the Year 2000.* Canberra: Australia-Japan Research Centre: Tokyo: Japan Center for Economic Research, 1989.

464. Drysdale, Peter, and Hironobu Kitaoji, eds. *Japan & Australia: Two Societies and Their Interaction.* Canberra; Miami, FL: Australian National University Press, 1981.

465. Frei, Henry P. *Japan's Southward Advance and Australia: From the Sixteenth Century to World War II.* Honolulu: University of Hawaii Press, 1991.

466. Hori, Takeaki. *The Japanese and the Australians: Business and Cultural Exchange.* Sydney; New York: Pergamon, 1982.

467. Rix, Alan. *Coming to Terms: The Politics of Australia's Trade with Japan 1945-57.* Sydney; London: Allen & Unwin, 1986.

468. Sheridan, Kyoko, ed. *The Australian Economy in the Japanese Mirror.* St. Lucia, Australia: University of Queensland Press, 1992.

Automation

See also: Industry—Electronics; Industry—High Technology; Information Technology; Robotics

469. Asai, K., S. Takashima, and P. R. Edwards. *Manufacturing, Automation System and CIM Factories.* London; New York: Chapman & Hall, 1994.

470. Galjaard, J. H. *A Technology Based Nation: An Inquiry into Industrial Organizing and Robotizing in Japan.* Scitech Publications, nr. 3. Delft, Netherlands: Eburon, 1985.

471. Hartley, John. *Flexible Automation in Japan.* Berlin, Germany; New York: Springer, 1984.

Banks and Banking

472. Aoki, Masahiko, and Hugh Patrick, eds. *The Japanese Main Bank System: Its Relevance for Developing and Transforming Economies.* Oxford, U.K.: Oxford University Press, 1994.

473. *The Banking System in Japan.* Tokyo: Federation of Bankers Associations of Japan, 1989.

474. Hanley, Thomas H., et al. *The Japanese Banks: Positioning for Competitive Advantage.* New York: Salomon Brothers, Stock Research, 1986.

475. Suzuki, Yoshio. *Money and Banking in Contemporary Japan: The Theoretical Setting and its Application.* Translated by John G. Greenwood. New Haven, CT: Yale University Press, 1980.

476. Tamaki, Norio. *Japanese Banking: A History, 1859-1959.* Studies in Monetary and Financial History. Cambridge, U.K.: Cambridge University Press, 1995.

477. Tatewaki, Kazuo. *Banking and Finance in Japan: An Introduction to the Tokyo Market.* London; New York: Routledge, 1991.

478. Tsutsui, William M. *Banking Policy in Japan: American Efforts at Reform During the Occupation.* Nissan Institute / Routledge Japanese Studies Series. London; New York: Routledge, 1988.

Banks and Banking—Dictionaries

479. Moriwaki, Akira, and Arno Moriwaki. *Banking Dictionary: English-Japanese, Japanese-English.* Bern, Switzerland: P. Haupt, 1990.

Basketry *See*: Art—Basketry

Baths

480. Clark, Scott. *Japan, A View from the Bath.* Honolulu, HI: University of Hawaii Press, 1994.

481. Grilli, Peter, and Dana Levy. *Furo, the Japanese Bath.* Tokyo; New York: Kodansha International, 1985.

Bibliography

482. Adami, Norbert R. *Russischsprachige Japanliteratur: ein Auswahlverzeichnis, 1980-1990 / Literature on Japan in Russian: A Selective Bibliography*. Munich, Germany: Iudicium, 1991.

483. Formanek, Susanne, and Peter Getreuer. *Verzeichnis des deutschsprachigen Japan-Schrifttums 1980-1987* [Bibliography of German Literature on Japan, 1980-1987]. Materialien zur Kultur- und Geistesgeschichte Asiens, 1. Vienna: Verlag der Österreichischen Akademie der Wissenschaften, 1989.

484. Gardner, James L. *Japan Access: A Bibliography of Bibliographies*. Salt Lake City, UT: Wings of Fire Press, 1990.

485. Getreuer, Peter. *Verzeichnis des deutschsprachigen Japan-Schrifttums 1988-1989: nebst Ergänzungen zu den Jahren 1980-1987* [Bibliography of German Literature on Japan, 1988-1989: Together with Additions for the Years 1980-1987]. Materialien zur Kultur- und Geistesgeschichte Asiens, 2. Vienna: Verlag der Österreichischen Akademie der Wissenschaften, 1991.

486. Hérail, Francine. *Eléments de Bibliographie Japonaise: Ouvrages Traduits du Japonais, Études en Langues Occidentales* [Elementary Japanese Bibliography: Works Translated from the Japanese, Studies in Occidental Languages]. Bibliothèque Japonaise. Paris: Publications Orientalistes de France, 1986.

487. *Japanese Publications in Foreign Languages, 1945-1990: Social Sciences & Humanities, Science & Technology, Arts, Hobbies & Sports, Children's Books*. Tokyo: Japan Book Publishers Association, 1990.

488. Makino, Yasuko, and Masaei Saito. *A Student Guide to Japanese Sources in the Humanities*. Michigan Papers in Japanese Studies, 24. Ann Arbor, MI: Center for Japanese Studies, University of Michigan, 1994.

489. Makino, Yasuko, and Mihoko Miki, comps. *Japan and the Japanese: A Bibliographic Guide to Reference Sources*. Bibliographies and Indexes in Asian Studies, no. 1. Westport, CT: Greenwood, 1996.

490. Olschleger, Hans-Dieter, and Jurgen Stalph. *Japanbezogene Bibliographien in &uropaischen Sprachen: eine Bibliographie* [Bibliographies in European Languages Related to Japan: A Bibliography]. Bibliographische Arbeiten (Philipp-Franz-von-Siebold-Stiftung. Deutsches Institut für Japanstudien), Bd. 1. Munich, Germany: Iudicium, 1990.

491. Rogala, Jozef. *Books on Japan in English: A Guide for Collectors, Librarians and Academics, Including a Selected List of over One Thousand Four Hundred Titles, Annotated and Indexed.* Citrus Heights, CA: Oriental Lost Art and Rare Books, 1991.

492. Shulman, Frank Joseph. *Japan.* World Bibliographic Series, v. 103. Oxford, U.K.; Santa Barbara, CA: Clio, 1989.

Biographies and Autobiographies

493. Craig, Albert M., and Shively, Donald H., eds *Personality in Japanese History.* Berkeley, CA: University of California Press, 1970. Reprint: Michigan Classics in Japanese Studies, 13. Ann Arbor, MI: Center for Japanese Studies, The University of Michigan, 1995.

494. Formanek, Susanne, and Sepp Linhart. *Japanese Biographies: Life Histories, Life Cycles, Life Stages.* Sitzungsberichte, 590. Bd. Beiträge zur Kultur- und Geistesgeschichte Asiens, Nr. 11. Vienna: Verlag der Österreichischen Akademie der Wissenschaften, 1992.

495. Morris, Ivan I. *The Nobility of Failure: Tragic Heroes in the History of Japan.* New York: Holt, Rinehart and Winston, 1975. Reprint: New York: Noonday Press, Farrar Straus Giroux, 1988.

496. Reischauer, Haru Matsukata. *Samurai and Silk: A Japanese and American Heritage.* Cambridge, MA: Belknap Press of Harvard University Press, 1986.

497. Richie, Donald. *Different People: Pictures of Some Japanese.* Tokyo; New York: Kodansha International, 1987.

Biographies—Arai, Hakuseki, 1657-1725

498. Arai, Hakuseki. *Told Round a Brushwood Fire: The Autobiography of Arai Hakuseki.* Translated by Joyce Ackroyd. UNESCO Collection of Representative Works. Japanese Series. Princeton, NJ: Princeton University Press, 1980.

499. Nakai, Kate Wildman. *Shogunal Politics: Arai Hakuseki and the Premises of Tokugawa Rule*. Harvard East Asian Monographs, 134. Cambridge, MA: Council on East Asian Studies, Harvard University, 1988.

Biographies—Fujita, Tsuguji, 1886-1968

500. Selz, Jean. *Foujita*. New York: Crown, 1981.

Biographies—Fukuchi, Gen'ichirō, 1841-1906

501. Huffman, James L. *Politics of the Meiji Press: The Life of Fukuchi Gen'ichiro*. Honolulu, HI: University Press of Hawaii, 1980.

Biographies—Fukuzawa, Yukichi, 1835-1901

502. Fukuzawa, Yukichi. *Autobiography*. Authorized edition. Translated by Eiichi Kiyooka. Tokyo: Hokuseido Press, 1948. Reprint: *The Autobiography of Yukichi Fukuzawa*. Revised translation. New York: Columbia University Press, 1966. Reprint: New York: Schocken Books, 1972.

Biographies—Higuchi, Ichiyō, 1872-1896

503. Danly, Robert Lyons. *In the Shade of Spring Leaves: The Life and Writings of Higuchi Ichiyō, a Woman of Letters in Meiji Japan*. New Haven, CT: Yale University Press, 1981.

Biographies—Kaneko, Fumiko, 1902-1926

504. Kaneko, Fumiko. *The Prison Memoirs of a Japanese Woman*. Translated by Jean Inglis. Foremother Legacies. Armonk, NY: Sharpe, 1991.

Biographies—Katō, Shizue, 1897-

505. Hopper, Helen M. *A New Woman of Japan: A Political Biography of Kato Shidzue*. Boulder, CO: Westview, 1996.

506. Ishimoto, Shidzue. *Facing Two Ways: The Story of my Life*. New York: Farrar & Rinehart, 1935. Reprint: Stanford, CA: Stanford University Press, 1984.

Biographies—Katsu, Kokichi, 1802-1850

507. Katsu, Kokichi. *Musui's Story: The Autobiography of a Tokugawa Samurai.* Translated by Teruko Craig. Tucson, AZ: University of Arizona Press, 1988.

Biograpies—Kawai, Eijirō, 1891-1944

508. Hirai, Atsuko. *Individualism and Socialism: Kawai Eijirō's Life and Thought (1891-1944).* Harvard East Asian Monographs, 127. Cambridge, MA: Council on East Asian Studies, Harvard University, 1986.

Biographies—Kido, Takayoshi, 1833-1877

509. Brown, Sidney Devere, and Akiko Hirota, trans. *The Diary of Kido Takayoshi.* 3 vols. Tokyo: University of Tokyo Press, 1983-1986.

Biographies—Kitaōji, Rosanjin, 1886-1959

510. Cardozo, Sidney B., and Masaaki Hirano. *The Art of Rosanjin.* Tokyo; New York: Kodansha International, 1987.

Biographies—Kobayashi, Hideo, 1902-

511. Konigsberg, Matthew. *Der junge Kobayashi Hideo: Leben und Werk eines japanischen Literatur kritikers der Moderne* [The Young Kobayashi Hideo: Life and Work of a Japanese Literary Critic of the Modern Age]. Mitteilungen der Deutschen Gesellschaft für Natur- und Völkerkunde Ostasiens, Bd. 118. Hamburg, Germany: Gesellschaft für Natur- und Völkerkunde Ostasiens, 1993.

Biographies—Koizumi, Setsu, 1868-1932

512. Hasegawa, Yoji. *Lafcadio Hearn's Japanese Wife: Her Memoirs and her Early Life.* Tokyo: Micro Printing, 1988.

Biographies—Konoye, Fumimaro, 1891-1945

513. Oka, Yoshitake. *Konoe Fumimaro, a Political Biography.* Translated by Shumpei Okamota and Patricia Murray. Tokyo: University of Tokyo Press, 1983.

Biographies—Kyōgoku, Tamekane, 1254-1332

514. Huey, Robert N. *Kyōgoku Tamekane: Poetry and Politics in Late Kamakura Japan*. Stanford, CA: Stanford University Press, 1989.

Biographies—Miyazaki, Tōten, 1870-1922

515. *My Thirty-Three Years' Dream: The Autobiography of Miyazaki Tōten*. Translated by Etō Shinkichi and Marius B. Jansen. Princeton Library of Asian Translations. Princeton, NJ: Princeton University Press, 1982.

Biographies—Naitō, Torajirō, 1866-1934

516. Fogel, Joshua A. *Politics and Sinology: The Case of Naitō Konan (1866-1934)*. Harvard East Asian Monographs, 114. Cambridge, MA: Council on East Asian Studies, Harvard University, 1984.

Biographies—Nakano, Makiko, 1890-1978

517. Nakano, Makiko. *Makiko's Diary: A Merchant Wife in 1910 Kyoto*. Translated by Kazuko Smith. Stanford, CA: Stanford University Press, 1995.

Biographies—Nakano, Seigō, 1886-1943

518. Oates, L. R. *Nakano Seigō (1886-1943)*. Leaders of Asia Series, 5. St. Lucia, Australia; New York: University of Queensland Press, 1982.

Biographies—Nakanoin Masatada no Musume, b. 1258

519. Nakanoin Masatada no Musume. *The Confessions of Lady Nijō*. Translated by Karen Brazell. Garden City, NY: Anchor Press / Doubleday, 1973. Reprint: Stanford, CA: Stanford University Press, 1976.

Biographies—Nitobe, Inazō, 1862-1933

520. Howes, John F., ed. *Nitobe Inazō: Japan's Bridge Across the Pacific*. Boulder, CO: Westview, 1995.

Biographies—Noguchi, Hideyo, 1876-1928

521. Plesset, Isabel Rosanoff. *Noguchi and his Patrons.* Rutherford, NJ: Fairleigh Dickenson University Press, 1980.

Biographies—Ō, Sadaharu, 1940-

522. Ō, Sadaharu, and David Falkner. *Sadaharu Oh: A Zen Way of Baseball.* New York: Times Books, 1984.

Biographies—Ōhira, Masayoshi, 1910-

523. Satō, Seizaburō, Ken'ichi Kōyama, and Kumon Shumpei. *Postwar Politician: The Life of Masayoshi Ōhira.* Tokyo; New York: Kodansha International, 1990.

Biographies—Oida, Yoshi

524. Oida, Yoshi, and Lorna Marshall. *An Actor Adrift.* London: Methuen, 1994.

Biographies—Ōkita, Saburō, 1914-

525. Ōkita, Saburō. *Japan's Challenging Years: Reflections on My Lifetime.* Translated by Graeme Bruce and Ann Nevile. Sydney, Australia; Boston, MA: G. Allen & Unwin, 1985.

Biographies—Ōshima, Hiroshi, 1886-1975

526. Boyd, Carl. *The Extraordinary Envoy: General Hiroshi Ōshima and Diplomacy in the Third Reich, 1934-1939.* Washington, DC: University Press of America, 1980.

Biographies—Ōsugi, Sakae, 1885-1923

527. Stanley, Thomas A. *Ōsugi Sakae, Anarchist in Taisho Japan: The Creativity of the Ego.* Harvard East Asian Monographs, 102. Cambridge, MA: Council on East Asian Studies, Harvard University, 1982.

Biographies—Ōyama, Sutematsu, 1860-1919

528. Kuno, Akiko. *Unexpected Destinations: The Poignant Story of Japan's First Vassar Graduate.* Translated by Kirsten McIvor. Tokyo; New York: Kodansha International, 1993.

Biographies—Saisho, Yuriko, 1926-

529. Saisho, Yuriko. *Women Executives in Japan: How I Succeeded in Business in a Male-Dominated Society.* Tokyo: YURI International, 1981.

Biographies—Sawada, Miki, 1901-1980

530. Hemphill, Elizabeth Anne. *The Least of These: Miki Sawada and her Children.* New York: Weatherhill, 1980.

Biographies—Shibue, Io, 1816-1884

531. McClellan, Edwin. *Woman in the Crested Kimono: The Life of Shibue Io and her Family.* Drawn from Mori Ōgai's *Shibue Chūsai.* New Haven, CT: Yale University Press, 1985.

Biographies—Shiotsuki, Masao, 1920-1979

532. Shiotsuki, Masao. *Doctor at Nagasaki: My First Assignment was Mercy Killing.* Tokyo: Kosei, 1987.

Biographies—Sugawara, Michizane, 845-903

533. Borgen, Robert. *Sugawara no Michizane and the Early Heian Court.* Harvard East Asian Monographs, 120. Cambridge, MA: Council on East Asian Studies, Harvard University, 1986.

Biographies—Tōjō, Hideki, 1884-1948

534. Hoyt, Edwin Palmer. *Warlord: Tojo Against the World.* Lanham, MD: Scarborough House, 1993.

Biographies—Tokugawa Ieyasu, 1542-1616

535. Sadler, Arthur Lindsay. *The Maker of Modern Japan: The Life of Tokugawa Ieyasu.* London: Allen & Unwin, 1937. Reprint: Rutland, VT: Tuttle, 1981.

536. Totman, Conrad D. *Tokugawa Ieyasu, Shogun: A Biography.* South San Francisco, CA: Heian, 1983.

Biographies—Tokugawa, Yoshichika, 1886-1976

537. Corner, Eldred John Henry. *The Marquis: A Tale of Syonan-To.* Singapore: Heineman Asia, 1981.

Biographies—Tokutomi, Iichirō, 1863-1957

538. Pierson, John D. *Tokutomi Sohō, 1863-1957, a Journalist for Modern Japan.* Princeton, NJ: Princeton University Press, 1980.

Biographies—Toyotomi, Hideyoshi, 1536?-1598

539. Berry, Mary Elizabeth. *Hideyoshi.* Harvard East Asian Series, 97. Cambridge, MA: Harvard University Press, 1982.

Biographies—Tsuda, Umeko, 1864-1929

540. Rose, Barbara. *Tsuda Umeko and Women's Education in Japan.* New Haven, CT: Yale University Press, 1992.

Biographies—Uragami, Gyokudō, 1745-1820

541. Addis, Stephen. *Tall Mountains and Flowing Waters: The Arts of Uragami Gyokudo.* Honolulu, HI: University of Hawaii Press, 1987.

Biographies—Yamada, Waka, 1879-1957

542. Yamazaki, Tomoko. *The Story of Yamada Waka: From Prostitute to Feminist Pioneer.* Translated by Wakako Hironaka and Ann Kostant. Tokyo; New York: Kodansha International, 1985.

Biographies—Yamagata, Daini, 1725-1767

543. Wakabayashi, Bob Tadashi. *Japanese Loyalism Reconstrued: Yamagata Daini's Ryushi Shinron of 1759.* Honolulu, HI: University of Hawaii Press, 1995.

Biographies—Yamamoto, Isoroku, 1884-1943

544. Hoyt, Edwin Palmer. *Yamamoto: The Man who Planned Pearl Harbor.* New York: McGraw-Hill, 1990.

Biographies—Yamazaki, Ikue, 1918-

545. Caillet, Laurence. *The House of Yamazaki: The Life of a Daughter of Japan*. Translated by Megan Backus. New York: Kodansha International, 1994.

Biographies—Yukawa, Hideki, 1907-1981

546. Yukawa, Hideki. *Tabibito / The Traveler*. Translated by L. Brown and R. Yoshida. Singapore: World Scientific, 1982.

Biology

547. Sasa, Manabu, and Mihoko Kikuchi. *Chironomidae (Diptera) of Japan*. Tokyo: University of Tokyo Press, 1995.

Biotechnology

548. Brock, Malcolm Vernon. *Biotechnology in Japan*. Nissan Institute / Routledge Japanese Studies series. London; New York: Routledge, 1989.

549. Dibner, Mark D., and R. Steven White. *Biotechnology Japan*. New York: McGraw-Hill, 1989.

550. Elkington, John. *Bio-Japan: The Emerging Japanese Challenge in Bio-Technology*. London: Oyez Scientific & Technical Services, 1985.

551. Schmid, Rolf. *Biotechnology in Japan: A Comprehensive Guide*. Berlin, Germany; New York: Springer, 1991.

552. Yuan, Robert T., and Mark D. Dibner. *Japanese Biotechnology: A Comprehensive Study of Government Policy, R & D and Industry*. Houndmills, U.K.: Macmillan, 1990.

Birth Control

553. Coleman, Samuel. *Family Planning in Japanese Society: Traditional Birth Control in a Modern Urban Culture*. Princeton, NJ: Princeton University Press, 1983.

554. Hodge, Robert William, and Naohiro Ogawa. *Fertility Change in Contemporary Japan*. Population and Development. Chicago, IL: University of Chicago Press, 1991.

Bonsai

555. Koide, Nobukichi, Saburō Katō, and Fusazō Takeyama. *The Masters' Book of Bonsai*. Tokyo; New York: Kodansha International, 1967. Reprint: 1983.

Book Illustration *See*: Art—Book Illustration

Brazil—Relations with

556. Mattos, João Metello de. *Kasuga-tai: Um Laço Entre o Brasil e o Japão* [Kasuga-tai: A Bond Between Brazil and Japan]. Sao Paulo, Brazil: Alianca Cultural Brasil-Japao, 1990.

Buddhism *See*: Religion—Buddhism

Buddhist Art *See*: Art—Buddhist

Buddhist Literature *See*: Literature—Buddhist

Bunraku *See*: Theater—Bunraku

Buraku *See*: Minorities—Buraku

Bureaucracy

557. *Japanese Models of Conflict Resolution*. Japanese Studies Series. London; New York: Kegan Paul International, 1990.

558. Kato, Junko. *The Problem of Bureaucratic Rationality: Tax Politics in Japan*. Princeton, NJ: Princeton University Press, 1994.

559. Kim, Paul S. *Japan's Civil Service System: Its Structure, Personnel, and Politics*. Contributions in Political Science, no. 202. New York: Greenwood, 1988.

560. Koh, B. C. *Japan's Administrative Elite*. Berkeley, CA: University of California Press, 1989.

561. Park, Yung H. *Bureaucrats and Ministers in Contemporary Japanese Government*. Japan Research Monograph, 8. Berkeley, CA: Institute of East Asian Studies, University of California, Berkeley, Center for Japanese Studies, 1986.

562. Ramseyer, J. Mark, and Frances M. Rosenbluth. *The Politics of Oligarchy: Institutional Choice in Imperial Japan*. Political Economy of Institutions and Decisions. Cambridge, U.K.; New York: Cambridge University Press, 1995.

563. Silberman, Bernard S. *Cages of Reason: The Rise of the Rational State in France, Japan, the United States, and Great Britain*. Chicago, IL: University of Chicago Press, 1993.

564. Steven, Rob. *Japan's New Imperialism*. Houndmills, U.K.: Macmillan, 1990.

Bushido

See also: 2088; 2089

565. Blomberg, Catharina. *The Heart of the Warrior: Origins and Religious Background of the Samurai System in Feudal Japan*. Sandgate, U.K.: Japan Library, 1994.

566. Day, Stacey B., and Kiyoshi Inokuchi. *The Wisdom of Hagakure: Way of the Samurai of Saga Domain*. Saga, Japan: Hagakure Society, 1994.

567. Donohue, John J. *The Forge of the Spirit: Structure, Motion, and Meaning in the Japanese Martial Tradition*. Garland Reference Library of Social Science, v. 702. New York: Garland, 1991.

568. Yamamoto, Tsunetomo. *The Hagakure: A Code to the Way of Samurai*. Translated by Takao Mukoh. Tokyo: Hokuseido, 1980.

Business *See*: Industrial Management

Business—Bibliographies

569. Jeffries, Francis M. *The English-Language Japanese Business Reference Guide*. Poolesville, MD: Jeffries & Associates, 1988.

Business—Dictionaries

570. Mitsubishi Corporation, comp. *Japanese Business Language: An Essential Dictionary*. London: KPI, 1987.

Calligraphy *See*: Art—Calligraphy

Canada—Relations with

571. Langdon, Frank. *The Politics of Canadian-Japanese Economic Relations, 1952-1983.* Vancouver, B.C.: University of British Columbia Press, 1983.

572. Pringsheim, Klaus H. *Neighbors Across the Pacific; The Development of Economic and Political Relations Between Canada and Japan.* Contributions in Political Science, no. 90. Global Perspectives in History and Politics. Westport, CT: Greenwood, 1983.

573. Schultz, John, and Miwa Kimitada. *Canada and Japan in the Twentieth Century.* Toronto; New York: Oxford University Press, 1991.

Capital Punishment

574. *The Death Penalty in Japan: Report of an Amnesty International Mission to Japan, 21 February - 3 March, 1983.* London: Amnesty International Publications, 1983.

Capitalism

575. Gould, Arthur. *Capitalist Welfare Systems: A Comparison of Japan, Britain and Sweden.* London; New York: Longman, 1993.

576. Ozaki, Robert S. *Human Capitalism: The Japanese Enterprise System as World Model.* Tokyo; New York: Kodansha International, 1991.

577. Sakakibara, Eisuke. *Beyond Capitalism: The Japanese Model of Market Economics.* Lanham, MD: University Press of America, 1993.

578. Suzuki, T. Morris, and T. Seiyama, eds. *Japanese Capitalism Since 1945: Critical Perspectives.* Armonk, NY: Sharpe, 1989.

579. Tsuru, Kotaro. *The Japanese Market Economy System: Its Strengths and Weaknesses.* LTCB International Library Selection, no. 4. Tokyo: LTCB International Library Foundation, 1996.

580. Tsuru, Shigeto. *Japan's Capitalism: Creative Defeat and Beyond.* Cambridge Surveys of Economic Policies and Institutions. Cambridge, U.K.: Cambridge University Press, 1993.

581. Yamamoto, Shichihei. *The Spirit of Japanese Capitalism and Selected Essays*. Library of Japan. Lanham, MD: Madison Books, 1992.

Carpentry *See*: Art—Furniture and Carpentry

Castles *See*: Architecture—Castles

Censorship

See also: Academic Freedom; Religious Freedom

582. Mitchell, Richard H. *Censorship in Imperial Japan*. Princeton, NJ: Princeton University Press, 1983.

583. Rubin, Jay. *Injurious to Public Morals: Writers and the Meiji State*. Seattle, WA: University of Washington Press, 1984.

Censorship—Bibliography

584. Yoshimura, Yoshiko, comp. *Censored Japanese Serials of the Pre-1946 Period: A Checklist of the Microfilm Collection*. Washington, DC: Library of Congress, 1994.

585. Yoshimura, Yoshiko, comp. *Japanese Government Documents and Censored Publications: A Checklist of the Microfilm Collection*. Washington, DC: Library of Congress, 1992.

Ceramics *See*: Arts—Ceramics

Chemistry—Dictionaries

586. Cao Huimin, and Bao Wenchu, eds. *Dictionary of Chemistry and Chemical Technology in Japanese, English, and Chinese*. Amsterdam; New York: Elsevier; Beijing: Chemical Industry Press, 1989.

Child Development

587. Hendry, Joy. *Becoming Japanese: The World of the Pre-school Child*. Japanese Studies. Manchester, U.K.: Manchester University Press, 1986.

588. Stevenson, Harold, Hiroshi Azuma, and Kenji Hakuta, eds. *Child Development and Education in Japan*. Series of Books in Psychology. New York: W. H. Freeman, 1986.

589. White, Merry I. *The Material Child: Coming of Age in Japan and America*. New York: Free Press, 1993.

China—Relations with

590. Bedeski, Robert E. *The Fragile Entente: The 1978 Japan-China Peace Treaty in a Global Context*. Westview Replica Edition. Boulder, CO: Westview, 1983.

591. Coble, Parks M. *Facing Japan: Chinese Politics and Japanese Imperialism, 1931-1937*. Harvard East Asian Monograph, 135. Cambridge, MA: Council on East Asian Studies, Harvard University, 1991.

592. Fogel, Joshua A. *The Cultural Dimension of Sino-Japanese Relations: Essays on the Nineteenth and Twentieth Centuries*. Armonk, NY: Sharpe, 1995.

593. Howe, Christopher, ed. *China and Japan: History, Trends and Prospects*. Studies on Contemporary China. New York: Oxford University Press, 1996.

594. Howland, Douglas. *Borders of Chinese Civilization: Geography and History at Empire's End*. Asia-Pacific. Durham, NC: Duke University Press, 1996.

595. Iriye, Akira. *China and Japan in the Global Setting*. Cambridge, MA: Harvard University Press, 1992.

596. Jansen, Marius B. *China in the Tokugawa World*. Cambridge, MA: Harvard University Press, 1992.

597. Lee, Chae-Jin. *China and Japan: New Economic Diplomacy*. Stanford, CA: Hoover Institute Press, 1984.

598. Li, Lincoln. *The China Factor in Modern Japanese Thought: The Case of Tachibana Shiraki, 1881-1945*. SUNY Series in Chinese Philosophy and Culture. Albany, NY: State University of New York Press, 1996.

599. Morton, William Fitch. *Tanaka Giichi and Japan's China Policy.* New York: St. Martin's Press, 1980.

600. Newby, Laura. *Sino-Japanese Relations: China's Perspective.* Chatham House Papers. London: Royal Institute of International Affairs; London; New York: Routledge, 1988.

601. Nish, Ian Hill. *Japan's Struggle with Internationalism: Japan, China, and the League of Nations, 1931-3.* London; New York: Kegan Paul International, 1993.

602. Ochi, Hisashi. *Der aussenpolitische Entscheidungsprozess Japans: der zur Normalisierung der Beziehungen zwischen Japan und der Volksrepublik China führende politische Entscheidungsprozess in Japan* [The Foreign-Political Decision Process of Japan: The Decision Process in Japan that Leads to Normalization of Relations Between Japan and the People's Republic of China]. Minerva-Fachserie Rechts- und Staatswissenschaften. Munich, Germany: Minerva Publikation, 1982.

603. Taylor, Robert. *China, Japan, and the European Community.* London: Athlone Press, 1990.

604. Taylor, Robert. *The Sino-Japanese Axis: A New Force in Asia?* London: Athlone Press, 1985.

605. Verschuer, Charlotte von. *Les Relations Officielles du Japon avec la Chine aux VIIIe et IXe Siècles* [Official Relations Between Japan and China in the 8th and 9th Centuries]. Hautes Études Orientales, 21. Geneva, Switzerland: Droz, 1985.

606. Whiting, Allen Suess. *China Eyes Japan.* Berkeley, CA: University of California Press, 1989.

Christianity *See*: Religion—Christianity

Civil Rights

607. Bowen, Roger W. *Rebellion and Democracy in Meiji Japan: A Study of Commoners in the Popular Rights Movement.* Berkeley, CA: University of California Press, 1980.

608. Buhman, Karin. *Civil and Political Rights in Japan; International and Constitutional Standards and National Practice*. Publications from the Danish Center of Human Rights, 0903-9961, no. 18. Copenhagen: Danish Center of Human Rights, 1989.

609. McCormack, Gavan, and Yoshio Sugimoto, eds. *Democracy in Contemporary Japan*. Armonk, NY: Sharpe, 1986.

Civilization

610. Aoki, Michiko Y., and Margaret B. Dardess, comps. and eds. *As the Japanese See It: Past and Present*. Honolulu, HI: University of Hawaii Press, 1981.

611. Barthes, Roland. *Empire of Signs*. Translated by Richard Howard. New York: Hill & Wang, 1982.

612. Benedict, Ruth. *The Chrysanthemum and the Sword: Patterns of Japanese Culture*. Cleveland, OH: Meridian Books, 1967. Reprint: Boston, MA: Houghton Mifflin, 1989.

613. Berque, Augustin, ed. *Dictionnaire de la Civilisation Japonaise* [Dictionary of Japanese Civilization]. Paris: Hazan, 1994.

614. Christopher, Robert C. *The Japanese Mind: The Goliath Explained*. New York: Linden Press / Simon & Schuster, 1983.

615. Collcutt, Martin, Marius Jansen, and Isao Kimakura. *Cultural Atlas of Japan*. Oxford, U.K.: Phaidon, 1988.

616. Cortazzi, Hugh. *The Japanese Achievement*. Great Civilizations Series. London: Sidgwick & Jackson; New York: St. Martin's Press, 1990.

617. Dalby, Liza, et al. *All-Japan: The Catalogue of Everything Japanese*. New York: Morrow, 1984.

618. De Mente, Boye. *Everything Japanese*. Lincolnwood, IL: Passport Books, 1989.

619. Ellwood, Robert S., Jr. *An Invitation to Japanese Civilization*. Wadsworth Civilization in Asia Series. Belmont, CA: Wadsworth, 1980.

620. Joseph, Joe. *The Japanese: Strange But Not Strangers*. London: Viking, 1993.

621. Lee, O-young. *Smaller is Better: Japan's Mastery of the Miniature.* Tokyo; New York: Kodansha International, 1984.

622. Naff, Clayton. *About Face: How I Stumbled onto Japan's Social Revolution.* New York: Kodansha America, 1994.

623. Passin, Herbert. *Encounter with Japan.* Tokyo; New York: Kodansha International, 1982.

624. Random, Michel. *Japan: Strategy of the Unseen.* Wellingborough, U.K.: Crucible, 1987.

625. Rauch, Jonathan. *The Outnation: A Search for the Soul of Japan.* Boston, MA: Harvard Business School Press, 1992.

626. Reingold, Edwin M. *Chrysanthemums and Thorns: The Untold Story of Modern Japan.* New York: St. Martin's Press, 1992.

627. Richie, Donald. *A Lateral View: Essays on Culture and Style in Contemporary Japan.* Berkeley, CA: Stone Bridge Press, 1992.

628. Singer, Kurt. *Mirror, Sword and Jewel: The Geometry of Japanese Life.* Edited by Richard Storry. London: Croom Helm, 1973. Reprint: Tokyo; New York: Kodansha International, 1981.

629. Statler, Oliver. *Japanese Inn.* New York: Random House, 1961. Reprint: Honolulu, HI: University of Hawaii Press, 1982.

630. Thomas, Roy. *Japan: The Blighted Blossom.* London: I. B. Tauris, 1989.

631. Watson, Burton. *The Rainbow World: Japan in Essays and Translations.* Seattle, WA: Broken Moon Press, 1990.

Civilization—Foreign Influences

632. Allen, G. C. *Modern Japan and Its Problems.* London; Atlantic Highlands, NJ: Athlone Press, 1990.

633. Burks, Ardath W., ed. *The Modernizers: Overseas Students, Foreign Employees, and Meiji Japan.* Boulder, CO: Westview, 1985.

634. Chapman, William. *Inventing Japan: The Making of a Postwar Civilization.* New York: Prenctice Hall, 1991.

635. Covell, Jon Carter, and Alan Covell. *Korean Impact on Japanese Culture: Japan's Hidden History*. Elizabeth, NJ: Hollym International, 1984.

636. Ishida, Takeshi. *Japanese Political Culture: Change and Continuity*. New Brunswick, NJ: Transaction Books, 1983.

637. Morishima, Michio. *Why has Japan 'Succeeded'?: Western Technology and the Japanese Ethos*. Cambridge, U.K.; New York: Cambridge University Press, 1982.

638. Pollack, David. *The Fracture of Meaning: Japan's Synthesis of China from the Eighth Through the Eighteenth Centuries*. Princeton, NJ: Princeton University Press, 1986.

639. Westney, D. Eleanor. *Imitation and Innovation: The Transfer of Western Organizational Patterns to Meiji Japan*. Cambridge, MA: Harvard University Press, 1987.

640. Yoshida, Mitsukuni. *The Hybrid Culture: What Happened when East and West Met*. Translated by Lynne E. Riggs and Takechi Manabu. Hiroshima, Japan: MAZDA, 1984.

Classical Literature *See*: Literature—Classical

Cloisonné *See*: Art—Cloisonné

Colombia—Relations with

641. González Vergara, Juan Carlos. *Historia y Perspectivas de las Relaciones Bilaterales entre Colombia y Japón* [History and Perspectives in the Bilateral Relations Between Colombia and Japan]. Serie Documentos Ocasionales, no. 27. Santafe de Bogota, Colombia: Centro de Estudios Internationales de la Universidad de los Andes, 1992.

Color Prints *See*: Art—Prints

Commerce

642. El-Agraa, A. M. *Japan's Trade Frictions: Realities or Misconceptions?* Basingstoke, U.K.: Macmillan, 1988.

643. Hirschmeier, Johannes, and Tsunehiko Yui. *The Development of Japanese Business, 1600-1980.* 2d ed. London; Boston, MA: G. Allen & Unwin, 1981.

644. Krugman, Paul. *Trade With Japan: Has the Door Opened Wider?* National Bureau of Economic Research Project Report. Chicago, IL: University of Chicago Press, 1991.

645. Ohno, Kenichi. *Dynamism of Japanese Manufacturing: Evidence From the Postwar Period.* Brookings Discussion Papers in International Economics, no. 96. Washington, DC: Brookings Institution, 1992.

646. Tilton, Mark. *Restrained Trade: Cartels in Japan's Basic Materials Industries.* Ithaca, NY: Cornell University Press, 1996.

647. Verschuer, Charlotte von. *Le Commerce Extérieur du Japon des Origines au XVIe Siècle* [Japan's Foreign Trade Since the 16th Century]. Bibliothèque de l'Institut des Hautes Études Japonaises. Paris: Maisonneuve & Larose, 1988.

Commercial Law *See*: Law—Commercial

Commercial Policy

648. Calder, Kent E. *Strategic Capitalism: Private Business and Public Purpose in Japanese Industrial Finance.* Princeton, NJ: Princeton University Press, 1993.

649. Fletcher, William Miles. *The Japanese Business Community and National Trade Policy, 1920-1942.* Chapel Hill, NC: University of North Carolina Press, 1989.

650. Higashi, Chikara. *Japanese Trade Policy Formulation.* New York: Praeger, 1983.

651. *Intra-firm Trade.* Trade Policy Issues, 1. Paris: Organisation for Economic Co-operation and Development, 1993.

652. Lincoln, Edward J. *Japan's Unequal Trade.* Washington, DC: Brookings Institution, 1990.

Communication

653. Barnlund, Dean C. *Communicative Styles of Japanese and Americans: Images and Realities.* Belmont, CA: Wadsworth, 1989.

654. Gudyskunst, William B. *Communication in Japan and the United States.* SUNY Series in Human Communication Processes. Albany: State University of New York, 1993.

655. Hendry, Joy. *Wrapping Culture: Politeness, Presentation, and Power in Japan and Other Societies.* Oxford Studies in the Anthropology of Cultural Forms. Oxford, U.K.: Clarendon Press, 1993.

Communism *See*: Socialism

Computers—Dictionaries

656. Ferber, Gene. *English-Japanese, Japanese-English Dictionary of Computer and Data-processing Terms / Ei-Wa Wa-Ei Konpyuta Deta Shori Yogo Jiten.* Cambridge, MA: MIT Press, 1989.

Confucianism

See also: 2086

657. Kassel, Marleen. *Tokugawa Confucian Education: The Kangien Academy of Hirose Tanso (1782-1856).* Studies of the East Asian Institute. Albany, NY: State University of New York Press, 1996.

658. Kracht, Klaus. *Studien zur Geschichte des Denkens im Japan des 17. bis 19. Jahrhunderts: Chu-Hsi-konfuzianische Geist-Diskurse* [Studies in the History of Thought in Japan of the 17th to the 19th Centuries: Chu-Hsi-Confucian Intellectual Discourse]. Veröffentlichungen des Ostasien-Instituts der Ruhr-Universität Bochum, Bd. 31. Wiesbaden, Germany: Harrassowitz, 1986.

659. Nosco, Peter, ed. *Confucianism and Tokugawa Culture.* Princeton, NJ: Princeton University Press, 1984.

660. Pfulb, Gerhard. *Soziale Ordnung als Problem: Auffassungen über soziale Ordnung im japanischen Konfuzianismus, 1660-1750* [Social Order as Problem: Opinions About Social Order in Japanese Confucianism, 1660-1750]. Sozialwissenschaftliche Studien, Bd. 49. Bochum, Germany: N. Brockmeyer, 1993.

661. Yamaga, Sokō. *Yamaga Sokōs "Kompendium der Weisenlehre" (Seikyō Yōroku): ein Wörterbuch des neoklassischen Konfuzianismus im Japan des 17. Jahrhunderts* [Yamaga Sokō's "Essentials of the Sacred Teachings" (Seikyō Yōroku): A Dictionary of Neo-Classical Confucianism in 17th Century Japan]. Translated by Gerhard Leinss. Izumi, Bd. 1. Wiesbaden, Germany: Harrassowitz, 1989.

Conglomerates

662. Downer, Lesley. *The Brothers: The Saga of the Richest Family in Japan.* London: Chatto & Windus, 1994.

663. Futatsugi, Yusaku. *Japanese Enterprise Groups.* Translated by Anthony Kaufmann. Monograph (Kobe Daigaku. Keiei Gakubu), no. 4. Kobe, Japan: School of Business Administration, Kobe University, 1986.

664. Havens, Thomas R. H. *Architects of Affluence: The Tsutsumi Family and the Seibu-Saison Enterprises in Twentieth-Century Japan.* Harvard East Asian Monographs, 166. Cambridge, MA: Council on East Asian Studies, Harvard University, 1994.

665. Miyashita, Kenichi, and David W. Russell. *Keiretsu: Inside the Hidden Japanese Conglomerates.* New York: McGraw-Hill, 1994.

666. Ohsono, Tomokazu. *Charting Japanese Industry: A Graphical Guide to Corporate and Market Structures.* London; New York: Cassell, 1995.

Corporate Culture

667. Abecasis-Phillips, J. A. S. *Doing Business With the Japanese.* Lincolnwood, IL: NTC Business Books, 1993.

668. Allison, Anne. *Nightwork: Sexuality, Pleasure, and Corporate Masculinity in a Tokyo Hostess Club.* Chicago, IL: University of Chicago Press, 1994.

669. Bacarr, Jina. *How to Succeed in a Japanese Company: Strategies for Bridging the Business and Culture Gap.* Secaucus, NJ: Carol Publishing Group, 1994.

670. Brannen, Christalyn, and Tracey Wilen. *Doing Business with Japanese Men: A Woman's Handbook.* Berkeley, CA: Stone Bridge Press, 1993.

671. De Mente, Boye. *Japanese Etiquette & Ethics in Business.* 5th ed. Lincolnwood, IL: Passport Books, 1987.

672. Durlabhji, Subhash, and Norton E. Marks, eds. *Japanese Business: Cultural Perspectives.* Albany, NY: State University of New York Press, 1993.

673. Gallo, Holly L., ed. *Profiting From Total Quality.* Conference Board Report, no. 1048. New York: Conference Board, 1993.

674. Gercik, Patricia. *On Track with the Japanese: A Case-by-Case Approach to Building Successful Relationships.* New York: Kodansha International, 1996.

675. Kamada, Mayumi. *Australia-Japan Business Cooperation Committees: Forging Channels of Communication.* Pacific Economic Papers, no. 219. Canberra, Australia: Australia-Japan Research Centre, 1993.

676. Katzenstein, Gary J. *Funny Business: An Outsider's Year in Japan.* New York: Soho Press, 1989.

677. Kinzley, William Dean. *Industrial Harmony in Modern Japan: The Invention of a Tradition.* Nissan Institute / Routledge Japanese Studies Series. London; New York: Routledge, 1991.

678. Kopp, Rochelle. *The Rice-paper Ceiling: Breaking through Japanese Corporate Culture.* Berkeley, CA: Stone Bridge Press, 1994.

679. Lanier, Alison Raymond. *The Rising Sun on Main Street: Working with the Japanese.* 2d ed. Yardley-Morrisville, PA: International Information Associates, 1992.

680. March, Robert M. *Reading the Japanese Mind: The Realities behind their Thoughts and Actions.* New York: Kodansha International, 1996.

681. Rowland, Diana. *Japanese Business Etiquette: A Practical Guide to Success with the Japanese.* New York: Warner Books, 1993.

682. Vardaman, James M., Jr., and Michiko Sasaki Vardaman. *Japanese Etiquette Today: A Guide to Business and Social Customs.* Rutland, VT: Tuttle, 1994.

683. Yamada, Haru. *American and Japanese Business Discourse: A Comparison of Interactional Styles.* Advances in Discourse Processes, v. 45. Norwood, NJ: Ablex, 1992.

Corporations

684. Abegglen, James C. *Kaisha, the Japanese Corporation.* New York: Basic Books, 1985.

685. *The Anatomy of Japanese Business.* Armonk, NY: Sharpe, 1984.

686. Aoki, Masahiko, ed. *The Economic Analysis of the Japanese Firm.* Contributions to Economic Analysis, 151. Amsterdam; New York: North-Holland, 1984.

687. Aoki, Masahiko, and Ronald Dore. *The Japanese Firm: The Sources of Competitive Strength.* Oxford, U.K.; New York: Oxford University Press, 1994.

688. Clough, Ronald, Chris Patrick, and Rosemary Yates. *Japanese Business Information: An Introduction.* Information in Focus. London: British Library, 1995.

689. Fruin, W. Mark. *The Japanese Enterprise System: Competitive Strategies and Cooperative Structures.* Oxford, U.K.: Clarendon Press; New York: Oxford University Press, 1992.

690. *How to Find Information about Japanese Companies and Industries.* International Series. Washington, DC: Washington Researchers, 1984.

691. Huddleston, Jackson N. *Gaijin Kaisha: Running a Foreign Business in Japan.* Armonk, NY: Sharpe, 1990.

692. Kamioka, Kazuyoshi. *Japanese Business Pioneers.* Union City, CA: Heian, 1988.

693. Kang, T. W. *Gaishi: The Foreign Company in Japan.* New York: Basic Books, 1990.

694. Khan, Sikander, and Hideki Yoshihara. *Strategy and Performance of Foreign Companies in Japan*. Westport, CT: Quorum Books, 1994.

695. Kishi, Nagami, and David Russell. *Successful Gaijin in Japan: How Foreign Companies are Making it in Japan*. Lincolnwood, IL: NTC Business Books, 1996.

696. Koren, Leonard. *Success Stories: How Eleven of Japan's most interesting Businesses came to be*. San Francisco, CA: Chronicle Books, 1990.

697. London, Nancy R. *Japanese Corporate Philanthropy*. New York: Oxford University Press, 1991.

698. Rafferty, Kevin. *Inside Japan's Power Houses: The Culture, Mystique and Future of Japan's Greatest Corporations*. London: Weidenfeld & Nicolson, 1995.

699. Sheard, Paul. *Japanese Firms, Finance and Markets*. Melbourne, Australia: Addison-Wesley, 1996.

700. Shimizu, Ryūei. *The Growth of Firms in Japan*. Tokyo: Keio Tsushin, 1980.

701. Tyrni, Ilari. *The Rate of Return, Risk, and the Financial Behaviour of the Japanese Industrial Firms*. Commentationes Scientiarum Socialium, 1984-26. Helsinki: Finnish Society of Sciences and Letters, 1984.

Costa Rica—Relations with

702. Nassar Soto, Ana Lucia. *Relaciones Japón-Costa Rica* [Relations Between Japan and Costa Rica]. San Jose, Costa Rica: VARITEC, 1991.

Costumes *See*: Art—Costumes

Crafts *See*: Art—Decorative

Criminal Justice

See also: Law

703. Castberg, A. Didrick. *Japanese Criminal Justice*. New York: Praeger, 1990.

68 AREA BIBLIOGRAPHY OF JAPAN

704. Parker, L. Craig. *The Japanese Police System Today: An American Perspective*. Tokyo; New York: Kodansha International, 1984.

705. Shikita, Minoru, and Shinichi Tsuchiya. *Crime and Criminal Policy in Japan: Analysis and Evaluation of the Showa Era, 1926-1988*. Research in Criminology. New York: Springer, 1992.

Criminals

706. Triplett, William. *Flowering of the Bamboo*. Kensington, MD: Woodbine House, 1985.

Dance

707. Alposta, Luis. *El Tango en Japón* [The Tango in Japan] Buenos Aires, Brazil: Corregidor, 1987.

708. Ashihara, Eiryo (Hidesato). *The Japanese Dance*. Tourist Library, new series 29. Tokyo: Japan Travel Bureau, 1964. Reprint: New York: Books for Libraries, 1980.

709. Holborn, Mark, et al. *Butoh, Dance of the Dark Soul*. Photographs, Ethan Hoffman. New York: Aperture Foundation, 1987.

710. Sellers-Young, Barbara. *Teaching Personality with Gracefulness: The Transmission of Japanese Cultural Values through Japanese Dance Theatre*. Lanham, MD: University Press of America, 1993.

Decorative Art *See*: Art—Decorative

Deflation

711. Wood, Christopher. *The End of Japan Inc.: And How the New Japan Will Look*. New York: Simon & Schuster, 1994.

Democracy

See also: 609

712. Hoshii, Iwao, and Peter J. Herzog. *Japan's Pseudo-Democracy*. Folkestone, U.K.: Japan Library, 1993.

713. Ishida, Takeshi, and Ellis S. Krauss, eds. *Democracy in Japan*. Pitt Series in Policy and Institutional Studies. Pittsburgh, PA: University of Pittsburgh Press, 1989.

714. Kersten, Rikki. *Democracy in Postwar Japan: Maruyama Masao and the Search for Autonomy.* Nissan Institute / Routledge Japanese Studies Series. London; New York: Routledge, 1996.

715. McNeil, Frank. *Democracy in Japan: The Emerging Global Concern.* New York: Crown, 1994.

Demography *See*: Population

Denmark—Relations with

716. Laderriere, Mette, ed. *Danes in Japan, 1868 to 1940: Aspects of Early Danish-Japanese Contacts.* Copenhagen: Akademisk Forlag, 1984.

Design *See*: Art—Design

Diaries

717. Bowring, Richard. *Murasaki Shikibu, her Diary and Poetic Memoirs: A Translation and Study.* Princeton Library of Asian Translations. Princeton, NJ: Princeton University Press, 1982.

718. Hérail, Francine. *Notes Journalières de Fujiwara no Michinaga, Ministre à la Cour de Hei.an (995-1018)* [Diary Notes of Fujiwara no Michinaga, Minister at the Heian Court (995-1018)]. Hautes Études Orientales, 23-24, etc. Geneva, Switzerland: Droz, 1987.

719. Keene, Donald. *Modern Japanese Diaries: The Japanese at Home and Abroad as Revealed through their Diaries.* New York: Henry Holt, 1995.

720. Keene, Donald. *Travelers of a Hundred Ages.* New York: Henry Holt, 1989.

721. Plutschow, Herbert, and Hideichi Fukuda, trans. *Four Japanese Travel Diaries of the Middle Ages.* Cornell University East Asia Papers, no. 25. Ithaca, NY: China-Japan Program, Cornell University, 1981.

722. Valensin, Giorgia, trans. *Diari di Dame di Corte nell'Antico Giappone* [Diaries of Court Ladies in Ancient Japan]. Struzzi, 375. Turin, Italy: Einaudi, 1990.

Dictionaries and Glossaries

723. *The AOTS Nihongo Dictionary for Practical Use.* Tokyo: Surie Nettowaku, 1993.

724. DeMente, Boye Lafayette. *NTC's Dictionary of Japan's Cultural Code Words.* National Textbook Language Dictionaries. Lincolnwood, IL: National Textbook, 1994.

725. Fujiwara, Shizuo, and Yuzuru Fujiwara. *The List of Multimeaning and Multidiscipline - Common Terms.* FID, 633. The Hague, Netherlands: FID, 1984.

726. Henshall, Kenneth G. *A Guide to Remembering Japanese Characters.* Rutland, VT: Tuttle, 1988.

727. *Kodansha's Furigana Japanese-English Dictionary: The Essential Dictionary for All Students of Japanese.* Tokyo; New York: Kodansha International, 1995.

728. Koine, Yoshio, ed. *Kenkyusha's New English-Japanese Dictionary.* 5th ed. Tokyo: Kenkyusha, 1980.

729. Masuda, Koh, ed. *Kenkyusha's New Japanese-English Dictionary.* 4th ed. Tokyo: Kenkyusha, 1974.

730. Nakao, Seigo, comp. *Random House Japanese-English English-Japanese Dictionary.* New York: Random House, 1995.

731. *The New Nelson: Japanese-English Character Dictionary: Based on the Classical Edition by Andrew N. Nelson.* Rutland, VT: Tuttle, 1997.

732. *The Oxford-Duden Pictorial English-Japanese Dictionary.* Oxford, U.K.; New York: Oxford University Press, 1989.

733. Spahn, Mark, Wolfgang Hadamitzky, and Kimiko Fujie-Winter. *The Kanji Dictionary.* Rutland, VT; Tokyo: Tuttle, 1996.

734. Vance, Timothy J. *Kodansha's Romanized Japanese-English Dictionary.* Tokyo; New York: Kodansha International, 1993.

735. Webb, James H. M. *A Guide to Modern Japanese Loanwords.* Tokyo: Japan Times, 1990.

Diplomacy

736. Chang, Richard T. *The Justice of the Western Consular Courts in Nineteenth-Century Japan.* Contributions in Intercultural and Comparative Studies, no. 10. Westport, CT: Greenwood, 1984.

737. Hirano, Minoru. *The Japanese Diplomacy, 1987-1993.* Tokyo, 1994.

738. Holland, Harrison M. *Managing Diplomacy: The United States and Japan.* Hoover Press Publications, 300. Stanford, CA: Hoover Institution Press, Stanford University, 1984.

Diplomatic Relations

739. Barnhart, Michael A. *Japan and the World Since 1868.* International Relations and the Great Powers. London; New York: Edward Arnold, 1995.

740. Drifte, Reinhard. *Japan's Foreign Policy.* Chatham House Papers. London: Royal Institute of International Affairs: Routledge, 1990.

741. Drifte, Reinhard. *Japan's Rise to International Responsibilities: The Case of Arms Control.* London: Athlone Press, 1990.

742. Fraser, T. G., and Peter Lowe. *Conflict and Amity in East Asia: Essays in Honor of Ian Nish.* Houndmills, U.K.: Macmillan Academic and Professional, 1992.

743. Giffard, Sidney. *Japan Among the Powers 1880-1990.* New Haven, CT: London: Yale University Press, 1994.

744. Inoguchi, Takashi. *Japan's International Relations.* Boulder, CO: Westview, 1991.

745. Ishihara, Shintaro. *The Japan That Can Say No.* Translated by Frank Baldwin. New York: Simon & Schuster, 1991.

746. Katz, Joshua D., and Tilly C. Friedman-Lichtschein, eds. *Japan's New World Role.* Boulder, CO: Westview, 1985.

747. Kitahara, Michio. *Children of the Sun: The Japanese and the Outside World.* Folkestone, U.K.: P. Norbury, 1989.

748. Lowe, Peter, and Herman Moeshart, eds. *Western Interactions with Japan: Expansion, the Armed Forces & Readjustment, 1859-1956.* Sandgate, U.K.: Japan Library, 1990.

749. Miyoshi, Masao, and H. D. Harootunian. *Japan in the World.* Durham, NC: Duke University Press, 1993.

750. Montgomery, Michael. *Imperialist Japan: The Yen to Dominate.* London: Christopher Helm, 1987.

751. Newland, Kathleen, ed. *The International Relations of Japan.* Houndmills, U.K.: Macmillan in association with Millenium: Journal of International Studies, 1990.

752. Wilkinson, Endymion Porter. *Japan Versus the West: Image and Reality.* Rev. ed. Harmondsworth, U.K.: Penguin, 1990.

Diplomatic Relations—Bibliography

753. Asada, Sadao, ed. *Japan and the World, 1853-1952: A Bibliographic Guide to Japanese Scholarship in Foreign Relations.* Studies of the East Asian Institute. New York: Columbia University Press, 1989.

Diplomatic Relations—Historical

754. Barr, Pat. *The Coming of the Barbarians: A Story of Western Settlement in Japan 1853-1870.* London; Melbourne, Australia: Macmillan, 1967. Reprint: Penguin Travel Library. London: Penguin, 1988.

755. Beasley, W. G. *Japan Encounters the Barbarian: Japanese Travelers in America and Europe, 1860-1873.* New Haven, CT: Yale University Press, 1995.

756. Beasley, W. G. *Japanese Imperialism, 1894-1945.* Oxford, U.K.: Clarendon Press; New York: Oxford University Press, 1987.

757. Hoare, James E. *Japan's Treaty Ports and Foreign Settlements: The Uninvited Guests, 1858-1899.* Meiji Japan Series, 1. Folkestone, UK: Japan Library, 1994.

758. Howe, Christopher. *The Origins of Japanese Trade Supremacy: Development and Technology in Asia from 1540 to the Pacific War.* Chicago, IL: University of Chicago Press, 1996.

Diplomatic Relations—Postwar

759. Akaha, Tsuneo, and Frank Langdon, eds. *Japan in the Posthegemonic World.* Boulder, CO: Rienner, 1993.

760. Chapman, J. W. M., R. Drifte, and I. T. M. Gow. *Japan's Quest for Comprehensive Security: Defence—Diplomacy—Dependence.* New York: St. Martin's Press, 1982.

761. Curtis, Gerald L., ed. *Japan's Foreign Policy after the Cold War: Coping with Change.* Studies of the East Asian Institute. Armonk, NY: Sharpe, 1993.

762. Edstrom, Bert. *Japan's Quest for a Role in the World: Roles ascribed to Japan Nationally and Internationally 1969-1982.* Edsbruk, Sweden: Akademitryck AB, 1988.

763. Friedman, George, and Meredith LeBard. *The Coming War With Japan.* New York: St. Martin's Press, 1991.

764. Garten, Jeffrey E. *A Cold Peace: America, Japan, Germany, and the Struggle for Supremacy.* New York: Times Books, 1992.

765. Horsley, William, and Roger Buckley. *Nippon: New Superpower: Japan since 1945.* London: BBC Books, 1990.

766. Saito, Shiro. *Japan at the Summit: Its Role in the Western Alliance and in Asian Pacific Co-operation.* London; New York: Routledge for the Royal Institute of International Affairs, London, 1990.

767. Sherwin, Martin J. *A World Destroyed: The Atomic Bomb and the Grand Alliance.* New York: Knopf, 1975. Reprint: *A World Destroyed: Hiroshima and the Origins of the Arms Race.* New York: Vintage Books, 1987.

Directories

768. Fields, Pamela L., ed. *On the Record re Japan: 1993 Media Directory of Japan Specialists in the United States.* Washington, DC: U.S.-Japan Conference on Cultural and Educational Interchange (CULCON), 1993.

769. Heginbotham, Erland, and Gretchen Shinoda, eds. *Focus Japan II: A Resource Guide to Japan-Oriented Organizations.* Washington, DC: Gateway Japan, 1993.

770. Japan Foundation. *Directory of Japan Specialists and Japanese Studies Institutions in the United States and Canada: Japanese Studies in the United States.* 3 vols. Japanese Studies Series, 24. Ann Arbor, MI: Association for Asian Studies, 1995.

771. *Overseas Japanese Studies Institutions / Kaigai Nihon Kenkyu Kikan Yoran.* 5th ed. Fukuoka, Japan: Fukuoka Unesco Association, 1994.

772. *Researchers, National Laboratories in Japan.* Saitama Prefecture, Japan: Research Development Corporation of Japan, 1993.

773. Shinoda, Gretchen, ed. *Academic Focus Japan: Programs and Resources in North America.* Washington, DC: Gateway Japan, 1994.

Dolls *See*: Art—Dolls

Drawing *See*: Art—Drawing

Dumping

774. Schwartzman, David. *The Japanese Television Cartel: A Study Based on Matsushita v. Zenith.* Studies in International Trade Policy. Ann Arbor, MI: University of Michigan Press, 1993.

Earthquakes

775. Miyamoto, Ryuji, and Akira Suzuki. *Kobe 1995: After the Earthquake.* Tokyo: Telescope / Workshop for Architecture and Urbanism, 1995.

776. Werner, Stuart D., and Stephen E. Dickenson, eds. *Hyogo-Ken Nanbu Earthquake of January 17, 1995: A Post-Earthquake Reconnaissance of Port Facilities.* New York: American Society of Civil Engineers, 1996.

East Asia—Relations with

777. Ellison, Herbert J. *Japan and the Pacific Quadrille: The Major Powers in East Asia.* Boulder, CO: Westview, 1987.

778. Nester, William R. *Japan's Growing Power over East Asia and the World Economy: End and Means.* Basingstoke, U.K.: Macmillan, 1990.

779. Seki, Mitsuhiro. *Beyond the Full-Set Industrial Structure: Japanese Industry in the New Age of East Asia.* LTCB International Library Selection, no. 2. Tokyo: LTCB International Library Foundation, 1994.

780. Toby, Ronald P. *State and Diplomacy in Early Modern Japan: Asia in the Development of the Tokugawa Bakufu.* Studies of the East Asian Institute. Princeton, NJ: Princeton University Press, 1984.

781. Wagner, Wieland. *Japans Aussenpolitik in der frühen Meiji-Zeit (1868-1894): die ideologische und politische Grundlegung des japanischen Führungsanspruchs in Ostasien* [Japan's Foreign Policy in the Early Meiji Period (1868-1894): The Ideological and Political Basis of Japan's Claim to Leadership in East Asia]. Beiträge zur Kolonial- und Überseegeschichte, Bd. 48. Stuttgart, Germany: F. Steiner, 1990.

Economic Assistance to Developing Nations

782. Arase, David. *Buying Power: The Political Economy of Japan's Foreign Aid.* Boulder, CO: Rienner, 1995.

783. Balessa, Bela A., and Marcus Noland. *Japan in the World Economy.* Washington, DC: Institute for International Economics, 1988.

784. Nester, William R. *Japan and the Third World: Patterns, Power, Prospects.* New York: St. Martin's Press, 1992.

785. Okita, Saburo. *The Developing Economies and Japan: Lessons in Growth.* Tokyo: University of Tokyo Press, 1980.

786. Okita, Saburo. *Japan in the World Economy of the 1980s.* Tokyo: University of Tokyo Press, 1989.

787. Rix, Alan. *Japan's Economic Aid: Policy-Making and Politics.* New York: St. Martin's Press, 1980.

788. Yasutomo, Dennis T. *The Manner of Giving: Strategic Aid and Japanese Foreign Policy.* Studies of the East Asian Institute. Lexington, MA: Lexington Books, 1986.

789. Yasutomo, Dennis T. *The New Multilateralism in Japan's Foreign Policy.* New York: St. Martin's Press, 1995.

Economic Development—Postwar

790. Allen, G. C. *The Japanese Economy.* New York: St. Martin's Press, 1981.

791. Allinson, Gary D., and Yasunori Sone. *Political Dynamics in Contemporary Japan.* Ithaca, NY: Cornell University Press, 1993.

792. *Economic Survey of Japan: 1990-1991.* Tokyo: Economic Agency, Japanese Government, 1992.

793. Hernadi, Andras. *Japan and the Pacific Region.* Iranyzatok a Vilaggazdasagban, sz. 42. Budapest, Hungary: Hungarian Scientific Council for World Economy, 1982.

794. Higashi, Chikara. *The Internationalization of the Japanese Economy.* 2d ed. Boston, MA: Kluwer Academic, 1990.

795. Hsu, Robert C. *The MIT Encyclopedia of the Japanese Economy.* Cambridge, MA: MIT Press, 1994.

796. Ishinomori, Shōtarō. *Japan Inc.: An Introduction to Japanese Economics: The Comic Book.* Translated by Betsey Scheiner. Berkeley, CA: University of California Press, 1988.

797. Itō, Takatoshi. *The Japanese Economy.* Cambridge, MA: MIT Press, 1992.

798. Itoh, Makoto. *The World Economic Crisis and Japanese Capitalism.* Houndmills, U.K.: Macmillan, 1990.

799. *Japan Marketing Handbook.* London: Euromonitor Publications, 1988.

800. Kosai, Yutaka, and Yoshitaro Ogino. *The Contemporary Japanese Economy.* Translated by Ralph Thompson. Armonk, NY: Sharpe, 1984.

801. Lincoln, Edward J. *Japan: Facing Economic Maturity.* Washington, DC: Brookings Institution, 1988.

802. McCormack, Gavan. *The Emptiness of Japanese Affluence.* Japan in the Modern World. Armonk, NY: Sharpe, 1996.

803. Mourdoukoutas, Panos. *Japan's Turn: The Interchange in Economic Leadership.* Lanham, MD: University Press of America, 1993.

804. Nakamura, Takafusa. *The Postwar Japanese Economy: Its Development and Structure, 1937-1994.* 2d ed. Tokyo: University of Tokyo Press, 1995.

805. Okabe, Mitsuaki, ed. *The Structure of the Japanese Economy: Changes in the Domestic and International Character.* Studies in the Modern Japanese Economy. New York: St. Martin's Press, 1995.

806. Okimoto, Daniel I., and Thomas P. Rohlen, eds. *Inside the Japanese System: Readings on Contemporary Society and Political Economy.* Stanford, CA: Stanford University Press, 1988.

807. Oppenheim, Phillip. *Japan Without Blinders: Coming to Terms with Japan's Economic Success.* Tokyo; New York: Kodansha International, 1992.

808. *The Political Economy of Japan.* Stanford, CA: Stanford University Press, 1987.

809. Shreshtha, Badri Prasad. *Post-war Economic Development of Japan: A Brief Review.* Bombay, India: Himalaya Publishing House, 1988.

810. Smith, Dennis B. *Japan Since 1945: The Rise of an Economic Superpower.* New York: St. Martin's Press, 1995.

811. Tabb, William K. *The Postwar Japanese System: Cultural Economy and Economic Transformation.* New York: Oxford University Press, 1995.

812. Tachi, Ryōichirō. *The Contemporary Japanese Economy: An Overview.* Translated by Richard Walker. Tokyo: University of Tokyo Press, 1993.

813. Takenaka, Heizo. *Contemporary Japanese Economy and Economic Policy.* Ann Arbor, MI: University of Michigan Press, 1991.

814. Uchino, Tatsurō. *Japan's Postwar Economy: An Insider's View of its History and its Future.* Translated by Mark A. Harbison. Tokyo; New York: Kodansha International, 1983.

815. Wood, Christopher. *The Bubble Economy: The Japanese Economic Collapse.* London: Sidgwick & Jackson, 1992.

816. Yamazawa, Ippei. *Economic Development and International Trade: The Japanese Model.* Honolulu, HI: Resource Systems Institute, East-West Center, 1990.

817. Ziemba, William T., and Sandra L. Schwartz. *Power Japan: How and Why the Japanese Economy Works.* Chicago, IL: Probus, 1992.

Economic Development—Prewar

818. Allen, G. C. *A Short Economic History of Modern Japan.* 4th ed. London: Macmillan, 1981.

819. Dore, Ronald, Radha Sinha, and Mari Sako, eds. *Japan and World Depression: Then and Now: Essays in Memory of E.F. Penrose.* Basingstoke, U.K.: Macmillan; New York: St. Martin's Press, 1987.

820. Lockwood, William W. *The Economic Development of Japan: Growth and Structural Change, 1868-1938.* Princeton, NJ: Princeton University Press, 1954. Reprint: Michigan Classics in Japanese Studies, no. 10. Ann Arbor, MI: Center for Japanese Studies, University of Michigan, 1993.

821. McPherson, W. J. *The Economic Development of Japan c. 1868-1941.* Studies in Economic and Social History. Houndmills, U.K.: Macmillan Education, 1987.

822. Minami, Ryōshin. *The Economic Development of Japan: A Quantitative Study.* 2d ed. Translated by Ralph Thompson, Kumie Fujimori, and Ryōshin Minami. New York: St. Martin's Press, 1986.

823. Nakamura, Takafusa, and Bernard R. G. Grace. *Economic Development of Modern Japan.* Tokyo: Ministry of Foreign Affairs, Japan, 1985.

824. Nakamura, Takafusa. *Economic Growth in Prewar Japan.* Translated by Robert A. Feldman. New Haven, CT: Yale University Press, 1983.

825. Nakamura, Takafusa. *Lectures on Modern Japanese Economic History, 1926-1994.* LTCB International Library Selection, no. 1. Tokyo: LTCB International Library Foundation, 1994.

826. Nariai, Osamu. *History of the Modern Japanese Economy.* Rev. ed. "About Japan" Series, 2. Tokyo: Foreign Press Center, Japan, 1994.

827. Tsuru, Shigeto. *The Economic Development of Modern Japan.* Aldershot, U.K.: Elgar, 1995.

828. Yoshihara, Kunio. *Japanese Economic Development: A Short Introduction.* 2d ed. Tokyo; New York: Oxford University Press, 1986.

Economic Forecasting

829. Fingleton, Eamonn. *Blindside: Why Japan is Still on Track to Overtake the U.S. by the Year 2000.* Boston, MA: Houghton Mifflin, 1995.

830. Hadfield, Peter. *Sixty Seconds that will Change the World: The Coming Tokyo Earthquake.* London Sidgwick & Jackson, 1991.

831. Makino, Noboru, ed. *Total Forecast: Japan, 1990s.* Cassell Asia Pacific Business Reference. London: Cassell, 1993.

832. Takahashi, K. *Limits of Survival: Forecasting the Future of Japan.* New Delhi; New York: Amerind, 1985.

Economic Foreign Relations

833. Bridges, Brian. *Japan: Hesitant Superpower.* Conflict Studies, 264. London: Research Institute for the Study of Conflict, 1993.

834. Emmott, Bill. *Japan's Global Reach: The Influences, Strategies, and Weaknesses of Japan's Multinational Companies.* London: Century, 1991.

835. Emmott, Bill. *The Sun Also Sets: Why Japan will not be Number One.* London: Simon & Schuster, 1989.

836. Garby, Craig, and Mary Brown Bullock, eds. *Japan: A New Kind of Superpower?* Washington, DC: Woodrow Wilson Center Press; Baltimore, MD: Johns Hopkins University Press, 1994.

837. Hatch, Walter. *Asia in Japan's Embrace: Building a Regional Production Alliance.* Cambridge Asia-Pacific Studies. Cambridge; New York: Cambridge University Press, 1996.

838. Leitch, Richard D., Akira Kato, and Martin E. Weinstein. *Japan's Role in the Post-Cold War World.* Contributions in Political Science, no. 361. Westport, CT: Greenwood, 1995.

839. Levine, Solomon B., and Koji Taira, eds. *Japan's External Economic Relations: Japanese Perspectives*. Annals of the American Academy of Political and Social Science, v. 513. Newbury Park, CA: Sage, 1991.

840. Lincoln, Edward J. *Japan's New Global Role*. Washington, DC: Brookings Institute, 1993.

841. Oppenheim, Phillip. *Trade Wars: Japan Versus the West*. London: Weidenfeld & Nicolson, 1992.

842. Suzuki, Yoshio. *Japan's Economic Performance and International Role*. Tokyo: University of Tokyo Press, 1989.

843. Takamiya, Susumu, and Keith Thurley, eds. *Japan's Emerging Multinationals: An International Comparison of Policies and Practices*. Tokyo: University of Tokyo Press, 1985.

844. Unger, Danny, and Paul Blackburn. *Japan's Emerging Global Role*. Boulder, CO: Rienner, 1993.

845. Uno, Kimio. *Technology, Investment, and Trade*. New York: Elsevier, 1991.

846. Woronoff, Jon. *Japan's Commercial Empire*. Armonk, NY: M. E. Sharpe; Houndmills, U.K.: Macmillan, 1984.

847. Woronoff, Jon. *World Trade War*. Tokyo: Lotus Press, 1983. Reprint: New York: Praeger, 1984.

Economic Policy

848. Allen, G. C. *Japan's Economic Policy*. New York: Holmes & Meier, 1980.

849. Angel, Robert C. *Explaining Economic Policy Failure: Japan in the 1969-71 International Monetary Crisis*. Studies of the East Asian Institute, Columbia University. New York: Columbia University Press, 1991.

850. Dore, Ronald Philip. *Taking Japan Seriously: A Confucian Perspective on Leading Economic Issues*. London: Athlone Press, 1987.

851. Fukui, Haruhiro, et al. *The Politics of Economic Change in Postwar Japan and West Germany*. New York: St. Martin's Press in association with St. Anthony's College, Oxford, 1993.

852. Huber, Thomas M. *Strategic Economy in Japan*. Boulder, CO: Westview, 1994.

853. Johnson, Chalmers A. *Japan, Who Governs?: The Rise of the Developmental State*. New York: Norton, 1995.

854. Kernell, Samuel, ed. *Parallel Politics: Economic Policymaking in the United States and Japan*. Tokyo: Japan Center for International Exchange; Washington, DC: Brookings Institution, 1991.

855. Komiya, Ryutaro. *The Japanese Economy: Trade, Industry, and Government*. Tokyo: University of Tokyo Press, 1990.

856. Kosai, Yutaka. *The Era of High-Speed Growth: Notes on the Postwar Japanese Economy*. Tokyo: University of Tokyo Press, 1986.

857. The Long Term Outlook Committee, Economic Council, Economic Planning Agency. *Japan in the Year 2000: Preparing Japan for an Age of Internationalization, the Aging Society and Maturity*. Tokyo: Japan Times, 1983.

858. Miyazaki, Isamu. *The Japanese Economy: What Makes it Tick*. Tokyo: Simul Press, 1990.

859. Nafziger, E. Wayne. *Learning from the Japanese: Japan's Pre-War Development and the Third World*. Armonk, NY: Sharpe, 1995.

860. Ohkawa, Kazushi, and Hirohisa Kohama. *Lectures on Developing Economies: Japan's Experience and its Relevance*. Tokyo: University of Tokyo Press, 1989.

861. Okimoto, Daniel I., ed. *Japan's Economy: Coping with Change in the International Environment*. Westview Special Studies on East Asia. Boulder, CO: Westview, 1982.

862. Osumi, Keisuke. *Economic Planning and Agreeability: An Investigation of Agreeable Plans in a General Class of Dynamic Economic Models*. Fukuoka, Japan: Kyushu University Press, 1986.

863. Schmiegelow, Michele, and Henrik Schmiegelow. *Strategic Pragmatism: Japanese Lessons in the Use of Economic Theory*. New York: Praeger, 1989.

864. Sheridan, Kyoko. *Governing the Japanese Economy*. Aspects of Political Economy. Cambridge, U.K.: Polity Press, 1993.

865. Shiraishi, Takashi. *Japan's Trade Policies 1945 to the Present Day*. London: Athlone Press, 1989.

866. Shishido, Toshio, and Ryuzo Sato, eds. *Economic Policy and Development: New Perspectives*. Dover, MA: Auburn House; London: Croom Helm, 1985.

867. Sugiyama, Chūhei. *Origin of Economic Thought in Modern Japan*. London; New York: Routledge, 1994.

868. Thurow, Lester C. *Head to Head: The Coming Economic Battle Among Japan, Europe and America*. New York: Morrow, 1992.

869. Woronoff, Jon. *Inside Japan, Inc*. 3d ed. Tokyo: Lotus Press, 1983.

870. Yoshikawa, Hiroshi. *Macroeconomics and the Japanese Economy*. Oxford, U.K.; New York: Oxford University Press, 1995.

Economy

871. Albritton, Robert, and Thomas T. Sekine, eds. *A Japanese Approach to Political Economy: Unoist Variations*. New York: St. Martin's Press, 1995.

872. Albritton, Robert. *A Japanese Reconstruction of Marxist Theory*. New York: St. Martin's Press, 1986.

873. Engler, Robert, and Yuriko Hayashi. *The Way of No Thinking: The Prophecies of Japan's Kunihiro Yamate*. Tulsa, OK: Council Oak Books, 1995.

874. Hosono, Kōichi. *Revolutional Thought About Economics*. Tokyo: Optima Press, 1993.

875. Morris-Suzuki, Tessa. *A History of Japanese Economic Thought*. Nissan Institute / Routledge Japanese Studies Series. London; New York: Routledge, 1989.

876. Sato, Ryuzo, and Takashi Negishi, eds. *Developments in Japanese Economics*. Boston, MA: Academic Press, 1989.

877. Sugiyama, Chūhei, and Hiroshi Mizuta, eds. *Enlightenment and Beyond: Political Economy Comes to Japan.* Tokyo: University of Tokyo Press, 1988.

878. Sugiyama, Chūhei. *Origins of Economic Thought in Modern Japan.* London; New York: Routledge, 1994.

879. Vogel, Ezra F. *Japan as Number One: Lessons for America.* Cambridge, MA: Harvard University Press, 1979. Reprint: Harper Torchbooks. New York: Harper & Row, 1985.

880. Woronoff, Jon. *The Japanese Economic Crisis.* 2d ed. Houndmills, U.K.: Macmillan; New York: St. Martin's Press, 1996.

881. Woronoff, Jon. *Japan as - anything but - Number One.* 2d ed. Houndmills, U.K.: Macmillan; Armonk, NY: Sharpe, 1996.

Economy—Bibliography

882. Alma, W. D. *Politics and Economics of Japan: An Annotated Bibliography.* Commack, NY: Nova Science, 1992.

883. Boger, Karl. *Postwar Industrial Policy in Japan: An Annotated Bibliography.* Metuchen, NJ: Scarecrow, 1988.

884. Jeffries, Francis M. *The English-Language Japanese Business Reference Guide.* Poolesville, MD: Jeffries & Associates, 1988.

885. Keresztesi, Michael, and Gary Cocozzoli. *Japan's Economic Challenge: A Bibliographic Sourcebook.* Garland Reference Library of Social Science; v. 425. New York: Garland, 1988.

886. Wray, William D. *Japan's Economy: A Bibliography of its Past and Present.* New York: Markus Wiener, 1989.

Education

See also: 588

887. Beauchamp, Edward R., and Richard Rubinger. *Education in Japan: A Source Book.* Garland Reference Library of Social Science, v. 329. Reference Books in International Education, vol. 5. New York: Garland, 1989.

888. Beauchamp, Edward R., ed. *Windows on Japanese Education.* Contributions to the Study of Education, no. 43. New York: Greenwood Press, 1991.

889. Goodman, Roger. *Japan's "International Youth": The Emergence of a New Class of Schoolchildren.* Oxford, U.K.: Clarendon Press; New York; Oxford University Press, 1990.

890. Leestma, Robert, and Herbert J. Walberg. *Japanese Educational Productivity.* Michigan Papers in Japanese Studies, no. 22. Ann Arbor, MI: Center for Japanese Studies, University of Michigan, 1992.

891. *The Modernization of Japanese Education.* 2 vols. Tokyo: International Society for Educational Information, 1986.

892. Passin, Herbert. *Society and Education in Japan.* Tokyo; New York: Kodansha International, 1982.

893. Shields, James J., Jr., ed. *Japanese Schooling: Patterns of Socialization, Equality, and Political Control.* 2 vols. University Park, PA: Pennsylvania State University Press, 1989.

894. Tokutake, Yasushi. *Education in Japan.* 2d revision. "About Japan" Series, 8. Tokyo: Foreign Press Center, Japan, 1995.

895. Tsukada, Mamoru. *Yobiko Life: A Study of the Legitimation Process of Social Stratification in Japan.* Japan Research Monograph, 11. Berkeley, CA: Institute of East Asian Studies, University of California, 1991.

896. White, Merry I. *The Japanese Educational Challenge: A Commitment to Children.* New York: Free Press; London: Collier Macmillan, 1987.

Education—Adults

897. Dore, Ronald Philip, Mari Sako. *How the Japanese Learn to Work.* The Nissan / Routledge Japanese Studies Series. London; New York: Routledge, 1989.

898. Okano, Kaori. *School to Work Transition in Japan: An Ethnographic Study.* The Language and Education Library, 3. Clevedon, U.K.; Philadelphia, PA: Multilingual Matters, 1993.

899. Thomas, J. E. *Learning Democracy in Japan: The Social Education of Japanese Adults*. London; Beverly Hills, CA: Sage, 1985.

900. Thomas, J. E. *Making Japan Work: The Origins, Education and Training of the Japanese Salaryman*. Sandgate, U.K.: Japan Library, 1993.

Education—Bibliography

901. Stevenson, Michael I. *Education in Japan: A Bibliography of Materials in English Since 1973*. Public Administration Series -- Bibliography, P-2093. Monticello, IL: Vance Bibliographies, 1987.

Education—Biography

902. Duke, Benjamin C., comp. and ed. *Ten Great Educators of Modern Japan: A Japanese Perspective*. Tokyo: University of Tokyo Press, 1989.

Education—Economic Aspects

903. Bowman, Mary Jean, Hideo Ikeda, and Yasumasa Tomoda. *Educational Choice and Labor Markets in Japan*. Chicago, IL: University of Chicago Press, 1981.

904. Kaneko, Motohisa. *Enrollment Expansion in Postwar Japan*. International Publication Series, no. 1. Higashi Senda-Machi, Hiroshima, Japan: Research Institute for Higher Education, Hiroshima University, 1987.

905. Stephens, Michael Dawson. *Japan and Education*. Houndmills, U.K.: Macmillan, 1991.

Education—Higher

906. Amano, Ikuo. *Education and Examination in Modern Japan*. Translated by William K. Cummings and Fumiko Cummings. Tokyo: University of Tokyo Press, 1990.

907. Haiducek, Nicholas J. *Japanese Education: Made in the U.S.A.* New York: Praeger, 1991.

Education—Preschool

See also: 587

908. Lewis, Catherine C. *Educating Hearts and Minds: Reflections on Japanese Preschool and Elementary Education.* Cambridge, U.K.; New York: Cambridge University Press, 1995.

909. Peak, Lois. *Learning to Go to School in Japan: The Transition from Home to Preschool Life.* Berkeley, CA: University of California Press, 1991.

Education—Private Schools

910. James, Estelle, and Gail Benjamin. *Public Versus Private Education: The Japanese Experiment.* PONPO Working Paper, 81. ISPS Working Paper, 2081. New Haven, CT: Institution for Social and Policy Studies, Yale University, 1984.

911. Rubinger, Richard. *Private Academies of Tokugawa Japan.* Princeton, NJ: Princeton University Press, 1982.

Education—School Discipline

912. Schoolland, Ken. *Shogun's Ghost: The Dark Side of Japanese Education.* New York: Bergin & Garvey, 1990.

Education—Secondary

913. Feiler, Bruce S. *Learning to Bow: An American Teacher in a Japanese School.* New York: Ticknor & Fields, 1991.

914. George, Paul S., Evan George, and Tadahiko Abiko. *The Japanese Junior High School: A View From the Inside.* Columbus, OH: National Middle School Association, 1989.

915. Rohlen, Thomas P. *Japan's High Schools.* Berkeley, CA: University of California Press, 1983.

Education—Vocational

916. Inoue, Ken. *The Education and Training of Industrial Manpower in Japan.* World Bank Staff Working Paper, no. 729. Washington, DC: World Bank, 1985.

917. Ishikawa, Toshio. *Vocational Training*. Rev. ed. Japanese Industrial Relations series, 7. Tokyo: Japan Institute of Labour, 1991.

918. Levine, Solomon Bernard, and Hisashi Kawada. *Human Resources in Japanese Industrial Development*. Princeton, NJ: Princeton University Press, 1980.

919. Lorriman, John, and Takashi Kenjo. *Japan's Winning Margins: Management, Training, and Education*. Oxford, U.K.; New York: Oxford University Press, 1994.

920. Thomas, J. E. *Making Japan Work: The Origins, Education and Training of the Japanese Salaryman*. Sandgate, U.K.: Japan Library, 1993.

Educational Anthropology

921. Finkelstein, Barbara, Anne E. Imamura, and Joseph J. Tobin, eds. *Transcending Stereotypes: Discovering Japanese Culture and Education*. Yarmouth, ME: Intercultural Press, 1991.

Educational Change

922. Stephens, Michael Dawson. *Education and the Future of Japan*. Sandgate, UK: Japan Library, 1991.

Educational Equalization

923. Cummings, William K. *Education and Equality in Japan*. Princeton, NJ: Princeton University Press, 1980.

Educational History

924. Beauchamp, Edward R., and James M. Vardaman. *Japanese Education Since 1945: A Documentary Study*. Armonk, NY: Sharpe, 1993.

925. Brunton, R. Henry. *Schoolmaster to an Empire: Richard Henry Brunton in Meiji Japan, 1868–1876*. Edited by Edward R. Beauchamp. Contributions in Asian Studies, 1053-1866, no. 1. New York: Greenwood, 1991.

926. Cummings, William K. *Education and Equality in Japan*. Princeton, NJ: Princeton University Press, 1980.

927. Kiyooka, Eiichi, trans., ed. *Fukuzawa Yukichi on Education: Selected Works*. Tokyo: University of Tokyo Press, 1985.

928. Lincicome, Mark Elwood. *Principle, Praxis, and the Politics of Educational Reform in Meiji Japan*. Honolulu, HI: University of Hawaii Press, 1995.

929. Roden, Donald F. *Schooldays in Imperial Japan: A Study in the Culture of a Student Elite*. Berkeley, CA: University of California Press, 1980.

930. Simmons, Cyril. *Growing Up and Going to School in Japan: Tradition and Trends*. Milton Keynes, U.K.; Philadelphia, PA: Open University Press, 1990.

Educational Policy

931. Aso, Makoto, and Ikuo Amano. *Education and Japan's Modernization*. Tokyo: Japan Times, 1983.

932. James, Estelle, and Gail Benjamin. *Public Policy and Private Education in Japan*. New York: St. Martin's Press, 1988.

933. *Mombusho, the Ministry of Education, Science and Culture, Japan*. Tokyo: Printing Bureau, Ministry of Finance, 1981.

934. Nishi, Toshio. *Unconditional Democracy: Education and Politics in Occupied Japan, 1945-1952*. Education and Society Series. Hoover Press Publication, 244. Stanford, CA: Hoover Institution Press, 1982.

Educational Reform

935. Schoppa, Leonard J. *Education Reform in Japan: A Case of Immobilist Politics*. Nissan Institute / Routledge Japanese Studies Series. London; New York: Routledge, 1991.

936. Tsuchimochi, Gary Hoichi. *Education Reform in Postwar Japan: The 1946 U.S. Education Mission*. Tokyo: University of Tokyo Press, 1993.

Elderly

937. Butler, Robert N., and Kenzo Kiikuni, eds. *Who is Responsible for my Old Age?* New York: Springer, 1993.

938. Campbell, John Creighton. *How Policies Change: The Japanese Government and the Aging Society.* Princeton, NJ: Princeton University Press, 1992.

939. Clark, Robert Louis. *Retirement Systems in Japan.* Ralph H. Blanchard Memorial Endowment Series, v. 4. Homewood, IL: Irwin for the Pension Research Council of the Wharton School, 1991.

940. Formanek, Susanne. *Denn dem Alter kann keiner entfliehen: altern und Alter im Japan der Nara- und Heian-Zeit* [For No-one Can Escape Old Age: Aging and Old Age in Japan of the Nara and Heian Period]. Sitzungsberichte Österreichische Akademie der Wissenschaften Philosophisch-Historische Klasse, 618. Bd; Beiträge zur Kultur und Geistesgeschichte Asiens, Nr. 13. Vienna: Verlag der Österreichischen Akademie der Wissenschaften, 1994.

941. Getreuer-Kargl, Ingrid. *Ende der Dynamik?: eine Expertenbefragung zur Alterung der japanischen Gesellschaft* [The End of the Dynamic: A Survey of Experts on the Change of Japanese Society]. Beiträge zur Japanologie, Bd. 28. Vienna: Institut für Japanologie der Universität Wien, 1990.

942. Getreuer-Kargl, Ingrid. *Old Age in Japan: Long-term Statistics.* Beiträge zur Japanologie, Bd. 24. Vienna: Institute für Japanologie, Universität Wien, 1987.

943. Hakuhodo Institute of Life and Living. *Japanese Seniors, Pioneers in their Era of Aging Populations.* Changing Lifestyles in Japan, v. 4. Tokyo: Hakuhodo Institute of Life and Living, 1984.

944. Kinoshita, Yasuhito, and Christie W. Kiefer. *Refuge of the Honored: Social Organization in a Japanese Retirement Community.* Berkeley, CA: University of California Press, 1992.

945. Linhart, Sepp. *Organisationsformen alter Menschen in Japan: Selbstverwirklichung durch Hobbies, Weiterbildung, Arbeit* [Organizational Forms of Elderly People in Japan: Fulfillment through Hobbies, Continued Education, and Work]. Beiträge zur Japanologie, Bd. 19. Vienna: Institute für Japanologie, Universität Wien, 1983.

946. Ohbuchi, Hiroshi, et al. *Aging of the Japanese Economy.* Edited by the Institute of Economic Research, Chuo University. Tokyo: Chuo University Press, 1992.

947. Palmore, Erdman Ballagh, and Daisaku Maeda. *The Honorable Elders Revisited: A Revised Cross-Cultural Analysis of Aging in Japan*. Durham, NC: Duke University Press, 1985.

948. Schulz, James H. *When "Life-time Employment" ends: Older Worker Programs in Japan: Final Report*. Waltham, MA: Policy Center on Aging, Heller School, Brandeis University, 1988.

949. Takayama, Noriyuki. *The Greying of Japan: An Economic Perspective on Public Pensions*. Economic Research Series, no. 30. Tokyo: Kinokuniya, 1992.

Elderly—Bibliography

950. Linhart, Sepp, and Fleur Woss. *Old Age in Japan: An Annotated Bibliography of Western-language Materials*. Beiträge zur Japanologie, Bd. 20. Vienna: Institut für Japanologie, Universität Wien, 1984.

951. Maderdonner, Megumi. *Old Age in Japan: An Annotated Bibliography of Japanese Books*. Beiträge zur Japanologie, Bd. 25. Vienna: Institute für Japanologie, Universität Wien, 1987.

Elections

952. Campbell, John Creighton, ed. *Parties, Candidates, and Voters in Japan: Six Quantitative Studies*. Michigan Papers in Japanese Studies, no. 2. Ann Arbor, MI: Center for Japanese Studies, University of Michigan, 1981.

953. Curtis, Gerald L. *Election Campaigning Japanese Style*. Tokyo; New York: Kodansha International, 1983.

954. Flanagan, Scott C., et al. *The Japanese Voter*. New Haven, CT: Yale University Press, 1991.

955. Reed, Steven R. *Japan Election Data: The House of Representatives, 1947-1990*. Ann Arbor, MI: Center for Japanese Studies, University of Michigan, 1992.

Embroidery *See*: Art—Embroidery

Encyclopedias

956. *The Cambridge Encyclopedia of Japan.* Cambridge, U.K.; New York: Cambridge University Press, 1993.

957. *Japan: An Illustrated Encyclopedia.* 2 vols. Tokyo; New York: Kodansha, 1993.

958. *Kodansha Encyclopedia of Japan.* 9 vols. Tokyo; New York: Kodansha, 1983.

959. *Kodansha Encyclopedia of Japan: Supplement.* Tokyo; New York: Kodansha International, 1986.

960. Perkins, Dorothy. *Encyclopedia of Japan: Japanese History and Culture, from Abacus to Zori.* New York: Facts on File, 1991.

Environment

961. Barrett, Brendan F. D., and Riki Therivel. *Environmental Policy and Impact Assessment in Japan.* Natural Environment - Problems and Management Series. London; New York: Routledge, 1991.

962. Foljanty-Jost, Gesine. *Kommunale Umweltpolitik in Japan: Alternativen zur rechtsformlichen Steuerung* [Local Environmental Policy in Japan: Alternatives to Legal Control]. Mitteilungen des Instituts für Asienkunde Hamburg, Nr.167. Hamburg, Germany: Institut für Asienkunde, 1988.

963. Gresser, Julian. *Environmental Law in Japan.* Studies in East Asian Law. Harvard Studies in East Asian Law. Cambridge, MA: MIT Press, 1981.

964. Huddle, Norie, Michael Reich, and Nahum Stiskin. *Island of Dreams: Environmental Crisis in Japan.* Rochester, VT: Schenkman Books, 1987.

965. McKean, Margaret A. *Environmental Protest and Citizen Politics in Japan.* Berkeley, CA; London: University of California Press, 1981.

966. Mishima, Akio. *Bitter Sea: The Human Cost of Minamata Disease.* Tokyo: Kosei, 1992.

967. Tsuru, Shigeto, and Helmut Weidner, eds. *Environmental Policy in Japan.* Berlin: Edition Sigma, 1989.

968. Ui, Jun, ed. *Industrial Pollution in Japan*. Technology Transfer, Transformation, and Development. Tokyo: United Nations University Press, 1992.

Erotica *See*: Art—Prints—Erotica

Espionage

969. Deacon, Richard. *Kempei Tai: A History of the Japanese Secret Service*. New York: Beaufort Books, 1983.

970. Hansen, James H. *Japanese Intelligence: The Competitive Edge*. Washington, DC: National Intelligence Book Center, 1996.

971. Mader, Julius. *Dr.-Sorge-Report: ein Dokumentarbericht über Kundschafter des Friedens mit ausgewählten Artikeln von Richard Sorge* [Dr. Sorge-Report: A Documentary Report about Peacetime Spies, with Selected Articles by Richard Sorge]. Berlin, Germany: Militärverlag der Deutschen Demokratischen Republik, 1984.

972. Matthews, Tony. *Shadows Dancing: Japanese Espionage Against the West, 1939-1945*. London: Hale, 1993.

973. Prange, Gordon, Donald M. Goldstein, and Katherine V. Dillon. *Target Tokyo: The Story of the Sorge Spy Ring*. New York: McGraw-Hill, 1984.

Ethnic Relations—Jews

974. Goodman, David G., and Masanori Miyazawa. *Jews in the Japanese Mind: The History and Uses of a Cultural Stereotype*. New York: Free Press, 1995.

975. Shillony, Ben-Ami. *The Jews & the Japanese: The Successful Outsiders*. Rutland, VT: Tuttle, 1992.

Ethnology

976. Akazawa, Takeru, and C. Melvin Aikens, eds. *Prehistoric Hunter-Gatherers in Japan: New Research Methods*. Bulletin (Tokyo Daigaku, Sogo Kenkyu Shiryokan), no. 27. Tokyo: University of Tokyo Press, 1986.

977. Ben-Ari, Eyal, Brian Moeran, and James Valentine, eds. *Unwrapping Japan: Society and Culture in Anthropological Perspective.* Japanese Studies. Manchester, U.K.: Manchester University Press, 1990.

978. Crawford, Gary W. *Paleoethnobotany of the Kameda Peninsula Jomon.* Anthropological Papers, Museum of Anthropology, University of Michigan, no. 73. Ann Arbor, MI: Museum of Anthropology, University of Michigan, 1983.

979. Dale, Peter N. *The Myth of Japanese Uniqueness.* Nissan Institute / Croom Helm Japanese Studies Series. London: Croom Helm; Oxford, U.K.: Nissan Institute for Japanese Studies, 1986.

980. Hendry, Joy, and Jonathan Webber, eds. *Interpreting Japanese Society: Anthropological Approaches.* JASO Occasional Papers, no. 5. Oxford, U.K.: JASA, 1986.

981. Houchins, Chang-su. *Artifacts of Diplomacy: Smithsonian Collections from Commodore Mathew Perry's Japan Expedition (1853-1854).* Smithsonian Contributions to Anthropology, no. 37. Washington, DC: Smithsonian Institution Press, 1995.

982. Ivy, Marilyn. *Discourses of the Vanishing: Modernity, Phantasm, Japan.* Chicago, IL: University of Chicago Press, 1995.

983. Moeran, Brian. *Ōkubo Diary: Portrait of a Japanese Valley.* Stanford, CA: Stanford University Press, 1985.

984. Oblas, Peter B. *Perspectives on Race and Culture in Japanese Society: The Mass Media and Ethnicity.* Lewiston, ME: Mellen Press, 1995.

985. Ohnuki-Tierney, Emiko. *Rice as Self: Japanese Identities through Time.* Princeton, NJ: Princeton University Press, 1993.

986. Tobin, Joseph J., ed. *Re-Made in Japan: Everyday Life and Consumer Taste in a Changing Society.* New Haven, CT: Yale University Press, 1992.

Ethnopsychology

987. Buruma, Ian. *The Wages of Guilt: Memories of War in Germany and Japan.* New York: Farrar, Straus, Giroux, 1994.

Europe—Relations with

988. Andersson, Thomas, ed. *Japan, a European Perspective*. London: Macmillan; New York: St. Martin's Press, 1993.

989. Bownas, Geoffrey. *Japan and the New Europe: Industrial Strategies and Options in the 1990's*. Special Report, no. 2072. London; New York: Economist Intelligence Unit, 1991.

990. Conte-Helm, Marie. *The Japanese and Europe: Economic and Cultural Encounters*. London; Atlantic Highlands, NJ: Athlone Press, 1996.

991. Daniels, Gordon, and Reinhard Drifte, eds. *Europe and Japan: Changing Relationships Since 1945*. Woodchurch, U.K.: Paul Norbury, 1986.

992. Massarella, Derek. *A World Elsewhere: Europe's Encounter with Japan in the Sixteenth and Seventeenth Centuries*. New Haven, CT: Yale University Press, 1990.

993. Maull, Hans W., and Volker Fuhrt, eds. *Japan und Europa — getrennte Welten?* [Japan and Europe — Separate Worlds?]. Schriften des Forschungsinstituts der Deutschen Gesellschaft für Auswärtige Politik e.V. Frankfurt, Germany; New York: Campus, 1993.

994. Nester, William R. *European Power and the Japanese Challenge*. New York: New York University Press, 1993.

995. Rothacher, Albrecht. *Economic Diplomacy Between the European Community and Japan, 1959-1981*. Aldershot, U.K.: Gower, 1983.

996. Rothermund, Dietmar. *Asian Trade and European Expansion in the Age of Mercantilism*. Perspectives in History, v. 1. New Delhi: Manohar, 1981.

997. Tsoukalis, Loukas, and Maureen White, eds. *Japan and Western Europe: Conflict and Cooperation*. Studies in International Political Economy. London: Frances Pinter, 1982.

998. Wilkinson, Endymion. *Japan Versus Europe: A History of Misunderstanding*. Harmondsworth, U.K.: Penguin, 1983.

Exports

999. March, Robert M. *The Honourable Customer.* London: Pitman, 1991.

1000. Marsh, Felicity. *Japan's Next Export Success: The Financial Services Industry.* EIU Special Report, no. 1066. London; New York: Crawford's The Economist Publications, 1986.

1001. Sugiyama, S. *Japan's Industrialization in the World Economy, 1859-1899: Export Trade and Overseas Competition.* London; Atlantic Highlands, NJ: Athlone Press, 1988.

Family

1002. Cowan, Philip A., ed. *Family, Self, and Society: Toward a New Agency for Family Research.* Hillsdale, NJ: Lawrence Erlbaum, 1993.

1003. Hamabata, Matthews Masayuki. *Crested Kimono: Power and Love in the Japanese Business Family.* Ithaca, NY: Cornell University Press, 1990.

1004. Jeremy, Michael, and M. E. Robinson. *Ceremony and Symbolism in the Japanese Home.* Japanese Studies. Manchester, U.K.; New York: Manchester University Press, 1989.

1005. Long, Susan Orpett. *Family Change and the Life Course in Japan.* Cornell University East Asia Papers, no. 44. Ithaca, NY: China-Japan Program, Cornell University, 1987.

1006. *Population and the Family in Japan.* "Population and Development" Series, no. 9. Tokyo: Asian Population and Development Association, 1989.

1007. Wagatsuma, Hiroshi, and George De Vos. *Heritage of Endurance: Family Patterns and Delinquency Formation in Urban Japan.* Berkeley, CA: University of California Press, 1984.

1008. White, Merry I. *The Japanese Overseas: Can They Go Home Again?* New York: Free Press, London: Collier Macmillan, 1988.

1009. Yuzawa, Yasuhiko. *Japanese Families.* "About Japan" Series, 19. Tokyo: Foreign Press Center, Japan, 1994.

Fans *See*: Art—Fans

Farming

1010. Fukuoka, Masanobu. *The Natural Way of Farming: The Theory and Practice of Green Philosophy.* Rev. ed. Translated by Frederic P. Metreaud. Tokyo: Japan Publications, 1987.

1011. Jussaume, Raymond Adelard. *Japanese Part-time Farming: Evolution and Impacts.* Henry A. Wallace Series on Agricultural History and Rural Studies. Ames, IA: Iowa State University Press, 1991.

1012. McClure, H. Elliott. *Inago — Children of Rice.* San Diego, CA: Libra, 1993.

1013. Rutherford, John. *Rice Dominant Land Settlement in Japan: A Study of Systems within Systems.* Sydney, Australia: Department of Geography, University of Sydney, 1984.

Fascism

1014. Masao, Nishikawa, and Miyachi Masato, eds. *Japan zwischen den Kriegen: eine Auswahl japanischer Forschungen zu Faschismus und Ultranationalismus* [Japan Between the Wars: A Selection of Japanese Studies on Fascism and Ultra-Nationalism]. Mitteilungen der Deutschen Gesellschaft für Natur- und Völkerkunde Ostasiens, Bd. 108. Hamburg, Germany: Gesellschaft für Natur- und Völkerkunde Ostasiens, 1990.

Fauna

1015. Massey, Joseph A., et al. *A Field Guide to the Birds of Japan.* Edited by Jane Washburn Robinson. Tokyo: Wild Bird Society of Japan; Tokyo; New York: Kodansha International, 1982.

Feudalism

1016. Jansen, Marius B. *Warrior Rule in Japan.* New York: Cambridge University Press, 1995.

1017. Mass, Jeffrey P., and William B. Hauser, eds. *The Bakufu in Japanese History.* Stanford, CA: Stanford University Press, 1985.

1018. Taranczewski, Detlev. *Lokale Grundherrschaft und Ackerbau in der Kamakura-Zeit: dargestellt anhand des Nitta no shō in der Provinz Kōzuke* [Local Land Control and Agriculture in the Kamakura period: Compiled by Means of the Nitta no Shō in the Kōzuke Province]. Bonner Zeitschrift für Japanologie, Bd. 10. Bonn, Germany: Förderverein "Bonner Zeitschrift für Japanologie," 1988.

Finance

1019. Ballon, Robert J., and Iwao Tomita. *The Financial Behavior of Japanese Corporations.* Tokyo; New York: Kodansha International, 1988.

1020. Bronte, Stephen. *Japanese Finance: Markets and Institutions.* London: Euromoney Publications, 1982.

1021. Burstein, Daniel. *Yen! Japan's New Financial Empire and its Threat to America.* New York: Simon & Schuster, 1988.

1022. Fabozzi, Frank J., ed. *The Japanese Bond Markets: An Overview & Analysis.* Chicago, IL: Probus, 1990.

1023. Feldman, Robert Alan. *Japanese Financial Markets: Deficits, Dilemmas, and Deregulation.* Cambridge, MA: MIT Press, 1986.

1024. Foundation for Advanced Information and Research, Japan (FAIR). *Japan's Financial Markets.* 2d ed. FAIR Fact Series, 2. Tokyo: FAIR, 1991.

1025. Goldsmith, Raymond William. *The Financial Development of Japan, 1868-1977.* New Haven, CT: Yale University Press, 1983.

1026. Goodhart, Charles A. E., and George Sutija, eds. *Japanese Financial Growth.* Basingstoke, U.K.: Macmillan, 1990.

1027. Horne, James. *Japan's Financial Markets: Conflict and Consensus in Policymaking.* Sydney; Boston, MA: Allen & Unwin in association with Australia-Japan Research Center, Australian National University, 1985.

1028. *Japan Laws and Regulations Concerning Duties and Customs Procedures.* Tokyo: Japan Tariff Association, 1981.

1029. *Japan's Financial Markets.* 2d ed. FAIR Fact series II. Tokyo: Foundation for Advanced Information and Research, 1991.

1030. Katō, Kōzō, et al. *Policy-Based Finance: The Experience of Postwar Japan.* World Bank Discussion Papers, 221. Washington, DC: World Bank, 1994.

1031. McKenzie, Colin, and Michael Stutchbury. *Japanese Financial Markets and the Role of the Yen.* North Sydney, Australia: Allen & Unwin in association with Australia-Japan Research Centre, Australian National University, 1992.

1032. Moran, Michael. *The Politics of the Financial Services Revolution: The USA, UK, and Japan.* Houndmills, U.K.: Macmillan, 1991.

1033. Robins, Brian. *Tokyo: A World Financial Centre.* London: Euromoney Publications, 1987.

1034. Rosenbluth, Frances McCall. *Financial Politics in Contemporary Japan.* Studies of the East Asian Institute. Ithaca, NY: Cornell University Press, 1989.

1035. Shibata, Tokue, ed. *Public Finance in Japan.* Tokyo: University of Tokyo Press, 1986.

1036. Suzuki, Yoshio. *The Japanese Financial System.* Oxford, U.K.: Clarendon Press; New York: Oxford University Press, 1992.

1037. Suzuki, Yoshio. *Money, Finance, and Macroeconomic Performance in Japan.* Translated by Robert Alan Feldman. New Haven, CT: Yale University Press, 1986.

1038. Tatewaki, Kazuo. *Banking and Finance in Japan: An Introduction to the Tokyo Market.* London: Routledge, 1991.

1039. Troughton, Helen. *Japanese Finance: The Impact of Deregulation.* London: Euromoney, 1986.

1040. Viner, Aron. *The Emerging Power of Japanese Money.* Homewood, IL: Dow Jones-Irwin, 1988.

1041. Viner, Aron. *Inside Japanese Financial Markets.* Homewood, IL: Dow Jones-Irwin, 1988.

1042. *What's What in Japan's Financial System.* Tokyo: Japan Times, 1990.

Financial Law *See*: Law—Financial

Fishery

1043. Howell, David Luke. *Capitalism from Within: Economy, Society, and the State in a Japanese Fishery.* Berkeley, CA: University of California Press, 1995.

1044. Kalland, Arne. *Shingū: A Japanese Fishing Community.* Scandinavian Institute of Asian Studies Monograph Series, 0069-1712, no. 44. London: Curzon Press, 1980.

1045. Kasuya, Toshio, and Yasuharu Izumizawa. *The Fishery-Dolphin Conflict in the Iki Island Area of Japan.* Washington, DC: U.S. Marine Mammal Commission, 1981.

1046. Statistics and Information Dept. Ministry of Agriculture, Forestry and Fisheries, Government of Japan, ed. *The Eighth Fishery Census of Japan, 1988.* Tokyo: Association of Agriculture-Forestry Statistics, 1991.

Flora

1047. Itō, Ihē, and John L. Creech. *A Brocade Pillow: Azaleas of Old Japan.* Translated by Kaname Katō. New York: Weatherhill, 1984.

1048. Takama, Shinji. *Bamboo of Japan: Splendor in Four Seasons.* Tokyo: Graphic-sha / Japan Publications, 1986.

Folk Art *See*: Art—Folk

Folk Literature *See*: Literature—Folk

Folk Religion *See*: Religion—Folk

Folklore

1049. Crump, Thomas. *The Japanese Numbers Game: The Use and Understanding of Numbers in Modern Japan.* Nissan Institute/Routledge Japanese Studies Series. London; New York: Routledge, 1992.

1050. Dorson, Richard Mercer, ed. *Studies in Japanese Folklore.* Indiana University Folklore Series, no. 17. Bloomington, IN: Indiana University Press, 1963. Reprint: Folklore of the World. New York: Arno Press, 1980.

1051. Ishida, Eiichirō. *The Kappa Legend.* Asian Folklore and Social Life Monographs, v. 123. Taipei, Taiwan, Republic of China: Chinese Association for Folklore, 1984.

1052. Iwasaka, Michiko, and Barre Toelken. *Ghosts and the Japanese: Cultural Experience in Japanese Death Legends.* Logan, UT: Utah State University Press, 1994.

1053. Kawada, Minoru. *The Origin of Ethnography in Japan: Yanagita Kunio and his Times.* Translated by Toshiko Kishida-Ellis. Japanese Studies. London; New York: Kegan Paul International, 1993.

1054. Koschman, J. Victor, Ōiwa Keibō, and Yamanashita Shinji, eds. *International Perspectives on Yanagita Kunio and Japanese Folklore Studies.* Cornell University East Asia Papers, no. 37. Ithaca, NY: China-Japan Program, Cornell University, 1985.

1055. Morse, Ronald A. *Yanagita Kunio and the Folklore Movement: The Search for Japan's National Character and Distinctiveness.* Garland Folklore Library, 2. Garland Reference Library of the Humanities, vol. 1286. New York: Garland, 1990.

Folktales

1056. Antoni, Klaus J. *Der weisse Hase von Inaba: vom Mythos zum Märchen Analyse eines japanischen "Mythos der ewigen Wiederkehr" vor dem Hintergrund altchinesischen und zirkumpazifischen Denkens* [The White Hare of Inaba: From Myth to Fairy Tale, Analysis of a Japanese "Myth of Eternal Return" Against the Background of Ancient Chinese and Pacific Ring Thought]. Münchener Ostasiatische Studien, Bd. 28. Wiesbaden, Germany: Franz Steiner, 1982.

1057. Kawai, Hayao. *The Japanese Psyche: Major Motifs in the Fairy Tales of Japan.* Dallas, TX: Spring Publications, 1988.

1058. Mayer, Fanny Hagin, comp., trans. *Ancient Tales in Modern Japan: An Anthology of Japanese Folk Tales.* Bloomington, IN: Indiana University Press, 1985.

1059. Mayer, Fanny Hagin, trans., ed. *The Yanagita Kunio Guide to the Japanese Folk Tale.* Bloomington, IN: Indiana University Press, 1986.

1060. Tyler, Royall, ed., trans. *Japanese Tales.* Pantheon Fairy Tale & Folklore Library. New York: Pantheon Books, 1987.

Food and Drink

1061. Antoni, Klaus J. *Miwa - der heilige Trank: Zur Geschichte und religiösen Bedeutung des Alkoholischen Getrankes (Sake) in Japan* [Miwa - the Sacred Drink: On the History and Religious Meaning of the Alcoholic Beverage (Sake) in Japan]. Munchener Ostasiatische Studien, Bd. 45. Stuttgart, Germany: Franz Steiner Verlag Wiesbaden, 1988.

1062. Fruin, W. Mark. *Kikkoman: Company, Clan, and Community.* Harvard Studies in Business History, 35. Cambridge, MA: Harvard University Press, 1983.

1063. Kondō, Hiroshi. *Sake: A Drinker's Guide.* Tokyo; New York: Kodansha International, 1984.

1064. Otsuka, Shigeru. *Japanese Food Past and Present.* "About Japan" Series, 21. Tokyo: Foreign Press Center, Japan, 1996.

1065. Richie, Donald. *A Taste of Japan: Food Fact and Fable: What the People Eat: Customs and Etiquette.* Tokyo; New York: Kodansha International, 1985.

1066. Shurtleff, William, and Akiko Aoyagi, comps. *Kikkoman and other Major Japanese Soy Sauce Manufacturers: Bibliography and Sourcebook, 1645 to 1994: Detailed Information on 484 Published Documents (Extensively Annotated Bibliography), 46 Commercial Soy Products, 45 Original Interviews (many full text) and Overviews, 43 Unpublished Archival Documents.* Bibliographies and Sourcebooks on Soya series. Lafayette, CA: Soyfoods Center, 1994.

1067. Shurtleff, William, and Akiko Aoyagi, comps. *Bibliography of Soy Sauce: From A.D. 535 to 1988: With 2150+ References, Subject and Country Index, Partially Annotated.* Bibliographies of Soya, vol. 6. Lafayette, CA: Soyfoods Center, 1988.

Foreign Exchange

1068. Athukoralge, Premachandra, and Jayant Menon. *Exchange Rate Changes and Export Pricing Behavior in Japan.* Pacific Economic Paper, no. 222. Canberra: Australia-Japan Research Centre, 1993.

1069. Iwami, Tōru. *Japan in the International Financial System.* Studies in the Modern Japanese Economy. Translation edited by Colin McKenzie. New York: St. Martin's Press, 1995.

1070. Komiya, Ryūtarō, Miyako Suda. *Japan's Foreign Exchange Policy, 1971-1982.* North Sydney, Australia: Allen L. Unwin, 1991.

1071. Kwan, C.H. *Economic Interdependence in the Asia-Pacific Region: Towards a Yen Bloc.* London; New York: Routledge, 1994.

Foreign Relations *See*: Diplomatic Relations

Foreign Views on Japan

1072. Bartu, Friedemann. *The Ugly Japanese: Nippon's Economic Empire in Asia.* Singapore; New York: Longman, 1992.

1073. Breger, Rosemary Anne. *Myth and Stereotype: Images of Japan in the German Press and in Japanese Self-perception.* Europäische Hochschulschriften. Reihe XXII, Soziologie, Bd. 199. Frankfurt am Main, Germany; New York: P. Lang, 1990.

1074. Butor, Michel. *Le Japon depuis la France: un Rêve à l'Ancre* [Japan Since France: An Anchored Dream]. Brèves Littérature. Paris: Hatier, 1995.

1075. Constantino, Renato, ed. *Southeast Asian Perceptions of Japan.* Tokyo: Zensei; Quezon City: Karrel, 1991.

1076. Johnson, Sheila K. *The Japanese Through American Eyes.* Stanford, CA: Stanford University Press, 1988.

1077. Littlewood, Ian. *The Idea of Japan: Western Images, Western Myths.* London: Secker & Warburg, 1996.

1078. Pound, Ezra. *Ezra Pound & Japan: Letters & Essays.* Redding Ridge, CT: Black Swan Books, 1987.

1079. Wilkinson, Endymion Porter. *Japan Versus the West: Image and Reality.* Rev. ed. London; New York: Penguin, 1990.

1080. Yokoyama, Toshio. *Japan in the Victorian Mind: A Study of Stereotyped Images of a Nation, 1850-80.* Basingstoke, U.K.: Macmillan, 1987.

Foreigners in Japan

1081. Allen, G. C. *Appointment in Japan: Memories of Sixty Years.* London: Athlone Press, 1983.

1082. Ballescas, Ma. Rosario Piquero. *Filipino Entertainers in Japan: An Introduction.* Quezon City: Foundation for Nationalist Studies, 1992.

1083. Barr, Pat. *The Deer Cry Pavilion: A Story of Westerners in Japan 1868-1905.* London: Macmillan, 1968. Reprint: London: Penguin, 1988.

1084. Beauchamp, Edward R., and Akira Iriye, eds. *Foreign Employees in Nineteenth-Century Japan.* Westview Special Studies on East Asia. Boulder, CO: Westview, 1990.

1085. Brunton, R. Henry. *Building Japan, 1868-1876.* Sandgate, U.K.: Japan Library, 1991.

1086. Cooper, Michael. *They Came to Japan: An Anthology of European Reports on Japan, 1543-1640.* University of California, Berkeley. Center for Japanese and Korean Studies. Publications. Berkeley, CA: University of California Press, 1965. Reprint: Michigan Classics in Japanese Studies, 15. Ann Arbor, MI: Center for Japanese Studies, The University of Michigan, 1995.

1087. Cortazzi, Hugh, ed. *Mitford's Japan: The Memoirs and Recollections, 1866-1906, of Algernon Bertram Mitford, the first Lord Redesdale.* London; Dover, NH: Athlone Press, 1985.

1088. Cortazzi, Hugh. *Victorians in Japan: In and Around the Treaty Ports.* London; Atlantic Highlands, NJ: Athlone Press, 1987.

1089. East, Alfred. *A British Artist in Meiji Japan.* Brighton, U.K.: In Print, 1991.

1090. Elder, John. *Following the Brush: An American Family's Encounter with Classical Japanese Culture.* Boston, MA: Beacon Press, 1993.

1091. Fenter, Kenneth. *Gaijin! Gaijin!* Springfield, OR: Cross Cultural Press, 1984.

1092. Fraser, Mary Crawford. *A Diplomat's Wife in Japan: Sketches at the Turn of the Century.* Edited By Hugh Cortazzi. New York: Weatherhill, 1982.

1093. Gordon Smith, Richard. *The Japan Diaries of Richard Gordon Smith*. Edited by Victoria Manthorpe. Harmondworth, U.K.; New York: Viking, 1986.

1094. Hall, Francis. *Japan Through American Eyes: The Journal of Francis Hall, Kanagawa and Yokohama, 1859-1866: From the Cleveland Public Library, John G. White Collection of Orientalia*. Edited by F. G. Notehelfer. Princeton, NJ: Princeton University Press, 1992.

1095. Hearn, Lafcadio. *Writings From Japan: An Anthology*. Edited by Francis King. Penguin Travel Library. Harmondsworth, U.K.; New York: Penguin, 1984.

1096. Heine, Wilhelm. *With Perry to Japan: A Memoir*. Honolulu, HI: University of Hawaii Press, 1990.

1097. Higa Oshiro, Augusto. *Japón no da Dos Oportunidades* [Japan Does not Give Two Chances]. Lima, Peru: editorial Generación '94: Central de Cooperativas Kyodai, 1994.

1098. Hodson, Peregrine. *A Circle Round the Sun: A Foreigner in Japan*. London: Heinemann, 1992.

1099. Jones, H. J. *Live Machines: Hired Foreigners and Meiji Japan*. Vancouver, B.C.: University of British Columbia Press, 1980.

1100. Martins Janeira, Armando. *Figuras de Silencio: a Tradicão Cultural Portuguesa no Japão de Hoje* [Silent Figures: The Portuguese Cultural Tradition in Today's Japan]. Lisbon, Portugal: Junta de Investigacoes Cientificas do Ultramar, 1981.

1101. Morley, John David. *Pictures from the Water Trade: Adventures of a Westerner in Japan*. Boston, MA: Atlantic Monthly Press; London: A. Deutsch, 1985.

1102. Napier, Nancy K., and Sully Taylor. *Western Women Working in Japan: Breaking Corporate Barriers*. Westport, CT; London, U.K.: Quorum Books, 1995.

1103. Ohshima, Shizuko, and Carolyn Francis. *Japan Through the Eyes of Women Migrant Workers*. Tokyo: Japan Woman's Christian Temperance Union, 1989.

1104. Pedlar, Neil. *The Imported Pioneers: Westerners Who Helped Build Modern Japan.* Folkestone, U.K.: Norbury; New York: St. Martin's Press, 1990.

1105. Rosenstone, Robert A. *Mirror in the Shrine: American Encounters with Meiji Japan.* Cambridge, MA: Harvard University Press, 1988.

1106. Satow, Ernest Mason. *A Diplomat in Japan: The Inner History of the Critical Years in the Evolution of Japan when the Ports were Opened and the Monarchy Restored, Recorded by a Diplomatist who Took an Active Part in the Events of the Time, with an Account of his Personal Experiences during that Period.* London: Seeley, 1921. Reprint: Rutland, VT: Tuttle, 1983.

1107. Velde, Paul van der. *The Deshima Diaries: Marginalia 1700-1740.* Tokyo: The Japan-Netherlands Institute, 1992.

1108. White, Morton, and Lucia White. *Journeys to the Japanese, 1952-1979.* Vancouver, B.C.: University of British Columbia Press, 1986.

1109. Wright, Scott. *Japan Encountered: A Brief (and Highly Selective) Survey of Famous Westerners in the Land of the Rising Sun.* Lanham, MD: University Press of America, 1996.

Foreigners in Japan—Brooke, John Mercer, 1826-1906

1110. Brooke, John M. *John M. Brooke's Pacific Cruise and Japanese Adventure, 1858-1860.* Edited by George M. Brooke, Jr. Honolulu, HI: University of Hawaii Press, 1986.

Foreigners in Japan—Frois, Luis, d. 1597

1111. Jorissen, Engelbert. *Das Japanbild im "Traktat" (1585) des Luis Frois* [The Image of Japan in the "Treatise" (1585) of Luis Frois]. Portugiesische Forschungen der Gorresgesellschaft. Zweite Reihe, 7. Bd. Munster, Germany: Aschendorff, 1988.

Foreigners in Japan—Graeff van Polsbroek, Dirk de, 1833-1916

1112. Moeshart, Herman J., ed. *Journaal van Jonkheer Dirk de Graeff van Polsbroek, 1857-1870: Belevenissen van een Nederlands Diplomaat in het Negentiende Eeuwse Japan* [Diary of Master Dirk de Graeff van Polsbroek, 1857-1870: Adventures of a Dutch Diplomat in Nineteenth-century Japan]. Assen, Netherlands: Van Gorcum, 1987.

Foreigners in Japan—Hearn, Lafcadio, 1850-1904

See also: 512

1113. Cott, Jonathan. *Wandering Ghost: The Odyssey of Lafcadio Hearn*. London; New York: Knopf, 1991.

1114. Dawson, Carl. *Lafcadio Hearn and the Vision of Japan*. Baltimore, MD: Johns Hopkins University Press, 1992.

1115. *Lafcadio Hearn: Japan's Great Interpreter; a New Anthology of His Writings: 1894-1904*. Folkestone, U.K.: Japan Library, 1992.

1116. Murray, Paul. *Fantastic Journey: The Life and Literature of Lafcadio Hearn*. Sandgate, Folkestone, U.K.: Japan Library, 1993.

1117. Shapiro, Michael. *Japan: In the Land of the Brokenhearted*. New York: H. Holt, 1989.

Foreigners in Japan—Kaempfer, Engelbert, 1651-1716

1118. Hüls, Hans, and Hoppe, Hans, comps. *Engelbert Kaempfer zum 330. Geburtstag: gesammelte Beiträge zur Engelbert-Kaempfer-Forschung und zur Frühzeit der Asienforschung in Europa* [For Engelbert Kaempfer's 330th Birthday: Collected Contributions to Engelbert Kaempfer Research, and to the Early Days of Asian Research in Europe]. Lippische Studien, Bd. 9. Lemgo, Germany: Wagener, 1982.

Foreigners in Japan—Keene, Donald, 1922

1119. Keene, Donald. *On Familiar Terms: A Journey across Cultures*. New York: Kodansha International, 1994.

Foreigners in Japan—Kipling, Rudyard, 1865-1936

1120. Kipling, Rudyard. *Kipling's Japan: Collected Writings*. Edited by Hugh Cortazzi and George Webb. London; Atlantic Highlands, NJ: Athlone Press, 1988.

Foreigners in Japan—Mendenhall, Thomas C., 1841-1924

1121. Mendenhall, Thomas C. *An American Scientist in Early Meiji Japan: The Autobiographical Notes of Thomas C. Mendenhall*. Asian Studies at Hawaii, 35. Honolulu, HI: University of Hawaii Press, 1989.

Foreigners in Japan—Moraes, Wenceslau de, 1854-1929

1122. Feldmann, Helmut. *Wenceslau de Moraes (1854-1929) und Japan: eine Untersuchung zur Selbstdarstellung in der exotistischen Literatur des Fin de Siecle in Portugal* [Wenceslau de Moraes (1854-1929) and Japan: An Examination of Self-Protrayal in the Exotic-Style Literature of Turn of the Century Portugal]. Portugiesische Forschungen der Gorresgesellschaft, Zweite Reihe, 6. Bd. Munster, Germany: Aschendorffsche Verlagsbuchhandlung, 1987.

Foreigners in Japan—Reischauer, Edwin O., 1910-1990

1123. Reischauer, Edwin O. *My Life Between Japan and America.* New York: Harper & Row, 1986.

Foreigners in Japan—Schultze, Wilhelm, 1840-1924

1124. Schultze, Emma. *Letters from Meiji Japan: Correspondence of a German Surgeon's Wife, 1878-1881.* Translated by Charlotte T. Marshall and John Z. Bowers. New York: Josiah Macy, Jr. Foundation, 1980.

Foreigners in Japan—Sergeant, Harriet

1125. Sergeant, Harriet. *The Old Sow in the Back Room: An Englishwoman in Japan.* London: John Murray, 1994.

Foreigners in Japan—Siebold, Philipp Franz von, 1796-1866

1126. Friese, Eberhard. *Philipp Franz von Siebold als früher Exponent der Ostasienwissenschaften: ein Beitrag zur Orientalismusdiskussion und zur Geschichte der europäisch-japanischen Begegnung* [Philip Franz von Siebold as Early Exponent of East Asian Studies: A Contribution to the Discussion of Orientalism, and to the History of European-Japanese Encounters]. Berliner Beiträge zur sozial- und wirtschaftswissenschaftlichen Japan-Forschung, Bd. 15. Bochum, Germany: N. Brockmeyer, 1983.

1127. Genschorek, Wolfgang. *In Land der aufgehende Sonne: Das Leben des japanforschers Philipp Franz von Siebold* [In the Land of the Rising Sun: The Life of Japan Scholar Philipp Franz von Siebold]. Pioniere der Menschheit. Leipzig, Germany: F.A. Brockhaus, 1988.

1128. Vos, K. *Assignment Japan: Von Siebold, Pioneer and Collector.* The Hague: SDU, 1989.

Foreigners in Japan—Storry, Richard, 1913-1982

1129. Storry, Dorothie. *Second Country: The Story of Richard Storry and Japan, 1913-1982: A Biography.* Woodchurch, U.K.: Norbury, 1986.

Foreigners in Japan—Titsingh, Isaac, 1744-1812

1130. Titsingh, Isaac. *The Private Correspondence of Isaac Titsingh.* Edited by Frank Lequin. Japonica Neerlandica, v. 4, etc. Titsingh Studies, v. 1, etc. Amsterdam: J. C. Gieben, 1990.

Foreigners in Japan—Willis, William, 1837-1894

1131. Cortazzi, Hugh. *Dr. Willis in Japan, 1862-1877: British Medical Pioneer.* London; Dover, NH: Athlone Press, 1985.

Forests and Forestry

1132. Handa, R., ed. *Forest Policy in Japan.* Tokyo: Nippon Ringyō Chōsakai, 1988.

1133. Totman, Conrad D. *The Green Archipelago: Forestry in Preindustrial Japan.* Berkeley, CA: University of California Press, 1989.

1134. Totman, Conrad D. *The Origins of Japan's Modern Forests: The Case of Akita.* Asian Studies at Hawaii, no. 31. Honolulu, HI: Center for Asian and Pacific Studies, University of Hawaii: University of Hawaii Press, 1985.

Free Trade

1135. Korhonen, Pekka. *Japan and the Pacific Free Trade Area.* Sheffield Centre for Japanese Studies/Routledge Series. London; New York: Routledge, 1994.

Freedom of Speech

See also: Academic Freedom; Censorship

1136. Beer, Laurence Ward. *Freedom of Expression in Japan: A Study in Comparative Law, Politics, and Society.* Tokyo; New York: Kodansha International, 1984.

1137. Braw, Monica. *The Atomic Bomb Suppressed: American Censorship in Occupied Japan.* Asia and the Pacific. Armonk, NY: Sharpe, 1991.

1138. Horio, Teruhisa. *Educational Thought and Ideology in Modern Japan: State Authority and Intellectual Freedom.* Tokyo: University of Tokyo Press, 1988.

Furniture *See*: Art—Furniture and Carpentry

Gardens *See*: Architecture—Landscape

Geisha

1139. Cobb, Jodi. *Geisha: The Life, the Voices, the Art.* New York: Knopf, 1995.

1140. Dalby, Liza Crihfield. *Geisha.* Berkeley, CA: University of California Press, 1983.

1141. Guillain, Robert. *Les Geishas, ou, Le Monde des Fleurs et des Saules* [The Geishas, or, the World of Flowers and Willows]. Paris: Arléa: Diffusion, Le Seuil, 1988.

1142. Haylock, John. *One Hot Summer in Kyoto.* Berkeley, CA: Stone Bridge Press, 1993.

1143. Longstreet, Stephen, and Ethel Longstreet. *Yoshiwara: The Pleasure Quarters of Old Tokyo.* Yenbooks. Rutland, VT; Tokyo: Tuttle, 1988.

1144. Louis, Lisa. *Butterflies of the Night: Mama-sans, Geisha, Strippers, and the Japanese Men they Serve.* New York: Tengu Books, 1992.

1145. Lühl, Hendrick. *Geishas und Kurtisanen: Die Kunst der Unterhaltung im alten Japan* [Geishas and Courtisans: The Art of Entertainment in Old Japan]. Die Bibliophilen Taschenbücher, Nr. 404. Dortmund, Germany: Harenberg, 1983.

1146. Seigle, Cecilia Segawa. *Yoshiwara: The Glittering World of the Japanese Courtesan*. Honolulu, HI: University of Hawaii Press, 1993.

Geography

1147. *Geography of Japan*. Special Publication, Association of Japanese Geographers, no. 4. Tokyo: Teikoku-Shoin, 1980.

1148. Sargent, John, and Richard Wiltshire, eds. *Geographical Studies & Japan*. Folkestone, U.K.: Japan Library, 1993.

1149. Takeuchi, Keiichi, comp. and ed. *Languages, Paradigms, and Schools in Geography*. Japanese Contributions to the History of Geographical Thought, 2. Tokyo: Laboratory of Social Geography, Hitotsubashi University, 1984.

1150. Yoshikawa, Torao, Sohei Kaizuka, and Yoko Ota. *The Landforms of Japan*. Tokyo: University of Tokyo Press, 1981.

Geology

1151. Hashimoto, M., ed. *Geology of Japan*. Developments in Earth & Planetary Sciences; v. 8. Dordrecht, Netherlands; Boston, MA: Kluwer Academic, 1990.

1152. Kimura, Toshio, Itaru Hayami, and Shizuo Yoshida. *Geology of Japan*. 2d rev. ed. Tokyo: University of Tokyo Press, 1991.

1153. Martin, Charles W. *Geology and Geological Hazards of Japan*. Occasional Papers, v. 2, no. 5. Richmond, IN: Institute for Education on Japan, Earlham College, 1992.

1154. Sasaki, Akira, Shunso Ishihara, and Yotaro Seki, eds. *Mineral Resources and Engineering Geology*. Texts in Earth Sciences. Chichester, U.K.; New York: Wiley, 1985.

Germany—Relations with

1155. Hayashima, Akira. *Die Illusion des Sonderfriedens: deutsche Verstandigungspolitik mit Japan im ersten Weltkrieg* [The Illusion of a Special Peace: German Policy of Understanding with Japan during the First World War]. Studien zur Geschichte des neunzehnten Jahrhunderts, Bd. 11. Munich, Germany: Oldenbourg, 1982.

1156. Kracht, Klaus, Bruno Lewin, and Klaus Muller, eds. *Japan und Deutschland im 20. Jahrhundert* [Japan and Germany in the 20th Century]. Veröffentlichungen des Ostasien-Instituts der Ruhr-Universität Bochum, Bd. 32. Wiesbaden, Germany: Harrassowitz, 1984.

1157. Kreiner, Josef, ed. *Deutschland, Japan: historische Kontakte* [Germany, Japan: Historical Contact]. Studium Universale, Bd. 3. Bonn: Bouvier, 1984.

1158. Kreiner, Josef, ed. *Japan und die Mittelmachte im Ersten Weltkrieg und in den zwanziger Jahren* [Japan and the Central Powers During the First World War and the Twenties]. Studium Universale, Bd. 8. Bonn: Bouvier, 1986.

1159. Kreiner, Josef, and Regine Mathias, eds. *Deutschland-Japan in der Zwischenkriegszeit* [Germany-Japan during the Interwar Years]. Studium Universale, Bd. 12. Bonn: Bouvier, 1990.

1160. Martin, Bernd. *Japan and Germany in the Modern World.* Providence, RI: Berghahn Books, 1995.

1161. Stahncke, Holmer. *Die diplomatischen Beziehungen zwischen Deutschland und Japan 1854-1868* [Diplomatic Relations between Germany and Japan 1854-1868]. Studien zur modernen Geschichte, Bd. 33. Stuttgart, Germany: F. Steiner, 1987.

1162. Wippich, Rolf-Harald. *Japan und die deutsche Fernostpolitik, 1894-1898: vom Ausbruch des Chinesisch-Japanischen Krieges bis zur Besetzung der Kiautschou-Bucht: ein Beitrag zur wilhelminischen Weltpolitik* [Japan and the German Far East Policy, 1894-1898: From the Start of the Sino-Japanese War until the Occupation of the Kiao-Cho Bay: A Contribution to Wilhelminic World Politics. Beiträge zur Kolonial- und Überseegeschichte, Bd. 35. Stuttgart, Germany: F. Steiner, 1987.

Government *See*: Bureaucracy

Graphic Art *See*: Art—Graphic

Haiku *See*: Literature—Poetry—Haiku

Health Care *See*: Medicine

Higher Education   *See*: Education—Higher

Historical Fiction

1163.   Mori, Ōgai. *The Historical Fiction of Mori Ōgai.* UNESCO Collection of Representative Works. Japanese Series. Honolulu, HI: University Press of Hawaii, 1991.

1164.   Smith, Henry, ed. *Learning from Shogun: Japanese History and Western Fantasy.* Santa Barbara, CA: Program in Asian Studies, University of California, Santa Barbara, 1980.

1165.   Tsuji, Kunio. *The Signore: Shogun of the Warring States.* Tokyo; New York: Kodansha International, 1990.

Historiography

1166.   Kapitza, Peter, ed. *Japan in Europa: Texte und Bilddokumente zur europäischen Japankenntnis, von Marco Polo bis Wilhelm von Humboldt* [Japan in Europe: Textual and Visual Documents for European Japan Studies: From Marco Polo to Wilhelm von Humboldt]. 3 vols. Munchen, Germany: Iudicium, 1990.

1167.   Mehl, Margaret. *Eine Vergangenheit für die japanische Nation: die entstehung des historischen Forschungsinstituts Tōkyō daigaku Shiryō hensanjo (1869-1895)* [A Past for the Japanese Nation; The Origin of the Historical Research Institute Tōkyō Daigaku Shiryō Hensanjo (1869-1895)]. Europäische Hochschulschiften. Reihe III, Geschichte und ihre Hilfswissenschaften, Bd. 528. Frankfurt am Main, Germany; New York: P. Lang, 1992.

History

1168.   Hall, John W., et al. *The Cambridge History of Japan.* Cambridge, U.K.; New York: Cambridge University Press, 1988.

1169.   Harvey, Robert. *Undefeated: The Rise, Fall and Rise of Greater Japan.* London: Macmillan, 1994.

1170.   Jansen, Marius B., ed. *Changing Japanese Attitudes Toward Modernization.* Princeton, NJ: Princeton University Press, 1965. Reprint: Rutland, VT: Tuttle, 1982.

1171. Meyer, Milton Walter. *Japan: A Concise History.* Savage, MD: Rowman & Littlefield, 1993.

1172. Mitsukuni, Yoshida, Ikko Tanaka, and Sesoko Tsune, eds. *The People's Culture, from Kyoto to Edo.* Translated by Lynne E. Riggs. Hiroshima, Japan: Mazda Motor Corp., 1986.

1173. Morton, W. Scott. *Japan: Its History and Culture.* New York: McGraw-Hill, 1994.

1174. Reischauer, Edwin O., and Albert M. Craig. *Japan: Tradition & Transformation.* Boston, MA: Houghton Mifflin, 1989.

1175. Sansom, George Bailey. *A History of Japan.* 3 vols. The Cresset Historical Series. London; Cresset Press; Stanford Studies in the Civilizations of Eastern Asia. Stanford, CA: Stanford University Press, 1958-1963.

1176. Schirokauer, Conrad. *A Brief History of Japanese Civilization.* Fort Worth, TX: Harcourt Brace Jovanovich, 1993.

1177. Tsunoda, Ryusaku, Wm. Theodore de Bary, and Donald Keene, comps. *Sources of Japanese Tradition.* Edited by Ryusaku Tsunoda. Records of Civilization, Sources and Studies, no. 54. Introduction to Oriental Civilizations. New York: Columbia University Press, 1958. Reprint: UNESCO Collection of Representative Works. Japan Series. 1964.

1178. Varley, H. Paul. *Japanese Culture.* 3d ed. Honolulu, HI: University of Hawaii Press, 1984.

History—Bibliography

1179. Bunn, J. M., and A. D. S. Roberts, comps. *A Union List of Japanese Local Histories in British Libraries.* Oxford, U.K.: Bodleian Library, 1981.

1180. Dower, John W. *Japanese History & Culture From Ancient to Modern Times: Seven Basic Bibliographies.* 2d ed. New York: M. Wiener, 1995.

1181. Fukuda, Naomi, ed. *Japanese History: A Guide to Survey Histories.* 2 vols. Ann Arbor: Center for Japanese Studies, University of Michigan, 1984-1986.

1182. Perren, Richard, ed., comp. *Japanese Studies from Pre-History to 1990: A Bibliographical Guide*. History and Related Disciplines Select Bibliographies. New York: Manchester University Press, 1992.

History—Ashikaga through Momoyama (1392-1600)

1183. Arai, Hakuseki. *Lessons from History: The Tokushi Yoron*. Translated by Joyce Ackroyd. St. Lucia, Australia; New York: University of Queensland Press, 1982.

1184. Elison, George, and Bardwell L. Smith, eds. *Warlords, Artists, & Commoners: Japan in the Sixteenth Century*. Honolulu, HI: University Press of Hawaii, 1981.

1185. Grossberg, Kenneth Allan. *Japan's Renaissance: The Politics of the Muromachi Bakufu*. Harvard East Asian Monographs, 99. Cambridge, MA: Council on East Asian Studies, Harvard University, 1981.

1186. Hall, John Whitney, Nagahara Keiji, and Kozo Yamamura, eds. *Japan before Tokugawa: Political Consolidation and Economic Growth, 1500-1650*. Princeton, NJ: Princeton University Press, 1981.

1187. Keirstead, Thomas. *The Geography of Power in Medieval Japan*. Princeton, NJ: Princeton University Press, 1992.

1188. Mass, Jeffrey P. *Antiquity and Anachronism in Japanese History*. Stanford, CA: Stanford University Press, 1992.

1189. Tonomura, Hitomi. *Community and Commerce in Late Medieval Japan: The Corporate Villages of Tokuchin-ho*. Stanford, CA: Stanford University Press, 1992.

History—Intellectual

1190. Barshay, Andrew E. *State and Intellectual in Imperial Japan: The Public Man in Crisis*. Berkeley, CA: University of California Press, 1988.

1191. Harootunian, Harry D. *Things Seen and Unseen: Discourse and Ideology in Tokugawa Nativism*. Chicago, IL: University of Chicago Press, 1988.

1192. Honda, Katsuichi. *The Impoverished Spirit in Contemporary Japan: Selected Essays of Honda Katsuichi*. Edited by John Lie. Translated by Eri Fujieda, Masayuki Yamazaki, and John Lie. New York: Monthly Review Press, 1993.

1193. *Japan in Transition: Thought and Action in the Meiji Era, 1868-1912*. Rutherford, NJ: Fairleigh Dickinson University Press; London: Associated University Presses, 1984.

1194. Najita, Tetsuo. *Visions of Virtue in Tokugawa Japan: The Kaitokudo Merchant Academy of Osaka*. Chicago, IL: University of Chicago Press, 1987.

1195. Nolte, Sharon H. *Liberalism in Modern Japan: Ishibashi Tanzan and his Teachers, 1905-1960*. Berkeley, CA: University of California Press, 1986.

1196. Nosco, Peter. *Remembering Paradise: Nativism and Nostalgia in Eighteenth-Century Japan*. Harvard-Yenching Institute Monograph Series, 31. Cambridge, MA: Council on East Asian Studies, Harvard University, 1990.

1197. Rimer, J. Thomas, ed. *Culture and Identity: Japanese Intellectuals during the Interwar Years*. Princeton, NJ: Princeton University Press, 1990.

1198. Rubinger, Richard. *Private Academies of Tokugawa Japan*. Princeton, NJ: Princeton University Press, 1982.

1199. Sakai, Naoki. *Voices of the Past: The Status of Language in Eighteenth-Century Japanese Discourse*. Ithaca, NY: Cornell University Press, 1992.

1200. Tsurumi, Shunsuke. *An Intellectual History of Wartime Japan, 1931-1945*. Japanese Studies. London; New York: KPI, 1986.

1201. Wakabayashi, Bob Tadashi. *Anti-Foreignism and Western Learning in Early-Modern Japan: The New Theses of 1925*. Harvard East Asian Monographs, 126. Cambridge, MA: Council on East Asian Studies, Harvard University, 1986.

History—Kamakura and Yoshino (1185-1392)

1202. Hall, John W., and Jeffrey P. Mass. *Medieval Japan: Essays in Institutional History.* New Haven, CT: Yale University Press, 1974. Reprint: Stanford, CA: Stanford University Press, 1988.

1203. Mass, Jeffrey P., ed. *Court and Bakufu in Japan: Essays in Kamakura History.* New Haven, CT: Yale University Press, 1982.

1204. Mass, Jeffrey P. *Lordship and Inheritance in Early Medieval Japan: A Study of the Kamakura Soryo System.* Stanford, CA: Stanford University Press, 1989.

1205. Shimizu, Yoshiaki, ed. *Japan, the Shaping of Daimyo Culture, 1185-1868.* New York: Braziller; Washington, DC: National Gallery of Art, 1988.

1206. Varley, H. Paul, trans. *A Chronicle of Gods and Sovereigns: Jinno Shotoki of Kitabatake Chikafusa.* Translations from the Oriental Classics. New York: Columbia University Press, 1980.

History—Legal

1207. Ch'en, Paul Heng Chao. *The Formation of the Early Meiji Legal Order: The Japanese Code of 1871 and its Chinese Foundation.* London Oriental Series, v. 35. Oxford, U.K.; New York: Oxford University Press, 1981.

1208. Hess, Albert G., and Shigeyo Murayama. *Everyday Law in Japanese Folk Art: Daily Life in Meiji Japan, As Seen through Petty Law Violations: Woodcuts, c. 1878.* Aalen, Germany: Scientia, 1980.

1209. *The Laws of the Muromachi Bakufu: Kemmu Shikimoku (1336) & Muromachi Bakufu Tsuikaho.* Monumenta Nipponica Monograph, 56. Tokyo: Monumenta Nipponica, Sophia University, 1981.

1210. Mitchell, Richard H. *Janus-Faced Justice: Political Criminals in Imperial Japan.* Honolulu, HI: University of Hawaii Press, 1992.

1211. Steenstrup, Carl. *A History of Law in Japan until 1868.* Handbuch der Orientalistik, Funfte Abteilung, Japan, 6. Bd., 2. Abschnitt, 1. T. Leiden, Netherlands; New York: Brill, 1991.

History—Local

1212. Baxter, James C. *The Meiji Unification through the Lens of Ishikawa Prefecture.* Harvard East Asian Monographs, 165. Cambridge, MA: Harvard University Press, 1994.

1213. *The History of Kanagawa.* Yokohama, Japan; Kanagawa Prefectural Government, 1985.

1214. Kalland, Arne. *Fishing Villages in Tokugawa Japan.* Honolulu, HI: University of Hawaii Press, 1995.

1215. Kitamura, Yoshiaki. *De L'Identité Japonaise: Changements et Permanence d'une Communauté Rurale* [On Japanese Identity: Change and Permanency of a Rural Community]. Bibliothèque Japonaise. Paris: Publications Orientalistes de France, 1986.

1216. McClain, James L. *Kanazawa: A Seventeenth-Century Japanese Castle Town.* Yale Historical Publications. Miscellany, 128. New Haven, CT: Yale University Press, 1982.

1217. Robertson, Jennifer Ellen. *Native and Newcomer: Making and Remaking a Japanese City.* Berkeley, CA: University of California Press, 1991.

1218. Tsuboi, Kiyotari, and Migaku Tanaka. *The Historic City of Nara: An Archeological Approach.* Tokyo: The Centre for East Asian Cultural Studies; Paris: The United Nations Educational, Scientific and Cultural Organization, 1991.

1219. Ward, Philip. *Japanese Capitals: A Cultural, Historical and Artistic Guide to Nara, Kyoto, and Tokyo, Successive Capitals of Japan.* Cambridge, MA: Oleander Press, 1985.

1220. Wigen, Karen. *The Making of a Japanese Periphery, 1750-1920.* Twentieth-century Japan, 3. Berkeley, CA: University of California Press, 1995.

History—Local—Kyoto

1221. Berry, Mary Elizabeth. *The Culture of Civil War in Kyoto.* Berkeley, CA: University of California Press, 1994.

1222. Iyer, Pico. *The Lady and the Monk: Four Seasons in Kyoto.* New York: Knopf, 1991.

1223. Plutschow, Herbert E. *Historical Kyoto: With Illustrations and Guide Maps.* Tokyo: Japan Times, 1983

History—Local—Tōkyō

1224. Ashihara, Yoshinobu. *The Hidden Order: Tokyo through the Twentieth Century.* Translated by Lynne E. Riggs. Tokyo; London: Kodansha International, 1989.

1225. Cybriwsky, Roman A. *Historical Dictionary of Tokyo.* Historical Dictionaries of Cities, no. 1. Lanham, MD: Scarecrow Press, 1996.

1226. Cybriwsky, Roman A. *Tokyo: The Changing Profile of an Urban Giant.* World Cities Series. London: Belhaven Press, 1991.

1227. Jinnai, Hidenobu. *Tokyo, A Spatial Anthropology.* Translated by Kimiko Nishimura. Berkeley, CA: University of California Press, 1995.

1228. Pons, Philippe. *D'Edo à Tōkyō: Memoires et Modernités* [From Edo to Tōkyō: Memories and Modernities]. Bibliothèque des Sciences Humaines. Paris: Gallimard, 1988.

1229. Popham, Peter. *Tokyo: The City at the End of the World.* Tokyo; New York: Kodansha International, 1985.

1230. Seidensticker, Edward. *Low City, High City: Tokyo from Edo to the Earthquake.* New York: Knopf, 1983.

1231. Seidensticker, Edward. *Tokyo Rising: The City since the Great Earthquake.* New York: Knopf, 1990.

1232. *Tokyo: The Making of a Metropolis.* TMG Municipal Library, no. 27. Tokyo: Tokyo Metropolitan Government, 1993.

1233. Van Staaveren, Jacob. *An American in Japan, 1945-1948: A Civilian View of the Occupation.* Seattle, WA: University of Washington Press, 1994.

1234. Waley, Paul. *Tokyo Now & Then: An Explorer's Guide.* New York: Weatherhill, 1984.

History—Meiji (1868-1912)

1235. Conroy, Hilary, Sandra T. W. Davis, and Wayne Patterson. *Japan in Transition: Thought and Action in the Meiji Era, 1868-1912.* Rutherford, NJ: Fairleigh Dickinson University Press; London: Associated University Presses, 1984.

1236. Daikichi, Irokawa. *The Culture of the Meiji Period.* Translated by Marius B. Jansen. Princeton Library of Asian Translations. Princeton, NJ: Princeton University Press, 1985.

1237. Gluck, Carol. *Japan's Modern Myths: Ideology in the Late Meiji Period.* Princeton, NJ: Princeton University Press, 1985.

1238. Jansen, Marius. *The Emergence of Meiji Japan.* New York: Cambridge University Press, 1995.

1239. Wilson, George M. *Patriots and Redeemers in Japan: Motives in the Meiji Restoration.* Chicago, IL: University of Chicago Press, 1992.

History—Military

1240. Cleary, Thomas F. *The Japanese Art of War: Understanding the Culture of Strategy.* Boston, MA: Shambala, 1991.

1241. Farris, William Wayne. *Heavenly Warriors: The Evolution of Japan's Military, 500-1300.* Harvard East Asian Monographs, 157. Cambridge, MA: Council on East Asian Studies, Harvard University, 1992.

1242. Friday, Karl F. *Hired Swords: The Rise of Private Warrior Power in Early Japan.* Stanford, CA: Stanford University Press, 1992.

1243. Fuller, Richard. *Shokan: Hirohito's Samurai.* London: Arms & Armour, 1992.

1244. Harries, Meirion, and Susie Harries. *Soldiers of the Sun: The Rise and Fall of the Imperial Japanese Army.* London: Heinemann, 1991.

1245. Hook, Glenn D. *Militarisation and Demilitarisation in Contemporary Japan.* Nissan Institute / Routledge Japanese Studies Series. London; New York: Routledge, 1996.

1246. Hoyt, Edwin Palmer. *Japan's War: The Great Pacific Conflict, 1853-1952.* New York: McGraw-Hill, 1986.

1247. Humphreys, Leonard A. *The Way of the Heavenly Sword: The Japanese Army in the 1920's*. Stanford, CA: Stanford University Press, 1995.

1248. Maeda, Tetsuo. *The Hidden Army: The Untold Story of Japan's Military Forces*. Edited by David J. Kenney. Translated by Steven Karpa. Chicago, IL: Edition Q, 1995.

1249. Okazaki, Hisahiko. *A Grand Strategy for Japanese Defense*. Lanham, MD: University Press of America: Abt Books, 1986.

1250. Turnbull, Stephen R. *Battles of the Samurai*. London; New York: Arms & Armour, 1987.

History—Military—Bibliography

1251. Kondō, Shinji. *Japanese Military History: A Guide to the Literature*. Garland Reference Library of Social Science, v. 195. Military History Bibliographies, vol. 5. New York: Garland, 1984.

History—Modern

1252. Beasley, W. G. *The Modern History of Japan*. 3d ed. London: Weidenfeld & Nicolson, 1981.

1253. Beasley, W. G. *The Rise of Modern Japan*. 2d ed. London: Weidenfeld & Nicolson, 1995.

1254. Buckley, Roger. *Japan Today*. 2d ed. Cambridge, MA; New York: Cambridge University Press, 1990.

1255. Gluck, Carol, and Stephen R. Granbard, eds. *Showa: The Japan of Hirohito*. New York: Norton, 1992.

1256. Hane, Mikiso. *Modern Japan: A Historical Survey*. 2d ed. Boulder, CO: Westview, 1992.

1257. Henny, Sue, and Jean-Pierre Lehman, eds. *Themes and Theories in Modern Japanese History: Essays in Memory of Richard Storry*. London; Atlantic Highlands, NJ: Athlone Press, 1988.

1258. Hidaka, Rokurō. *The Price of Affluence: Dilemmas of Contemporary Japan*. Tokyo; New York: Kodansha International, 1984.

1259. Hunter, Janet. *Concise Dictionary of Modern Japanese History.* Berkeley, CA: University of California Press, 1984.

1260. Hunter, Janet. *The Emergence of Modern Japan: An Introductory History since 1853.* London; New York: Longman, 1989.

1261. McCormack, Gavan, and Yoshio Sugimoto, eds. *The Japanese Trajectory: Modernization and Beyond.* Cambridge, U.K.; New York: Cambridge University Press, 1988.

1262. Morris-Suzuki, Tessa. *Showa: An Inside History of Hirohito's Japan.* New York: Schocken Books, 1985.

1263. Najita, Tetsuo, and J. Victor Koschman, eds. *Conflict in Modern Japanese History: The Neglected Tradition.* Princeton, NJ: Princeton University Press, 1982.

1264. Neary, Ian, ed. *War Revolution and Japan.* Folkestone, U.K.: Japan Library, 1993.

1265. Pyle, Kenneth B. *The Making of Modern Japan.* 2d ed. Lexington, MA: D. C. Heath, 1996.

1266. Reading, Brian. *Japan: The Coming Collapse.* London: Weidenfeld and Nicolson, 1992.

1267. Waswo, Ann. *Modern Japanese Society, 1868-1994.* Oxford, U.K.; New York: Oxford University Press, 1996.

1268. Wilson, Dick. *The Sun at Noon: An Anatomy of Modern Japan.* London: H. Hamilton, 1986.

1269. Wray, Harry, and Hilary Conroy, eds. *Japan Examined: Perspectives on Modern Japanese History.* Honolulu, HI: University of Hawaii Press, 1983.

1270. Yoda, Yoshiie. *The Foundations of Japan's Modernization: A Comparison With China's Path Toward Modernization.* Translated by Kurt W. Radtke. Brill's Japanese Studies Library, v. 5. Leiden; New York: Brill, 1996.

History—Nara and Heian (645-1185)

1271. McCullough, Helen Craig. *Okagami, the Great Mirror: Fujiwara Michinaga (966-1027) and his Times: A Study and Translation.* Princeton Library of Asian Translation. Princeton, NJ: Princeton University Press, 1980.

1272. Morris, Ivan I. *The World of the Shining Prince: Court Life in Ancient Japan.* London: Oxford University Press; New York: Knopf, 1964. Reprint: New York: Kodansha International, 1994.

1273. Sakamoto, Tarō. *The Six National Histories of Japan.* Translated by John S. Brownlee. Vancouver, BC: University of British Columbia Press; Tokyo: University of Tokyo Press, 1991.

History—Naval

1274. Fuller, Richard. *Shokan, Hirohito's Samurai.* London: Arms & Armour, 1992.

1275. Howarth, Stephen. *The Fighting Ships of the Rising Sun: The Drama of the Imperial Japanese Navy, 1895-1945.* New York: Atheneum, 1983.

1276. Howarth, Stephen. *Morning Glory: A History of the Imperial Japanese Navy.* London: H. Hamilton, 1983.

1277. Marder, Arthur Jacob. *Old Friends, New Enemies: The Royal Navy and the Imperial Navy: Strategic Illusions, 1936-1941.* Oxford, U.K.: Clarendon; New York: Oxford University Press, 1981.

1278. Skulski, Janusz. *The Battleship Yamato.* London: Conway Maritime Press, 1988.

1279. Yoshida, Mitsuru. *Requiem for Battleship Yamato.* Translated by Richard Minear. Tokyo: Kodansha International, 1985.

History—Political

1280. Banno, Junji. *The Establishment of the Japanese Constitutional System.* Nissan Institute / Routledge Japanese Studies Series. New York: Routledge, 1992.

1281. Connors, Lesley. *The Emperor's Adviser: Saionji Kinmochi and Pre-War Japanese Politics.* Nissan Institute / Croom Helm Japanese Studies Series. London; Wolfeboro, NH: Croom Helm, 1987.

1282. *Democratizing Japan: The Allied Occupation.* Honolulu, HI: University of Hawaii Press, 1987.

1283. Fletcher, William Miles, III. *The Search for a New Order: Intellectuals and Fascism in Prewar Japan.* Chapel Hill, NC: University of North Carolina Press, 1982.

1284. Fraser, Andrew. *Japan's Early Parliaments, 1890-1905: Structure, Issues and Trends.* The Nissan Institute / Routledge Japanese Studies Series. London; New York: Routledge, 1995.

1285. Hall, John W., and Jeffrey P. Mass, eds. *Medieval Japan: Essays in Institutional History.* Stanford, CA: Stanford University Press, 1988.

1286. Ishii, Ryōsuke. *A History of Political Institutions in Japan.* Tokyo: University of Tokyo Press, 1980.

1287. Mass, Jeffrey P., and William B. Hauser, eds. *The Bakufu in Japanese History.* Stanford, CA: Stanford University Press, 1985.

1288. Minichiello, Sharon. *Retreat from Reform: Patterns of Political Behavior in Interwar Japan.* Honolulu, HI: University of Hawaii Press, 1984.

1289. Mitchell, Richard H. *Political Bribery in Japan.* Honolulu, HI: University of Hawaii Press, 1996.

1290. Ooms, Herman. *Tokugawa Ideology: Early Constructs, 1570-1680.* Princeton, NJ: Princeton University Press, 1985.

1291. Plotkin, Ira L. *Anarchism in Japan: A Study of the Great Treason Affair, 1910-1911.* Japanese Studies, v. 1. Lewiston, NY: Mellen Press, 1990.

1292. Pyle, Kenneth B. *The Japanese Question: Power and Purpose in a New Era.* 2d ed. Washington, DC: AEI Press, 1996.

1293. Ramsdell, Daniel B. *The Japanese Diet: Stability and Change in the Japanese House of Representatives, 1890-1990.* Lanham, MD: University Press of America, 1992.

1294. Shillony, Ben-Ami. *Politics and Culture in Wartime Japan.* Oxford, U.K.: Clarendon Press; New York: Oxford University Press, 1981.

1295. Sims, Richard L. *A Political History of Modern Japan, 1868-1952.* Afro-Asian Nations, History and Culture, 4. New Delhi: Vikas, 1991.

1296. Takeda, Kiyoko. *The Dual-Image of the Japanese Emperor.* London: Macmillan Education, 1988.

1297. Tokutomi, Sohō. *The Future Japan.* Translated by Vinh Sinh. Edited by Vinh Sinh, Matsuzawa Hiroaki, and Nicholas Wickenden. Edmonton, Alberta: University of Alberta Press, 1989.

1298. Totman, Conrad D. *Politics in the Tokugawa Bakufu, 1600-1843.* Berkeley, CA: University of California Press, 1988.

1299. Umegaki, Michio. *After the Restoration: The Beginning of Japan's Modern State.* New York: New York University Press, 1988.

1300. Ward, Robert E., and Sakamoto Yoshikazu. *Democratizing Japan: The Allied Occupation.* Honolulu, HI: University of Hawaii Press, 1987.

History—Prehistory and Early History (To 645)

1301. Aikens, C. Melvin, and Takayasu Higuchi. *Prehistory of Japan.* Studies in Archaeology. New York: Academic Press, 1981.

1302. Barnes, Gina Lee. *China, Korea and Japan: The Rise of Civilization in East Asia.* London: Thames & Hudson, 1993.

1303. Pearson, Richard J. *Ancient Japan.* Washington, DC: Arthur M. Sackler Gallery; New York: Braziller, 1992.

1304. Pearson, Richard J., Gina Lee Barnes, and Karl L. Hutterer, eds. *Windows on the Japanese Past: Studies in Archaeology and Prehistory.* Ann Arbor, MI: Center for Japanese Studies, University of Michigan, 1986.

1305. Vargo, Lars. *Social and Economic Conditions for the Formation of the Early Japanese State.* Japanological Studies, 1. Stockholm: Stockholm University, Institute of Oriental Languages, Department of Japanese and Korean, 1982.

History—Rural

1306. Bailey, Jackson H. *Ordinary People, Extraordinary Lives: Political and Economic Change in a Tohoku Village*. Honolulu, HI: University of Hawaii Press, 1991.

1307. Lewis, Michael Lawrence. *Rioters and Citizens: Mass Protest in Imperial Japan*. Berkeley, CA: University of California Press, 1990.

1308. Moon, Okpyo. *From Paddy Field to Ski Slope: The Revitalization of Tradition in Japanese Village Life*. Japanese Studies. Manchester, U.K.; New York: Manchester University Press, 1989.

History—Russo-Japanese War, 1904-1905

1309. Akashi, Motojirō. *Rakka Ryūsui: Colonel Akashi's Report on his Secret Cooperation with the Russian Revolutionary Parties during the Russo-Japanese War*. Selected chapters translated by Inaba Chiharu. Edited by Olavi K. Fält and Antti Kujala. Studia Historica, 31. Helsinki: SHA, 1988.

1310. Connaughton, R. M. *The War of the Rising Sun and Tumbling Bear: A Military History of the Russo-Japanese War, 1904-5*. London: Routledge, 1988.

1311. Esthus, Raymond A. *Double Eagle and Rising Sun: The Russians and Japanese at Portsmouth in 1905*. Durham, NC: Duke University Press, 1988.

1312. Nish, Ian Hill. *The Origins of the Russo-Japanese War*. Origins of Modern Wars. London; New York: Longman, 1985.

1313. Westwood, J. N. *Russia against Japan, 1904-1905: A New Look at the Russo-Japanese War*. Houndmills, U.K.: Macmillan, 1986.

History—Sino-Japanese War, 1894-1895

1314. Lone, Stewart. *Japan's First Modern War: Army and Society in The Conflict with China, 1894-95*. New York: St. Martin's Press, 1994.

1315. Mutsu, Munemitsu. *A Diplomatic Record of the Sino-Japanese War, 1894-95*. Edited and Translated by Gordon Mark Berger. Princeton Library of Asian Translations. Princeton, NJ: Princeton University Press; Tokyo: University of Tokyo Press, 1982.

History—Tokugawa (1600-1868)

1316. Brown, Philip C. *Central Authority and Local Autonomy in the Formation of Early Modern Japan: The Case of Kaga Domain.* Stanford, CA: Stanford University Press, 1993.

1317. Brownlee, John S. *Political Thought in Japanese Historical Writings: From Kojiki (712) to Tokushi Yoron (1712).* Waterloo, Ont.: Wilfrid Laurier University Press, 1991.

1318. Gerstle, C. Andrew, ed. *18th Century Japan: Culture and Society.* East Asia Series. Sydney, Australia; Boston: Allen & Unwin, 1989.

1319. Hane, Mikiso. *Peasants, Rebels and Outcasts: The Underside of Modern Japan.* New York: Pantheon, 1982.

1320. Hane, Mikiso. *Premodern Japan: A Historical Survey.* Boulder, CO: Westview, 1991.

1321. Huber, Thomas M. *The Revolutionary Origins of Modern Japan.* Stanford, CA: Stanford University Press, 1981.

1322. Jansen, Marius B., and Gilbert Rozman, eds. *Japan in Transition, from Tokugawa to Meiji.* Princeton, NJ: Princeton University Press, 1986.

1323. Koschman, J. Victor. *The Mito Ideology: Discourse, Reform, and Insurrection in Late Tokugawa Japan, 1790-1864.* Berkeley, CA: University of California Press, 1987.

1324. Lehman, Jean-Pierre. *The Roots of Modern Japan.* London: Macmillan, 1982.

1325. Nakane, Chie, and Shinzaburō Ōishi, eds. *Tokugawa Japan: The Social and Economic Antecedents of Modern Japan.* Tokyo: University of Tokyo Press, 1990.

1326. Totman, Conrad D. *The Collapse of the Tokugawa Bakufu, 1862-1868.* Honolulu, HI: University Press of Hawaii, 1980.

1327. Totman, Conrad D. *Japan Before Perry: A Short History.* Berkeley, CA: University of California Press, 1981.

1328. White, James W. *The Demography of Sociopolitical Conflict in Japan, 1721-1846.* Japan Research Monograph, vol. 12. Berkeley, CA: Institute for East Asian Studies, University of California, Berkeley, Center for Japanese Studies, 1992.

History—20th Century—Pacific War (1939-1945)

1329. Allen, Thomas B., and Norman Polmar. *Code-name Downfall: The Secret Plan to Invade Japan and why Truman Dropped the Bomb.* New York: Simon & Schuster, 1995.

1330. Best, Antony. *Britain, Japan and Pearl Harbor: Avoiding War in East Asia, 1936-41.* London; New York: Routledge: LSE, 1995.

1331. Dower, John W. *War Without Mercy: Race and Power in the Pacific War.* New York: Pantheon Books, 1986.

1332. Duus, Peter, Ramon H. Myers, and Mark R. Peattie, eds. *The Japanese Wartime Empire, 1931-1945.* Princeton, NJ: Princeton University Press, 1996.

1333. Edwards, Bernard. *Blood and Bushido: Japanese Atrocities at Sea 1941-1945.* Upton-upon-Severn, U.K.: Self Publishing Association, 1991.

1334. Evans, David C., ed., trans. *The Japanese Navy in World War II: In the Words of Former Japanese Naval Officers.* 2d ed. Annapolis, MD: Naval Institute Press, 1986.

1335. Feifer, George. *Tennozan: The Battle of Okinawa and the Atomic Bomb.* New York: Ticknor & Fields, 1992.

1336. Gow, Ian. *Okinawa, 1945: Gateway to Japan.* Garden City, NY: Doubleday, 1985.

1337. Hata, Ikuhiko, and Yasuho Izawa. *Japanese Naval Aces and Fighter Units in World War II.* Translated by Don Cyril Gorham. Annapolis, MD: Naval Institute Press, 1989.

1338. Hoyt, Edwin Palmer. *Closing the Circle: War in the Pacific, 1945.* New York: Van Nostrand Reinhold, 1982.

1339. Jones, Don. *Oba, the Last Samurai: Saipan 1944-45.* Novato, CA: Presidio Press, 1986.

1340. McCune, Shannon Boyd-Bailey. *Intelligence on the Economic Collapse of Japan in 1945*. Lanham, MD: University Press of America, 1989.

1341. Morley, James William, ed. *The Final Confrontation: Japan's Negotiations with the United States, 1941*. Translated by David A. Titus. Japan's Road to the Pacific War. Studies of the East Asian Institute. New York: Columbia University Press, 1994.

1342. Newell, William H., ed. *Japan in Asia, 1942-1945*. Singapore: Singapore University Press, 1981.

1343. Parillo, Mark P. *The Japanese Merchant Marine in World War II*. Annapolis, MD: Naval Institute Press, 1993.

1344. Passin, Herbert. *Encounter with Japan*. Tokyo; New York: Kodansha International, 1982.

1345. Prange, Gordon William, Donald M. Goldstein, and Katherine V. Dillon. *God's Samurai: Lead Pilot at Pearl Harbor*. Washington, DC: Brassey's, 1990.

1346. Quigley, Martin Schofield. *Peace Without Hiroshima: Secret Action at the Vatican in the Spring of 1945*. Lanham, MD: Madison Books, 1991.

1347. Spector, Ronald H. *Eagle Against the Sun: The American War with Japan*. New York: Free Press, 1985.

1348. Stephan, John J. *Hawaii Under the Rising Sun: Japan's Plans for Conquest After Pearl Harbor*. Honolulu: University of Hawaii Press, 1984.

1349. Stewart, Adrian. *The Underrated Enemy: Britain's War with Japan, December 1941-May 1942*. London: W. Kimber, 1987.

1350. Thorne, Christopher G. *The Issue of War: States, Societies, and the Far Eastern Conflict of 1941-1945*. London: Hamish Hamilton, 1985.

1351. Utley, Jonathan G. *Going to War with Japan, 1937-1941*. Knoxville, TN: University of Tennessee Press, 1985.

1352. Ward, Ian. *The Killer They Called a God*. Singapore: Media Masters, 1992.

1353. Willmott, H. P. *The Barrier and the Javelin: Japanese and Allied Pacific Strategies, February to June 1942*. Annapolis, MD: Naval Institute Press, 1983.

1354. Willmott, H. P. *Empires in the Balance: Japanese and Allied Pacific Strategies to April 1942*. Annapolis, MD: Naval Institute Press, 1982.

History—20th Century—Pacific War—Atomic Bomb

1355. Burchett, Wilfred G. *Shadows of Hiroshima*. London: Verso, 1983.

1356. Goldstein, Donald M., Katherine V. Dillon, and J. Michael Wenger. *Rain of Ruin: A Photographic History of Hiroshima and Nagasaki*. Washington, DC: Brassey's, 1995.

1357. Gordon, Thomas, and Max Morgan Witts. *Ruin From the Air: The Enola Gay's Atomic Mission to Hiroshima*. Chelsea, MI: Scarborough House, 1990.

1358. Hersey, John. *Hiroshima*. New York: Knopf, 1985.

1359. Kurzman, Dan. *Day of the Bomb: Countdown to Hiroshima*. New York: McGraw-Hill, 1986.

1360. Liebow, Averill A. *Encounter with Disaster: A Medical Diary of Hiroshima, 1945*. New York: Norton, 1985.

1361. Lifton, Betty, and Eiko Hosoe. *A Place Called Hiroshima*. Tokyo; New York: Kodansha International, 1985.

1362. Maddox, Robert James. *Weapons for Victory: The Hiroshima Decision Fifty Years Later*. Columbia, MO: University of Missouri Press, 1995.

1363. Newman, Robert P. *Truman and the Hiroshima Cult*. Rhetoric and Public Affairs Series. East Lansing, MI: Michigan State University Press, 1995.

1364. Nobile, Philip. *Judgment at the Smithsonian*. Banned History. New York: Marlowe, 1995.

1365. Ōe, Kenzaburō. *Hiroshima Notes*. Translated by David L. Swain and Toshi Yonezawa. New York: Marion Boyars, 1995.

1366. Pacific War Research Society. *The Day man Lost: Hiroshima, 6 August 1945*. Tokyo; Palo Alto, CA: Kodansha International, 1972. Reprint: Tokyo; New York,: Kodansha International, 1981.

1367. Schull, William J. *Song Among the Ruins*. Cambridge, MA: Harvard University Press, 1990.

1368. Selden, Kyoko, and Mark Selden, eds. *The Atomic Bomb: Voices from Hiroshima and Nagasaki*. Armonk, NY: Sharpe, 1989.

1369. Shono, Naomi. *The Legacy of Hiroshima: Its Past, Our Future*. Tokyo: Kosei, 1986.

1370. Takaki, Ronald T. *Hiroshima: Why America Dropped the Atomic Bomb*. Boston: Little, Brown, 1995.

1371. Wilcox, Robert K. *Japan's Secret War*. New York: Morrow, 1985.

1372. Wyden, Peter. *Day One: Before Hiroshima and After*. New York: Simon and Schuster, 1984.

History—20th Century—Pacific War—Atomic Bomb Victims

1373. Barker, Rodney. *The Hiroshima Maidens: A Story of Courage, Compassion, and Survival*. New York: Viking, 1985.

1374. *The Half-Life of Awareness: Photographs of Hiroshima and Nagasaki: 21 September-10 November, 1995, Tokyo Metropolitan Museum of Photography*. Tokyo: Tokyo Metropolitan Culture Foundation: Tokyo Metropolitan Museum of Photography, 1995.

1375. Hogan, Michael. *Hiroshima in History and Memory*. Cambridge, U.K.; New York: Cambridge University Press, 1996.

1376. Lifton, Robert Jay. *Death in Life: Survivors of Hiroshima*. Chapel Hill, NC: University of North Carolina Press, 1991.

1377. Lifton, Robert Jay, Greg Mitchell. *Hiroshima in America: Fifty Years of Denial*. New York: Putnam's Sons, 1995.

1378. Linner, Rachelle. *City of Silence: Listening to Hiroshima*. Maryknoll, NY: Orbis Book, 1995.

1379. Sekimori, Gaynor, trans. *Hibakusha, Survivors of Hiroshima and Nagasaki*. Tokyo, Kosei, 1986.

1380. Snider, Hideko Tamura. *One Sunny Day: A Child's Memories of Hiroshima.* Chicago, IL: Open Courts, 1996.

1381. Vance-Watkins, Lequita, and Mariko Aratani, eds, trans. *White Flash, Black Rain: Women of Japan Relive the Bomb.* Minneapolis, MN: Milkweed Editions, 1995.

1382. Weale, Adrian, ed. *Eye-Witness Hiroshima: First-Hand Accounts of the Atomic Terror that Changed the World.* New York: Carroll & Graf, 1995.

1383. Yamazaki, James N., and Lomis B. Fleming. *Children of the Atomic Bomb: An American Physician's Memoir of Nagasaki, Hiroshima and the Marshall Islands.* Asia Pacific. Durham, NC: Duke University Press, 1995.

History—20th Century—Pacific War—Biological Warfare

1384. Harris, Sheldon H. *Factories of Death: Japanese Biological Warfare 1932-45 and the American Cover-Up.* London; New York: Routledge, 1994.

1385. Williams, Peter, David Wallace. *Unit 731: The Japanese Army's Secret of Secrets.* London: Hodder & Stoughton, 1989.

History—20th Century—Pacific War—Bombardments

1386. Edoin, Hoito. *The Night Tokyo Burned.* New York: St. Martin's Press, 1987.

1387. Glines, Carroll V. *The Doolittle Raid: America's Daring First Strike Against Japan.* New York: Orion Books, 1988.

1388. Kerr, E. Bartlett. *Flames Over Tokyo: The U.S. Army Air Force's Incendiary Campaign Against Japan, 1944-45.* New York: D. I. Fince, 1991.

1389. Schultz, Duane P. *The Doolittle Raid.* New York: St. Martin's Press, 1988.

1390. Werrell, Kenneth P. *Blankets of Fire: U.S. Bombers over Japan during World War II.* Smithsonian History of Aviation Series. Washington, DC: Smithsonian Institution Press, 1996.

History—20th Century—Pacific War—Campaigns

1391. Alexander, Joseph H. *Closing in: Marines in the Seizure of Iwo Jima.* Marines in World War II Commemorative Series. Washington, DC: History and Museums Division, Headquarters, U.S. Marine Corps: 1994.

1392. Astor, Gerald. *Operation Iceberg: The Invasion and Conquest of Okinawa in World War II.* New York: D. I. Fine, 1995.

1393. Fisch, Arnold G. *Ryukyus.* The U.S. Army Campaigns of World War II CMH pub, 72-35. Washington, DC: U.S. Army Center of Military History, 1995.

1394. Hallas, James H. *Killing Ground on Okinawa: The Battle for Sugar Loaf Hill.* Westport, CT: Praeger, 1996.

1395. Leckie, Robert. *Okinawa: The Last Battle of World War II.* New York: Viking, 1995.

1396. Levine, Alan J. *The Pacific War: Japan Versus the Allies.* Westport, CT: Praeger, 1995.

1397. Miller, Edward S. *War Plan Orange: The U.S. Strategy to defeat Japan, 1897-1945.* Annapolis, MD: Naval Institute Press, 1991.

1398. Skates, John Ray. *The Invasion of Japan: Alternative to the Bomb.* Columbia, SC: University of South Carolina Press, 1994.

1399. Willmott, H. P. *Grave of a Dozen Schemes: British Naval Planning and the War Against Japan, 1943-1945.* Annapolis, MD: Naval Institute Press, 1996.

1400. Worth, Roland H. *No Choice but War: The United States Embargo against Japan and the Eruption of War in the Pacific.* Jefferson, NC: McFarland, 1995.

1401. Yahara, Hiromichi. *The Battle for Okinawa.* Translated by Roger Pineau, and Masatoshi Uehara. New York: Wiley, 1995.

History—20th Century—Pacific War—Foreign Fronts

1402. Buturlinov, V. F., A. M. Ledovsky, and A. A. Sveshnikov, eds. *Defeat of Militarist Japan and the USSR's Liberatory Mission in Asia: (documents).* Moscow: Novosti Press Agency Publishing House, 1985.

1403. Connaughton, R. M. *Shrouded Secrets: Japan's War on Mainland Australia, 1942-1944.* London; Washington, DC: Brassey's, 1994.

1404. Coox, Alvin D. *Nomonhan: Japan against Russia, 1939.* 2 vols. Stanford, CA: Stanford University Press, 1985.

1405. Drea, Edward J. *Nomonhan: Japanese-Soviet Tactical Combat, 1939.* Leavenworth Papers, no. 2. Fort Leavenworth, KA: Combat Studies Institute, U.S. Army Command and General Staff College, 1981.

History—20th Century—Pacific War—Intelligence Operations

1406. Boyd, Carl. *Hitler's Japanese Confidant: General Oshima Hiroshi and MAGIC Intelligence, 1941-1945.* Modern War Studies. Lawrence, KS: University Press of Kansas, 1993.

1407. Drea, Edward J. *MacArthur's ULTRA: Codebreaking and the War against Japan, 1942-1945.* Modern War Studies. Lawrence, KS: University of Kansas, 1992.

1408. Fujiwara, Iwaichi. *F. Kikan: Japanese Army Intelligence Operations in Southeast Asia during World War II.* Translated by Akashi Yoji. Asian Studies Series. Hong Kong: Heinemann Asia, 1983.

1409. Lee, Bruce. *Marching Orders: The Untold Story of World War II.* New York: Crown, 1995.

1410. Prados, John. *Combined Fleet Decoded: Secret History of American Intelligence and the Japanese Navy in World War II.* New York: Random House, 1995.

1411. Spector, Ronald H., ed. *Listening to the Enemy: Key Documents on the Role of Communications Intelligence in the War with Japan.* Wilmington, DE: Scholarly Resources, 1988.

History—20th Century—Pacific War—Kamikaze Fighters

1412. Hoyt, Edwin Palmer. *The Kamikazes.* New York: Arbor House, 1983.

1413. Naito, Hatsuho. *Thunder Gods: The Kamikaze Pilots Tell their Story.* Translated by Mayumi Ichikawa. Tokyo; New York: Kodansha International, 1989.

History—20th Century—Pacific War—Memoirs

1414. Cook, Haruko Taya, and Theodore F. Cook. *Japan at War: An Oral History*. New York: New Press, 1992.

1415. Guillain, Robert. *I Saw Tokyo Burning: An Eyewitness Narrative from Pearl Harbor to Hiroshima*. Translated by William Byron. Garden City, NY: Doubleday, 1981.

1416. Kanda, Mikio. *Widows of Hiroshima: The Life Stories of Nineteen Peasant Wives*. Translated by Taeko Midorikawa. New York: St. Martin's Press; Houndmills, UK: Macmillan, 1989.

1417. Kohchi, Akira. *Why I Survived the A-bomb*. Costa Mesa, CA: Institute for Historical Review, 1989.

1418. Korean Council for Women Drafted for Military Sexual Slavery by Japan, and the Research Association on the Women Drafted for Military Sexual Slavery by Japan. *True Stories of the Korean Comfort Women: Testimonies*. Translated by Young Joo Lee. Edited by Keith Howard. London; New York: Cassell, 1995.

1419. Minear, Richard H., ed., trans. *Hiroshima: Three Witnesses*. Princeton, NJ: Princeton University Press, 1990.

1420. Nagai, Takashi. *The Bells of Nagasaki*. Tokyo; New York: Kodansha International, 1984.

1421. Ugaki. Matome. *Fading Victory: The Diary of Admiral Matome Ugaki, 1941-1945*. Pittsburgh, PA: University of Pittsburgh Press, 1991.

History—20th Century—Pacific War—Naval Operations

1422. Boyd, Carl, and Akihiko Yoshida. *The Japanese Submarine Force and World War II*. Annapolis, MD: Naval Institute Press, 1995.

History—20th Century—Pacific War—Occupied Territories

1423. Duus, Peter, Ramon H. Myers, and Mark R. Peattie, eds. *The Japanese Wartime Empire, 1931-1945*. Princeton, NJ: Princeton University Press, 1996.

1424. Friend, Theodore. *The Blue-eyed Enemy: Japan Against the West in Java and Luzon, 1942-1945*. Princeton, NJ: Princeton University Press, 1988.

1425. Goodman, Grant K. *Japanese Cultural Policies in Southeast Asia during World War II*. New York: St. Martin's Press, 1991.

1426. Hsiung, James C., and Steven I. Levine, eds. *China's Bitter Victory: The War with Japan, 1937-1945*. Studies on Modern China. Armonk, NY: Sharpe, 1992.

1427. Morley, James William. *The Fateful Choice: Japan's Advance into Southeast Asia, 1939-1941: Selected Translations from Taiheiyo Senso e no Michi, Kaisen Gaiko Shi*. Japan's Road to the Pacific War. New York: Columbia University Press, 1980.

1428. Reynolds, E. Bruce. *Thailand and Japan's Southern Advance, 1940-1945*. New York: St. Martin's Press, 1994.

1429. Sareen, Tilak Raj. *Japan and the Indian National Army*. Delhi: Agam Prakashan, 1986.

History—20th Century—Pacific War—Peace

1430. Dunn, Frederic S. *Peace-Making and the Settlement with Japan*. Princeton, NJ: Princeton University Press, 1963. Reprint: Westport, CT: Greenwood, 1981.

History—20th Century—Pacific War—Prisoners of War

1431. Baynes, L. L. *Kept — The Other Side of Tenko*. Lewes, U.K.: Book Guild, 1984.

1432. Berry, William A. *Prisoner of the Rising Sun*. Norman, OK: University of Oklahoma Press, 1993.

1433. Burdick, Charles, and Ursula Moessner. *The German Prisoner-of-War in Japan, 1914-1920*. Lanham, MD: University Press of America, 1984.

1434. Clarke, Hugh V. *Last Stop Nagasaki!* London; Boston: G. Allen & Unwin, 1984.

1435. Corbet, P. Scott. *Quiet Passages: The Exchange of Civilians between the United States and Japan during the Second World War.* Kent, OH: Kent State University Press, 1987.

1436. Daws, Gavan. *Prisoners of the Japanese: POWs of World War II in the Pacific.* New York: William Morrow, 1994.

1437. Fujita, Frank. *Foo, a Japanese-American Prisoner of the Rising Sun: The Secret Prison Diary of Frank "Foo" Fujita.* War and the Southwest Series, no. 1. Denton, TX: University of North Texas Press, 1993.

1438. Giles, Donald T. *Captive of the Rising Sun: The POW Memoirs of Rear Admiral Donald T. Giles, USN.* Annapolis, MD: Naval Institute Press, 1994.

1439. Haney, Robert E. *Caged Dragons: An American P.O.W. in WW II Japan.* Ann Arbor, MI: Sabre Press, Division of Momentum Books, 1991.

1440. Kiyosaki, Wayne S. *A Spy in their Midst: The World War II Struggle of a Japanese-American Hero.* Lanham, MD: Madison Books, 1995.

1441. MacKay, James. *The Allied Japanese Conspiracy.* Edinburgh, U.K.: Pentland Press, 1995.

1442. Roy, Patricia, et al. *Mutual Hostages: Canadians and Japanese during the Second World War.* Toronto, Ont.: University of Toronto Press, 1990.

1443. Stellingwerff, Johannes. *Fat Man in Nagasaki: Nederlandse Krijgsgevangenen Overleefden de Atoombom* [Fat Man in Nagasaki: Dutch Prisoners of War Survived the Atomic Bomb]. Franeker, Netherlands: Wever, 1980.

1444. Waterford, Van. *Prisoners of the Japanese in World War II: Statistical History, Personal Narratives, and Memorials Concerning POWs in Camps and on Hellships, Civilian Internees, Asian Slave Laborers, and Other Captured in the Pacific Theater.* Jefferson, NC: McFarland, 1994.

History—20th Century—Postwar (Since 1945)

1445. Braddon, Russell. *The Other Hundred Years War: Japan's Bid for Supremacy 1941-2041*. London: Collins, 1983.

1446. Crump, Thomas. *The Death of an Emperor: Japan At the Crossroads*. London: Constable, 1989.

1447. Entwistle, Basil. *Japan's Decisive Decade: How a Determined Minority Changed the Nation's Course in the 1950s*. London; Bridgeport, CT: Grosvenor Books, 1985.

1448. Field, Norma. *In the Realm of a Dying Emperor*. New York: Pantheon Books, 1991.

1449. Gibney, Frank. *Japan, the Fragile Superpower*. 2d rev. ed. New York: New American Library, 1985.

1450. Gordon, Andrew, ed. *Postwar Japan as History*. Berkeley, CA: University of California Press, 1993.

1451. Hane, Mikiso. *Eastern Phoenix: Japan since 1945*. Boulder, CO: Westview, 1996.

1452. Havens, Thomas R. H. *Fire Across the Sea: The Vietnam War and Japan, 1965-1975*. Princeton, NJ: Princeton University Press, 1987.

1453. Hoyt, Edwin Palmer. *The Militarists: The Rise of Japanese Militarism since World War II*. New York: D. I. Fine, 1985.

History—20th Century—Postwar—Allied Occupation

1454. Cohen, Theodore. *Remaking Japan: The American Occupation as New Deal*. New York: Free Press, 1987.

1455. Finn, Richard B. *Winners in Peace: MacArthur, Yoshida, and Postwar Japan*. Berkeley, CA: University of California Press, 1992.

1456. Harries, Meirion, and Susie Harries. *Sheathing the Sword: The Demilitarization of Japan*. London: Hamish Hamilton, 1987.

1457. Schonberger, Howard B. *Aftermath of War: Americans and the Remaking of Japan, 1945-1952*. American Diplomatic History Series. Kent, OH: Kent State University Press, 1989.

History—20th Century—Postwar—Tokyo Trial

1458. Brackman, Arnold C. *The Other Nuremberg: The Untold Story of the Tokyo War Crimes Trials.* New York: Morrow, 1987.

1459. Ginn, John L. *Sugamo Prison; Tokyo: An Account of the Trial and Sentencing of Japanese War Criminals in 1948, by a U.S. Participant.* Jefferson, NC: McFarland, 1992.

1460. International Military Tribunal for the Far East. *The Tokyo War Crimes Trial: Index and Guide.* 5 vols. Compiled, and edited by R. John Pritchard and Sonia Magbanua Zaide. New York: Garland, 1981-1987.

1461. Röling, B. V. A. *The Tokyo Trial and Beyond: Reflections of a Peacemonger.* Edited by Antonio Cassese. Cambridge, U.K.: Polity, 1993.

History—20th Century—Prewar (To 1939)

1462. Barnhart, Michael A. *Japan Prepares for Total War: The Search for Economic Security, 1919-1941.* Cornell Studies in Security Affairs. Ithaca: Cornell University Press, 1987.

1463. Murakami, Hyoe. *Japan, the Years of Trial, 1919-52.* Tokyo: Japan Culture Institute, 1982.

1464. Myers, Ramon H., and Mark R. Peattie, eds. *The Japanese Colonial Empire, 1895-1945.* Princeton, NJ: Princeton University Press, 1984.

1465. Sun, You-Li. *China and the Origins of the Pacific War, 1931-41.* New York: St. Martin's Press, 1993.

Human Geography

1466. Schwind, Martin. *Japan, die neue Mitte Ostasiens: Erlebnisse, Forschungen, Begegnungen* [Japan, the New Center of East Asia: Experiences, Studies and Encounters]. Kleine Geographische Schriften, Bd. 7. Berlin, Germany: D. Reimer, 1987.

Human Rights

1467. Goodman, Roger, and Ian Neary, eds. *Case Studies on Human Rights in Japan.* Richmond, U.K.: Japan Library, 1996.

Humanism

1468. Nagatomo, Shigenori. *A Philosophical Foundation of Miki Kiyoshi's Concept of Humanism.* Studies in Asian Thought and Religion, v. 15. Lewiston, NY: Mellen Press, 1995.

Ikebana

1469. Coe, Stella. *Ikebana: A Practical and Philosophical Guide to Japanese Flower Arrangement.* Edited by Mary L. Stewart. New York: Gallery Books, 1988.

1470. Fusonie, Alan, and Judith Ho. *Ikebana: Rare Book Collection Located at the U.S. National Arboretum.* Beltsville, MD: Special Collections, National Agricultural Library, 1984.

1471. Herrigel, Gustie L. *Zen in the Art of Flower Arrangement: An Introduction to the Spirit of the Japanese Art of Flower Arrangement.* Translated by R. F. C. Hull. London; New York: Arkana, 1987.

1472. Kasuya, Akihiro, ed. *Ikebana, Ichiyo School.* Tokyo: Shufunotomo, 1991.

1473. Masanobu, Kudo. *The History of Ikebana.* Translated by Jay Gluck and Sumi Gluck. Tokyo: Shufunotomo, 1986.

1474. Ohno, Noriko. *The Poetry of Ikebana.* Tokyo; New York: Kodansha International, 1990.

1475. Okada, Kozan, and Hollistar Ferretti. *Ikebana with the Seasons.* Tokyo: Shufunotomo, 1989.

1476. Takenaka, Masao. *Consider the Flowers: Meditations in Ikebana.* Tokyo: Kyo Bun Kwan, 1990.

Incense

1477. Morita, Kiyoko. *The Book of Incense: Enjoying the Traditional Art of Japanese Scents.* Tokyo; New York: Kodansha International, 1992.

India—Relations with

1478. Bajpai, U.S., ed. *India and Japan: A New Relationship?* New Delhi: Lancer, 1988.

1479. Iqbal, Badar Alam. *India's Trade With Japan*. Delhi: Academic Foundation, 1990.

1480. Kanwar, Kamlendra, ed. *India-Japan: Towards a New Era*. New Delhi: UBS, 1992.

1481. Narasimha Murthy, P. A. *India and Japan: Dimensions of Their Relations: Economic and Cultural*. New Delhi: Lancers Books, 1993.

1482. Narasimha Murthy, P.A. *India and Japan: Dimensions of Their Relations: Historical and Political* with *India and Japan: Dimensions of Their Relations: Documents*. New Delhi: ABC Publishing House, 1986.

Individualism

1483. Miyanaga, Kuniko. *The Creative Edge: Emerging Individualism in Japan*. New Brunswick, NJ: Transaction, 1991.

1484. Reinhold, Gerd. *Familie und Beruf in Japan: zur Identitätsbildung in einer asiatischen Industriegesellschaft* [Family and Profession in Japan: Toward the Formation of Identity in an Asian Industrial Society]. Sozialwissenschaftliche Abhandlungen der Gorres-Gesellschaft, Bd. 7. Berlin, Germany: Duncker & Humblot, 1981.

Industrial Management

1485. Aoki, Masahiko. *Information, Incentives, and Bargaining in the Japanese Economy*. Cambridge, U.K.; New York: Cambridge University Press, 1988.

1486. Bratton, John. *Japanization at Work: Managerial Studies for the 1990s*. Basingstoke, U.K.: Macmillan, 1992.

1487. De Mente, Boye. *How to Do Business with the Japanese: A Complete Guide to Japanese Customs and Business Practices*. Lincolnwood, IL: NTC Business Books, 1987.

1488. Hayashi, Shuji. *Culture and Management in Japan*. Tokyo: University of Tokyo Press, 1988.

1489. Imai, Kenichi, and Ryutaro Komiya. *Business Enterprise in Japan: Views of Leading Japanese Economists*. Translation edited by Ronald Dore and Hugh Whittaker. Cambridge, MA: MIT Press, 1994.

1490. Imai, Masaaki. *Kaizen, the Key to Japanese Competitive Success.* New York: Random House Business Division, 1986.

1491. Katayama, Osamu. *Japanese Business Into the 21st Century: Strategies for Success.* London; Atlantic Highlands, NJ: Athlone Press, 1996.

1492. Levine, David I. *Reinventing the Workplace: How Business and Employees Can Both Win.* Washington, DC: Brookings Institution, 1995.

1493. McMillan, Charles J. *The Japanese Industrial System.* 2d rev. ed. De Gruyter Studies in Organization, 1. Berlin; New York: W. de Gruyter, 1985.

1494. Mito, Setsuo. *The Honda Book of Management: A Leadership Philosophy for High Industrial Success.* Rev. ed. London; Atlantic Highlands, NJ: Athlone Press, 1990.

1495. Nonaka, Ikujiro, and Hiro Takeuchi. *The Knowledge-Creating Company: How Japanese Companies Create the Dynamics of Innovation.* New York: Oxford University Press, 1995.

1496. Odagiri, Hiroyuki. *Growth through Competition, Competition through Growth: Strategic Management and the Economy in Japan.* Oxford, U.K.: Clarendon, 1992.

1497. Odaka, Kunio. *Japanese Management: A Forward-Looking Analysis.* Tokyo: Asian Productivity Organization, 1986.

1498. Ohmae, Kenichi. *The Mind of the Strategist: The Art of Japanese Business.* New York: McGraw-Hill, 1982.

1499. Sasaki, Naoto. *Management and Industrial Structure in Japan.* 2nd ed. Oxford, U.K.: New York: Pergamon, 1990.

1500. Sato, Kazuo, and Yasuo Hoshino, eds. *The Anatomy of Japanese Business.* Armonk, NY: M. E. Sharpe; London: Croom Helm, 1984.

1501. Shimizu, Ryūei. *Company Vitalization by Top Management in Japan.* Tokyo: Keio Tsushin, 1992.

1502. Sugimoto, Giichi. *Six-Sided Management: Righteousness, Gratitude, Compassion.* Mellon Studies in Business, v. 3. Lewiston, NY: Mellen Press, 1989.

1503. Suzuki, Yoshitaka. *Japanese Management Structures, 1920-80*. Studies in the Modern Japanese Economy. London: Macmillan, 1991.

1504. Tanaka, Hiroshi. *The Human Side of Japanese Enterprise*. Philadelphia, PA: University of Pennsylvania Press, 1988.

1505. Tateishi, Kazuma. *The Eternal Venture Spirit: An Executive's Practical Philosophy*. Cambridge, MA: Productivity Press, 1989.

1506. Thurow, Lester, ed. *The Management Challenge: Japanese Views*. Cambridge, MA: MIT Press, 1985.

1507. Whitehill, Arthur M. *Japanese Management: Tradition and Transition*. London; New York: Routledge, 1991.

1508. Yuzawa, Takeshi, ed. *Japanese Business Success: The Evolution of a Strategy*. Comparative and International Business. Modern Histories Series. New York; London: Routledge, 1994.

1509. Zimmerman, Mark. *How to do Business with the Japanese*. New York: Random House, 1985.

Industrial Organization

1510. Gerlach, Michael L. *Alliance Capitalism: The Social Organization of Japanese Business*. Berkeley, CA: University of California Press, 1992.

1511. Kobayashi, Maurie K. *Japan: The Most Misunderstood Country*. Tokyo: Japan Times, 1984.

1512. Kono, Toyohiro. *Strategy and Structure of Japanese Enterprises*. London: Macmillan; Armonk, NY: Sharpe, 1984.

1513. Miwa, Yoshiro. *Firms and Industrial Organization in Japan*. New York: New York University Press, 1996.

1514. Sheard, Paul, ed. *International Adjustment and the Japanese Firm*. St. Leonards, Australia: Allen Unwin in association with the Australia-Japan Research Centre, the Australian National University, 1992.

Industrial Policy

1515. Francks, Penelope. *Japanese Economic Development: Theory and Practice*. Nissan Institute / Routledge Japanese Studies Series. London; New York: Routledge, 1992.

1516. Friedman, David. *The Misunderstood Miracle: Industrial Development and Political Change in Japan.* Cornell Studies in Political Economy. Ithaca, NY: Cornell University Press, 1988.

1517. Hollerman, Leon. *Japan, Disincorporated: The Economic Liberalization Process.* Stanford, CA: Stanford University Press, 1988.

1518. Johnson, Chalmers A. *MITI and the Japanese Miracle: The Growth of Industrial Policy, 1925-1975.* Stanford, CA: Stanford University Press, 1982.

1519. Komiya, Ryutaro, Masahiro Okuno, and Kotaro Suzumura, eds. *Industrial Policy of Japan.* Tokyo; San Diego, CA: Academic Press, 1988.

1520. Kotabe, Masaaki. *Anticompetitive Practices in Japan: Their Impact on the Performance of Foreign Firms.* Westport, CT: Praeger, 1996.

1521. Oppenheim, Phillip. *The New Masters: Can the West Match Japan?* London: Business Books, 1991.

1522. Samuels, Richard J. *The Business of the Japanese State: Energy Markets in Comparative and Historical Perspective.* Cornell Studies in Political Economy. Ithaca, NY: Cornell University Press, 1987.

1523. Sato, Kazuo, ed. *Industry and Business in Japan.* White Plains, NY: M. E. Sharpe; London: Croom Helm, 1980.

1524. Vestal, James E. *Planning for Change: Industrial Policy and Japanese Economic Development, 1945-1990.* Oxford, U.K.: Clarendon Press; Oxford, U.K.; New York: Oxford University Press, 1993.

1525. Wilks, Stephen, and Maurice Wright, eds. *Promotion and Regulation of Industry in Japan.* New York: St. Martin's Press, 1991.

1526. Wolf, Marvin J. *The Japanese Conspiracy: The Plot to Dominate Industry Worldwide — And How to Deal with it.* New York: Empire Books, 1983.

Industrial Productivity

1527. Feinberg, Walter. *Japan and the Pursuit of a New American Identity: Work and Education in a Multicultural Age.* New York: Routledge, 1993.

1528. Johnson, Chalmers, Laura D'Andrea Tyson, and John Sysman, eds. *Politics and Productivity: The Real Story of Why Japan Works.* Cambridge, MA: Ballinger, 1989.

Industrial Research

1529. Bess, James L. *Creative R & D Leadership: Insights from Japan.* Westport, CT: Quorum Books, 1995.

1530. Clark, Rodney. *Aspects of Japanese Commercial Innovation.* London: Technical Change Centre, 1984.

1531. Eto, Hajime, and Konomu Matsui, eds. *R & D Management Systems in Japanese Industry.* Amsterdam; New York: North Holland, 1984.

1532. Minami, Ryoshin, et al. *Acquiring, Adapting, and Developing Technologies: Lessons from the Japanese Experience.* Studies in Modern Japanese Economy. New York: St. Martin's Press, 1995.

1533. Tatsuno, Sheridan M. *Created in Japan: From Imitators to World-Class Innovators.* New York: Harper & Row, 1990.

Industry

1534. Dore, Ronald Philip. *Flexible Rigidities: Industrial Policy and Structural Adjustment in the Japanese Economy, 1970-80.* Stanford, CA: Stanford University Press, 1986.

1535. Dore, Ronald Philip. *Structural Adjustment in Japan, 1970-82.* Employment, Adjustment, and Industrialization, 1. Geneva, Switzerland: International Labour Office, 1986.

1536. Ehrlich, Eva. *Japan, a Case of Catching-Up.* Budapest, Hungary: Akademiai Kiado, 1984.

1537. Murata, Kiyoji, ed. *An Industrial Geography of Japan.* New York: St. Martin's Press, 1980.

1538. Ohsono, Tomokazu. *Charting Japanese Industry: A Graphical Guide to Corporate and Market Structures.* London; New York: Cassell, 1995.

1539. Okuda, Yoshio. *Japan's Industrial Economy: Recent Trends and Changing Aspects.* Translated by James J. D. Hegarty. Understanding Japan, 52. Tokyo: International Society for Educational Information, 1987.

1540. Smith, Thomas C. *Native Sources of Japanese Industrialization, 1750-1920.* Berkeley, CA: University of California Press, 1988.

1541. Uriu, Robert M. *Troubled Industries: Confronting Economic Change in Japan.* Cornell Studies in Political Economy. A Studies of the East Asian Institute. Ithaca, NY: Cornell University Press, 1996.

1542. Woronoff, Jon. *The Japan Syndrome: Symptoms, Ailments, and Remedies.* New Brunswick, NJ: Transaction Books, 1986.

1543. Zengage, Thomas R. *The Japanese Century: Challenge and Response.* Hong Kong: Longman, 1988.

Industry—Automobile

1544. Kamata, Satoshi. *Japan in the Passing Lane: An Insider's Account of Life in a Japanese Auto Factory.* Translated and edited by Tatsuru Akimoto. New York: Pantheon Books, 1982.

1545. Mair, Andrew. *Honda's Global Local Corporation.* New York: St. Martin's Press, 1994.

1546. Smitka, Michael. *Competitive Ties: Subcontracting in the Japanese Automotive Industry.* Studies of the East Asian Institute. New York: Columbia University Press, 1991.

1547. Togo, Yukiyasu, and William Wartman. *Against All Odds: The Story of the Toyota Motor Corporation and the Family that Created It.* New York: St. Martin's Press, 1993.

1548. Wokutch, Richard E. *Worker Protection, Japanese Style: Occupational Safety and Health in the Auto Industry.* Cornell International Industrial and Labor Relations Reports, no. 21. Ithaca, NY: ILR Press, 1992.

1549. Womack, James P., Daniel T. Jones, and Daniel Roos. *The Machine that Changed the World: How Japan's Secret Weapon in the Global Auto Wars will Revolutionize Western Industry.* New York: Harper Perennial, 1991.

Industry—Automobile—Bibliography

1550. Chao, Sheau-yueh J., comp. *The Japanese Automobile Industry: An Annotated Bibliography.* Bibliographies and Indexes in Economics and Economic History, no. 15. Westport, CT: Greenwood, 1994.

Industry—Construction

See also: 1710

1551. Hasegawa, Fumio, and the Shimizu Group SS. *Built By Japan: Competitive Strategies of the Japanese Construction Industry.* New York: Wiley, 1988.

1552. Levy, Sidney M. *Japanese Construction: An American Perspective.* New York: Van Nostrand Reinhold, 1990.

1553. Levy, Sidney M. *Japan's Big Six: Case Studies of Japan's Largest Contractors.* New York: McGraw-Hill, 1993.

1554. Webster, Anthony C. *Technological Advance in Japanese Building Design and Construction.* New York: ASCE Pressers, 1994.

1555. Woodhall, Brian. *Japan Under Construction: Corruption, Politics, and Public Works.* Berkeley, CA: University of California Press, 1996.

Industry—Electronics

1556. Cusumano, Michael A. *Japan's Software Factories: A Challenge to U.S. Management.* New York: Oxford University Press, 1991.

1557. Fransman, Martin. *Japan's Computer and Communications Industry: The Evolution of Industrial Giants and Global Competitiveness.* New York: Oxford University Press, 1995.

1558. Kobayashi, Koji. *The Rise of NEC: How the World's Greatest C & C Company is Managed.* Development Management. Cambridge, MA: B. Blackwell Business, 1991.

1559. Mead, Graham P., Harry Carrel, and Julia Miezejeski. *NEC in Telecom: A Strategic Analysis.* New York: McGraw-Hill, 1993.

1560. Morita, Akio, Edwin M. Reingold, and Mitsuko Shimomura. *Made in Japan: Akio Morita and Sony.* New York: Dutton, 1986.

Industry—Food

1561. Bergin, Anthony, and Marcus Haward. *Japan's Tuna Fishing Industry: A Setting Sun or a New Dawn?* Commack, NY: Nova Science, 1996.

1562. George, Aurelia, and David Rapkin. *GATT Negotiations and the Opening of Japan's Rice Market: A Two-Level Game Approach.* Pacific Economic Papers, no. 215. Canberra: Australia-Japan Research Centre, 1993.

1563. Hayami, Yujiro. *Japanese Agriculture Under Siege: The Political Economy of Agricultural Policies.* Studies in the Modern Japanese Economy. London: Macmillan, 1988.

1564. Howell, David Luke. *Capitalism from Within: Economy, Society, and the State in a Japanese Fishery.* Berkeley, CA: University of California Press, 1995.

1565. Longworth, John W. *Beef in Japan: Politics, Production, Marketing & Trade.* St. Lucia, Australia; New York: University of Queensland Press, 1983.

1566. O'Rourke, A. Desmond, ed. *Understanding the Japanese Food and Agrimarket: A Multifaceted Opportunity.* New York: Food Products Press, 1994.

1567. Rothacher, Albrecht. *Japan's Agro-food Sector: The Politics and Economics of Excess Protection.* Basingstoke, U.K.: Macmillan, 1989.

Industry—High Technology

1568. Callon, Scott. *Divided Sun: MITI and the Breakdown of Japanese High-tech Industrial Policy, 1975-1993.* Stanford, CA: Stanford University Press, 1995.

1569. *High Tech in Japan.* Tokyo: High Tech Research Institute, 1985.

1570. Kodama, Fumio. *Analyzing Japanese High Technologies: The Techno-Paradigm Shift.* London; New York: Pinter, 1991.

1571. Okimoto, Daniel I. *Between MITI and the Market: Japanese Industrial Policy for High Technology.* Stanford, CA: Stanford University Press, 1989.

Industry—Lumber

1572. Totman, Conrad D. *The Lumber Industry in Early Modern Japan.* Honolulu, HI: University of Hawaii Press, 1995.

Industry—Military

1573. Drifte, Reinhard. *Arms Production in Japan: The Military Applications of Civilian Technology.* Westview Special Studies on East Asia. Boulder, CO: Westview, 1986.

1574. Soderberg, Marie. *Japan's Military Export Policy.* Japanological Studies, 6. Stockholm: University of Stockholm, 1986.

Industry—Mining

1575. Allen, Matthew. *Undermining the Japanese Miracle: Work and Conflict in a Coalmining Community.* Cambridge, UK; New York: Cambridge University Press, 1994.

Industry—Pharmaceutical

1576. Macarthur, Donald. *The Japanese Pharmaceutical Challenge.* Richmond, U.K.: PJB Publications, 1987.

Industry—Steel

1577. Subcommittee on Postwar History of Iron and Steel Technology, Iron and Steel Institute of Japan. *Technological Development in the Japanese Steel Industry During Its Postwar Reconstruction.* Tokyo: Iron and Steel Institute of Japan, 1993.

Industry—Textile

1578. Findlay, Christopher, and Motoshige Itoh, eds. *Wool in Japan: Structural Change in the Textile and Clothing Market.* Pymble, Australia: HarperEducational in association with the Australia-Japan Research Centre, the Australian National University, 1994.

1579. McNamara, Dennis L. *Textiles and Industrial Transition in Japan.* Ithaca, NY: Cornell University Press, 1995.

Information Technology

1580. Arnold, Stephen E. *The Information Factory: A Profile of Japan's Information and Database Infrastructure.* Infonortics in-depth Briefings. Calne, U.K.: Infonortics, 1991.

1581. Evers, Rolf. *Information Technology in Japan: State of the Art, Future Developments and Government Promotion.* GMD-Studien 0170-8120, Nr. 125. Sankt / Augustin, Germany: Gesellschaft für Mathematik und Datenverarbeiting, 1987.

1582. Feigenbaum, Edward, et al. *Advanced Software Applications in Japan.* Advanced Computing and Telecommunications Series. Park Ridge, NJ: Noyes Data Corp., 1994.

1583. Feigenbaum, Edward A., and Pamela McCorduck. *The Fifth Generation: Artificial Intelligence and Japan's Computer Challenge to the World.* Reading, MA: Addison-Wesley, 1983.

1584. Forrester, Tom. *Sillicon Samurai: How Japan Conquered the World's IT Industry.* Cambridge, MA: B. Blackwell Business, 1993.

1585. Hunt, Brian, and David Targett. *The Japanese Advantage?: Competitive IT Strategies Past, Present, and Future.* Oxford, U.K.; Boston, MA: Butterworth-Heinemann, 1995.

1586. Morris-Suzuki, Tessa. *Beyond Computopia: Information, Automation, and Democracy in Japan.* Japanese Studies. London; New York: Kegan Paul International, 1988.

1587. Vardaman, Jan, ed. *Surface Mount Technology: Recent Japanese Developments.* New York: Institute of Electrical and Electronics Engineers, 1993.

Innovation

1588. Herbig, Paul A. *Innovation Japanese Style: A Cultural and Historical Perspective*. Westport, CT: Quorum Books, 1995.

1589. Kodama, Fumio. *Emerging Patterns of Innovation: Sources of Japan's Technological Edge*. Management of Innovation and Change Series. Boston, MA: Harvard Business School Press, 1995.

Input-output Analysis

1590. Uno, Kimio. *Measurement of Services in an Input-Output Framework*. Amsterdam; New York: North-Holland, 1989.

Inro *See*: Art—Netsuke and Inro

Insurance

1591. Japan Business History Institute, ed. *The 100-Year History of Nippon Life: Its Growth and Socioeconomic Setting 1889-1989*. Osaka, Japan: Nippon Life Insurance Co., 1991.

1592. Niwata, Noriaki. *Insurance, its Principles and Practice in Japan: Second Series*. Tokyo: Insurance Institute of the Keio University, 1993.

1593. Niwata, Noriaki. *The Theory of Insurance and Social Security in Japan*. Tokyo: The Insurance Institute of the Keio University, 1986.

Intelligence *See*: Espionage

Interior Design *See*: Architecture—Interior Design

International Relations *See*: Diplomatic Relations

Investments

1594. Alletzhauser, Al. *The House of Nomura: The Rise to Power of the World's Wealthiest Company: The Inside Story of the Legendary Japanese Dynasty*. New York: Arcade, 1990.

1595. Dattel, Eugene R. *The Sun that Never Rose: The Inside Story of Japan's Failed Attempt at Global Financial Dominance*. Chicago, IL: Probus, 1994.

1596. Isaacs, Jonathan, and Takashi Ejiri. *Japanese Securities Market*. London: Euromoney, 1990.

1597. Matsumoto, Toru. *Japanese Stocks: A Basic Guide for the Intelligent Investor*. Tokyo; New York: Kodansha International, 1989.

1598. Morris, Jonathan. *Japan and the Global Economy: Issues and Trends in the 1990s*. London; New York: Routledge, 1991.

1599. Murphy, R. Taggart. *The Weight of the Yen: How Denial Imperils America's Future and Ruins an Alliance*. New York: Norton, 1996.

1600. Nakao, Shigeo. *The Political Economy of Japan Money*. Tokyo: University of Tokyo Press, 1995.

1601. Nison, Steve. *Beyond Candlesticks: More Japanese Charting Techniques Revealed*. Wiley Finance Editions. New York: Wiley, 1994.

1602. Ohmae, Ken'ichi. *The Borderless World: Power and Strategy in the Interlinked World Economy*. New York: Harper Business, 1990.

1603. Sakakibara, Shigeki, et al. *The Japanese Stock Market: Pricing Systems and Accounting Information*. New York: Praeger, 1988.

1604. *Savings and Savings Promotion Movement in Japan*. Tokyo: Central Council for Savings Promotion, 1981.

1605. *Selling in Japan: The World's Second Largest Market*. Tokyo: JETRO, 1985.

1606. Steven, Rob. *Japan and the New World Order: Global Investments, Trade and Finance*. New York: St. Martin's Press, 1996.

1607. Strange, Roger. *Japanese Manufacturing Investments in Europe: Its Impact on the UK Economy*. International Business Series. London; New York: Routledge, 1993.

1608. Turner, Charlie G. *Japan's Dynamic Efficiency in the Global Market: Trade, Investment, and Economic Growth*. New York: Quorum Books, 1991.

1609. Wood, Christopher. *The Bubble Economy: The Japanese Economic Collapse*. London: Sidgwick & Jackson, 1992.

1610. Yamashita, Shoichi. *Transfer of Japanese Technology and Management to the ASEAN Countries.* Tokyo: University of Tokyo Press, 1991.

1611. Ziemba, William T., and Sandra L. Schwartz. *Invest Japan: The Structure, Performance and Opportunities of Japan's Stock, Bond and Fund Markets.* Institutional Investor Publication. Chicago, IL: Probus, 1992.

1612. Ziemba, William T., Warren Bailey, and Yasushi Hamao. *Japanese Financial Market Research.* Contributions to Economic Analysis, 205. Amsterdam; New York: North-Holland, 1991.

Investments—Foreign

1613. Borton, James W. *Venture Japan: How Growing Companies Worldwide Can Tap Into the Japanese Venture Capital Markets.* Chicago, IL: Probus, 1992.

1614. Brown, J. Robert. *Opening Japan's Financial Markets.* London; New York: Routledge, 1994.

1615. Christelow, Dorothy B. *When Giants Converge: The Role of U.S.-Japan Direct Investment.* Armonk, NY: Sharpe, 1995.

1616. Hines, Mary Alice. *Investing in Japanese Real Estate.* New York: Quorum Books, 1987.

1617. Ishizumi, Kanji. *Acquiring Japanese Companies: Mergers and Acquisitions in the Japanese Market.* Rev. ed. Oxford, U.K.; Cambridge, MA: Blackwell, 1990.

1618. Matsushita, Mitsuo. *Japanese International Trade and Investment Law.* Tokyo: University of Tokyo Press, 1989.

1619. Yoshitomi, Masaru, and Edward M. Graham, eds. *Foreign Direct Investment in Japan.* New Horizons in International Business. Cheltenham, U.K.; Brookfield, VT: E. Elgar, 1996.

Islam *See:* Religion—Islam

Japanese Studies outside Japan

1620. Befu, Harumi, and Josef Kreiner, eds. *Othernesses of Japan: Historical and Cultural Influences on Japanese Studies in Ten Countries*. Monographien, Bd. 1. Munchen, Germany: Iudicium, 1992.

1621. Boscaro, Adriana, Franco Gatti, and Massino Raveri, eds. *Rethinking Japan*. 2 vols. New York: St. Martin's Press, 1990-1991.

1622. Cogan, John J., and Donald O. Schneider, eds. *Perspectives on Japan: A Guide for Teachers*. Washington, DC: National Council for the Social Studies, 1983.

1623. *Japan Information Resources in the United States, 1995*. 4th ed. Tokyo: Keizai Koho Center, 1995.

1624. *Japanese Studies in Europe*. Directory Series, 7. Tokyo: Japan Foundation, 1985.

1625. Kirby, E. Stuart. *Russian Studies of Japan: An Exploratory Survey*. London: Macmillan, 1981.

Job Security

1626. Beck, John C., and Martha N. Beck. *The Change of a Lifetime: Employment Patterns Among Japan's Managerial Elite*. Honolulu, HI: University of Hawaii Press, 1994.

Joruri *See*: Theater—Joruri

Joint Ventures

1627. Tung, Rosalie L. *Business Negotiations with the Japanese*. Lexington, MA: Lexington Books, 1984.

Justice *See*: Criminal Justice; Law

Just-in-Time Systems

1628. Japan Management Association, ed. *Kanban Just-in-Time at Toyota: Management Begins at the Workplace*. Translated by David J. Lu. Cambridge, MA: Productivity Press, 1989.

1629. Ohno, Taiichi, and Setsuo Mito. *Just-in-Time for Today and Tomorrow*. Cambridge, MA: Productivity Press, 1988.

Juvenile Delinquency

1630. Sato, Ikuya. *Kamikaze Biker: Parody and Anomy in Affluent Japan*. Chicago, IL: University of Chicago Press, 1991.

1631. Wagatsuma, Hiroshi, and George DeVos. *Heritage of Endurance: Family Patterns and Delinquency Formation in Urban Japan*. Berkeley, CA: University of California Press, 1984.

Kabuki *See*: Theater—Kabuki

Korea—Relations with

1632. Bridges, Brian. *Japan and Korea in the 1990s: From Antagonism to Adjustment*. Aldershot, U.K.; Brookfield, VT: Elgar, 1993.

1633. Calman, Donald. *The Nature and Origins of Japanese Imperialism: A Reinterpretation of the Great Crisis of 1873*. London; New York: Routledge, 1992.

1634. Cheong, Sung-hwa. *The Politics of Anti-Japanese Sentiment in Korea: Japanese-South Korean Relations under American Occupation, 1945-1952*. Contributions to the Study of World History, no. 24. New York: Greenwood, 1991.

1635. Duus, Peter. *The Abacus and the Sword: The Japanese Penetration of Korea, 1895-1910*. Twentieth Century Japan, 4. Berkeley, CA: University of California Press, 1995.

1636. Hong, Wontack. *Relationship Between Korea and Japan in Early Period: Paekche and Yamato Wa*. Ancient Korean-Japanese History. Seoul: ILSIMMSA, 1988.

1637. Lee, Chong-Sik. *Japan and Korea: The Political Dimension*. Hoover Press Publication, 318. Stanford, CA: Hoover Institution Press, 1985.

1638. Moon, Tae-Woon. *Die japanisch-koreanischen Beziehungen nach dem Zweiten Weltkrieg unter besonderer Berucksichtigung der Nationalstereotypen* [Japanese-Korean Relations after World War II with Particular Consideration of National Stereotypes]. Reihe Geschichtswissenschaft, Bd. 11. Pfaffenweiler, Germany: Centaurus-Verlagsgesellschaft, 1989.

1639. Shin, Jung Hyun. *Japanese-North Korean Relations: Linkage Politics in the Regional System of East Asia.* Seoul: Kyunghee University Press, 1981.

1640. Yun, Ki-Whang. *Die Rolle der Friedenslinie (Rhee Line) im Normalizierungsprozess der Beziehungen zwischen Korea und Japan in der Nachkriegsära: in der Perzeptions- und Aktionsstruktur der südkoreanischen Regierung* [The Role of the (Rhee) Peace line in the Process of Normalization of Relationships between Korea and Japan in the Postwar Era: In the Perception and Action Structure of the South Korean Government]. Frankfurt am Main, Germany: P. Lang, 1983.

Koreans *See*: Minorities—Koreans

Kyogen *See*: Theater—Kyogen

Kyoto *See*: History—Local—Kyoto

Labor

See also: Law—Labor

1641. Chalmers, Norma. *Industrial Relations in Japan: The Peripheral Workforce.* Routledge Japanese Studies Series. London: New York: Routledge, 1989.

1642. Connaghan, Charles J. *The Japanese Way: Contemporary Industrial Relations.* Ottawa, Ont.: Labour Canada, 1982.

1643. Dore, Ronald, Jean Bonnine-Cabalé, and Kari Tapiola. *Japan at Work: Markets, Management and Flexibility.* Paris: OECD, 1989.

1644. Dore, Ronald Philip. *Structural Adjustment in Japan, 1970-82.* Employment, Adjustment and Industrialization, 0257-3415, 1. Geneva: International Labour Office, 1986.

1645. Ernst, Angelika. *Japans langer Abschied von der Vollbeschäftigung: Arbeitsmarktstrukturen und Arbeitsmarktentwicklung* [Japan's Long Farewell from Full Employment: Labor Market Structures and Labor Market Development]. Mitteilungen des Instituts für Asienkunde Hamburg, Nr. 147. Hamburg, Germany: Institut für Asienkunde, 1986.

1646. Garon, Sheldon M. *The State and Labor in Modern Japan.* Berkeley, CA: University of California Press, 1987.

1647. Mosk, Carl. *Competition and Cooperation in Japanese Labour Markets.* Studies in the Modern Japanese Economy. New York: St. Martin's Press, 1995.

1648. Nishikawa Shunsaku, ed. *The Labor Market in Japan: Selected Readings.* Translated by Ross Mouer. Tokyo: University of Tokyo Press, 1980.

1649. Reed, Steven R. *Making Common Sense of Japan.* Pitt Series in Policy and Institutional Studies. Pittsburgh, PA: University of Pittsburgh Press, 1993.

1650. Shirai, Taishiro, ed. *Contemporary Industrial Relations in Japan.* Madison, WI: University of Wisconsin Press, 1983.

1651. Takezawa, S., et al. *Improvements in the Quality of Working Life in Three Japanese Industries.* Geneva, Switzerland: International Labour Office, 1982.

Labor—Alien

1652. Beauchamp, Edward R., and Akira Iriye, eds. *Foreign Employees in Nineteenth-Century Japan.* Boulder, CO: Westview, 1990.

1653. Shimada, Haruo. *Japan's "Guest Workers": Issues and Public Policies.* Translated by Roger Northridge. Tokyo: University of Tokyo Press, 1994.

Labor—Bibliography

1654. Ford, Bill, Millicent Easther, and Ann Brewer. *Japanese Employment and Employee Relations: An Annotated Bibliography.* Canberra: Australian Government Publishing Service, 1984.

Labor—History

1655. Calvetti, Paolo. *The Ashio Copper Mine Revolt (1907): A Case Study on the Changes of the Labor Relations in Japan at the Beginning of the XX Century.* Series Minor, 29. Naples, Italy: Istituto Universitorio Orientale, Dipartimento di Studi Asiatici, 1987.

1656. Deck, David Deyo. *The General Strike of February 1, 1947: A Turning Point in America's Occupational Labor Policy toward Japan.* S.l.: s.n., 198-

1657. Gordon, Andrew. *The Evolution of Labor Relations in Japan: Heavy Industry, 1853-1955.* Harvard East Asian Monographs, 117. Harvard East Asian Monographs. Subseries on the History of Japanese Business and Industry. Cambridge, MA: Council on East Asian Studies, Harvard University, 1985.

1658. Gordon, Andrew. *Labor and Imperial Democracy in Prewar Japan.* Berkeley, CA: University of California Press, 1991.

1659. Leupp, Gary P. *Servants, Shophands, and Laborers in the Cities of Tokugawa Japan.* Princeton, NJ: Princeton University Press, 1992.

1660. Park, Sung-Jo. *U.S. Labor Policy in Postwar Japan.* Berlin: Express Edition, 1985.

Labor—Trade Unions

1661. Koike, Kazuo. *The Economics of Work in Japan.* LTCB International Library Selection, no. 3. Tokyo: LTCB International Library Foundation, 1996.

1662. Kuwahara, Yasuo. *Industrial Relations System in Japan: A New Interpretation.* Japanese Industrial Relations Series, 16. Tokyo: Japan Institute of Labour, 1989.

1663. Maekawa, Kaichi. *Labour Administration and Trade Unionism in Japan: After World War II.* Kyoto, Japan: Keibunsha, 1984.

1664. Marsland, Stephen E. *The Birth of the Japanese Labor Movement: Takano Fusataro and the Rodo Kumiai Kiseikai.* Honolulu, HI: University of Hawaii Press, 1989.

1665. Williamson, Hugh. *Coping with the Miracle: Japan's Unions Explore New International Relations*. International Labour Series. London; Boulder, CO: Pluto Press, 1994.

Labor—Wages

1666. Tachibanaki, Toshiaki. *Wage Determination and Distribution in Japan*. Oxford, U.K.; New York: Clarendon, 1996.

Lacquer *See*: Art—Lacquer

Land Use

1667. Haley, John Owen, and Kozo Yamamura. *Land Issues in Japan: A Policy Failure?* Seattle, WA: Society for Japanese Studies, 1992.

1668. Iwata, Shingo, Toshio Tabuchi, and Benno P. Warkentin. *Soil-Water Interactions: Mechanisms and Applications*. 2d ed. Books in Soils, Plants, and the Environment. New York: M. Dekker, 1995.

1669. Kornhauser, David Henry. *Japan, Geographical Background to Urban-Industrial Development*. 2d ed. World's Landscapes. London; New York: Longman, 1982.

Landscape Architecture *See*: Architecture—Landscape

Language

1670. Habein, Yaeko Sato. *The History of the Japanese Written Language*. Tokyo: University of Tokyo Press, 1984.

1671. Miller, Roy Andrew. *The Japanese Language*. History and Structure of Languages. Chicago, IL; London: University of Chicago Press, 1967. Reprint: 1980.

1672. Miller, Roy Andrew. *Japan's Modern Myth: The Language and Beyond*. New York: Weatherhill, 1982.

1673. Miyagawa, Shigeru, and Chisato Kitagawa, eds. *Studies in Japanese Language Use*. Current Inquiry into Language, Linguistics, and Human Communication, 48. Carbondale, IL: Linguistic Research, 1984.

1674. Mizutani, Osamu. *Japanese, the Spoken Language in Japanese Life*. Translated by Janet Ashby. Tokyo: Japan Times, 1981.

1675. Shibatani, Masayoshi. *The Languages of Japan*. Cambridge Language Surveys. Cambridge, U.K.; New York: Cambridge University Press, 1990.

1676. Suzuki, Takao. *Reflections on Japanese Language and Culture*. Studies in the Humanities and Social Relations, v. 15. Tokyo: Institute of Cultural and Linguistic Studies, Keio University, 1987.

Language—Children

1677. Miyata, Susanne. *Japanische Kinderfragen: zum Erwerb von Form, Inhalt, Funktion von Frageausdrücken* [Japanese Children's Questions: Toward the Acquisition of Form, Content and Function of Expressions of Enquiry]. Mitteilungen der Deutschen Gesellschaft für Natur- und Völkerkunde Ostasiens, 117. Hamburg, Germany: Gesellschaft für Natur- und Völkerkunde Ostasiens, 1993.

Language—Etymology

1678. Martin, Samuel Elmo. *The Japanese Language through Time*. Yale Language Series. New Haven, CT: Yale University Press, 1987.

Language—Foreign Elements

1679. Haarmann, Harald. *Prestigefunktionen europäischer Sprachen im modernen Japan: Betrachtungen zum Multilingualismus in japanischen Massenmedien* [Functions of Prestige of European Languages in Modern Japan: Attempts to Multilingualism in Japanese Mass Media]. Hamburg, Germany: H. Buske, 1986.

1680. Loveday, Leo J. *Language Contact in Japan: A Socio-Linguistic History*. Oxford Studies in Language Contact. New York: Clarendon, 1996.

Language—Negation

1681. McGloin, Naomi Hanaoka. *Negation in Japanese*. Current Inquiry into Language, Linguistics, and Human Communication, 49. USA: Boreal Scholarly Publishers, 1986.

Language—Proverbs

1682. Galef, David, comp., trans. *"Even Monkeys fall from Trees" and Other Japanese Proverbs.* Rutland, VT: Tuttle, 1987.

1683. Ragle, Nina Shire. *Even Monkeys Fall Out of Trees: John Naka's Collection of Japanese Proverbs.* Laguna Beach, CA: Nippon Art Forms, 1987.

1684. Roper, Trey. *Japanese-English Idioms.* Las Vegas, NV: US-Asia Research, 1994.

Language—Social Aspects

1685. Bachnik, Jane M., and Charles J. Quinn, Jr., eds. *Situated Meaning: Inside and Outside in Japanese Self, Society, and Language.* Princeton, NJ: Princeton University Press, 1994.

1686. Maher, John C., and Gaynor Macdonald, eds. *Diversity in Japanese Culture and Language.* Japanese Studies. London; New York: Kegan Paul International, 1995.

1687. Passin, Herbert. *Japanese and the Japanese: Language and Culture Change.* Tokyo: Kinseido, 1980.

1688. Swenki, Takao. *Japanese and the Japanese.* Translated by Akira Miura. Tokyo; New York: Kodansha International, 1978. Reprinted as *Words in Context: A Japanese Perspective on Language and Culture.* Tokyo; New York: Kodansha International, 1984.

Language—Women

1689. Ide, Sachiko, and Naomi Hanaoka McGloin, eds. *Aspects of Japanese Women's Language.* Tokyo: Kurosio, 1990.

1690. Kittredge, Cherry. *Womansword: What Japanese Words Say About Women.* Tokyo; New York: Kodansha International, 1987.

1691. Shibamoto, Janet S. *Japanese Women's Language.* Orlando, FL: Academic Press, 1985.

Language Policy

1692. Gottlieb, Nanette. *Kanji Politics: Language Policy and Japanese Script*. Japanese Studies. London; New York: Kegan Paul International, 1995.

1693. Twine, Nanette. *Language and the Modern State: The Reform of Written Japanese*. Nissan Institute / Routledge Japanese Studies Series. London; New York: Routledge, 1991.

Language Teaching

1694. Kaiser, Stefan, ed. *Japanese Language Teaching in the Nineties: Materials and Course Design*. Folkestone, U.K.: Japan Library, 1993.

Latin America—Relations with

See also: 2636

1695. Purcell, Susan Kaufman, and Robert M. Immerman, eds. *Japan and Latin America in the New Global Order*. Boulder, CO; London: Rienner, 1992.

Law

1696. Clifford, W. *Crime Control in Japan*. Lexington, MA: Lexington Books, 1976.

1697. Haley, John Owen. *Authority Without Power: Law and the Japanese Paradox*. Studies on Law and Social Control. New York: Oxford University Press, 1991.

1698. Hamilton, V. Lee, and Joseph Sanders. *Everyday Justice: Responsibility and the Individual in Japan and the United States*. New Haven, CT: Yale University Press, 1992.

1699. Itoh, Hiroshi. *The Japanese Supreme Court: Constitutional Policies*. New York: M. Wiener, 1989.

1700. *Justice in Japan*. Tokyo: Supreme Court of Japan, 1988.

1701. Upham, Frank K. *Law and Social Change in Postwar Japan*. Cambridge, MA: Harvard University Press, 1987.

Law—Alien

1702. *Living with the Japanese Law: A Guide to Foreigners in Japan: Q & A.* Tokyo: Japan Legal Aid Association, 1991.

Law—Antitrust

1703. *Guidelines for the Regulation of Unfair Trade Practices with Respect to Patent and Know-How Licensing Agreements.* Tokyo: Kosei Torihiki Kyokai, 1989.

1704. Iyori, Hiroshi, and Akinori Uesugi. *The Antimonopoly Laws of Japan.* New York: Federal Legal Publications, 1983.

1705. Oda, Hiroshi, and R. Jeffrey Grice. *Japanese Banking, Securities and Anti-Monopoly Law.* London: Boston, MA: Butterworths, 1988.

Law—Bibliography

1706. Scheer, Matthias K. *Japanisches Recht in westlichen Sprachen, 1974-1989: Eine Bibliographie / Japanese Law in Western Languages, 1974-1989: A Bibliography.* Hamburg, Germany: Deutsch-Japanische Juristen-Vereinigung, 1992.

Law—Building

1707. *The Building Standard Law of Japan.* 2d ed. Tokyo: Building Center of Japan, 1990.

1708. Matsushita, Fumio. *Design and Construction Practice in Japan: A Practical Guide.* Tokyo: Kaibunsha, 1994.

Law—Commercial

1709. *Doing Business in Japan.* Ernst & Young's International Business Series. New York: Ernst & Young International, 1993.

1710. Hahn, Elliot J. *Japanese Business Law and the Legal System.* Westport, CT: Quorum Books, 1984.

1711. Ishizumi, Kanji. *Acquiring Japanese Companies: Mergers and Acquisitions in the Japanese Market.* Rev. ed. Oxford, U.K.; Cambridge, MA: Blackwell, 1990.

Law—Constitutional

1712. Inoue, Kyoko. *MacArthur's Japanese Constitution: A Linguistic and Cultural Study of Its Making*. Chicago, IL: University of Chicago Press, 1991.

1713. Yamagami, Ken'ichi, and Eijun Suketake. *Japan's Constitution and Civil Law*. "About Japan" Series, 20. Tokyo: Foreign Press Center, Japan, 1994.

Law—Financial

1714. *Japan Laws and Regulations Concerning Customs Duties and Customs Procedures*. Tokyo: Japan Tariff Association, 1981.

Law—Intellectual Property

1715. Doi, Teruo. *The Intellectual Property Law of Japan*. Alphen aan de Rijn, Netherlands; Germantown, MD: Sijthoff & Noordhoff, 1980.

Law—Labor

1716. Hanami, Tadashi. *Labour Law and Industrial Relations in Japan*. 2d ed. Deventer, Netherlands; Boston, MA: Kluwer Law and Taxation, 1985.

1717. Woodiwiss, Anthony. *Law, Labour, and Society in Japan: From Repression to Reluctant Recognition*. London; New York: Routledge, 1992.

Law—Maritime

1718. Akaha, Tsuneo. *Japan in Global Ocean Politics*. Honolulu, HI: University of Hawaii Press and Law of the Sea Institute, University of Hawaii, 1985.

Law—Patent

1719. Hanabusa, Masami. *An Analysis of Japanese Patent Law: Translated from the Original Treatise*. Lawrenceville, VA: Brunswick, 1992.

Leather *See*: Art—Leather

Legal Dictionaries

1720. Jarman, Samuel. *English-Japanese Legal Dictionary and Handbook*. London; New York: Cassell, 1995.

Legal History *See*: History—Legal

Leisure

1721. *Leisure and Recreational Activities*. 3d ed. "About Japan" Series, 4. Tokyo: Foreign Press Center, Japan, 1993.

1722. Manzenreiter, Wolfram. *Leisure in Contemporary Japan: An Annotated Bibliography and List of Books and Articles*. Beiträge zur Japanologie, Bd. 33. Vienna: Institute der Japanologie der Universität Wien, 1995.

1723. Plath, David W. *The After Hours: Modern Japan and the Search for Enjoyment*. Berkeley, CA: University of California, 1964.

Liberalism

1724. Nolte, Sharon H. *Liberalism in Modern Japan: Ishibashi Tanzan and his Teachers, 1905-1960*. Berkeley, CA: University of California Press, 1986.

Librarianship

1725. Editorial Committee of Librarianship in Japan, ed. *Librarianship in Japan*. Tokyo: Japan Organizing Committee of IFLA Tokyo, 1986.

1726. Findley, Naomi, Tomoko Hermsmeier, and Sharon Domier. *Library of Congress Subject Headings Related to Japan Topical Headings*. New York: Subcommittee on Technical Processing, Committee on East Asian Libraries, Association for Asian Studies, 1994.

Library Catalogs

1727. *Early Japanese Books at Harvard-Yenching Library, Harvard University / Habado Enkei Toshokan Washo Mokuroku.* Bibliographical Series (Harvard-Yenching Library), 4. Shoshi Shomoku Shirizu, 36. Tokyo: Yumani Shobo, 1994.

1728. Gardner, Kenneth B., comp. *Descriptive Catalogue of Japanese Books in the British Library printed before 1700.* London: British Library; Tenri-shi, Japan: Tenri Central Library, Tenri University, 1993.

1729. Hayashi, Nozomu, and Peter Kornicki. *Early Japanese Books in Cambridge University Library: A Catalogue of the Aston, Satow, and Von Siebold Collections.* University of Cambridge Oriental Publications, no. 40. Cambridge, U.K.; New York: Cambridge University Press, 1991.

Limnology

1730. Horie, Shoji, ed. *Lake Biwa.* Monographiae Biologicae, v. 54. Dordrecht, Netherlands; Boston, MA: Dr. W. Junk Publishers, 1984.

1731. Mori, Syuiti, ed. *An Introduction to Limnology of Lake Biwa.* Kyoto, Japan, 1980.

1732. Okuda, Setsuo, Jörg Imberger, and Michio Kumagai, eds. *Physical Processes in a Large Lake: Lake Biwa, Japan.* Coastal and Estuarine Studies, 0733-9569, 48. Washington, DC: American Geophysical Union, 1995.

Linguistics—Discourse Analysis

1733. Fujii, Noriko. *Historical Discourse Analysis: Grammatical Subject in Japanese.* Discourse Perspective on Grammar, 3. Berlin, Germany; New York: Mouton de Gruyter, 1991.

1734. Iwasaki, Shōichi. *Subjectivity in Grammar and Discourse: Theoretical Considerations and Case Study of Japanese Spoken Discourse.* Studies in Discourse and Grammar, v. 2. Amsterdam; Philadelphia, PA: John Benjamins, 1993.

1735. Maynard, Senko K. *Discourse Modality: Subjectivity, Emotion, and Voice in the Japanese Language.* Pragmatics and Beyond, 0922-842X, new ser. 24. Amsterdam; Philadelphia, PA: J. Benjamins, 1993.

1736. Maynard, Senko K. *Japanese Conversation: Self-Contextualization through Structure and Interactional Management.* Advances in Discourse Processes, v. 35. Norwood, NJ: Ablex, 1989.

Linguistics—Ellipsis

1737. Hinds, John. *Ellipsis in Japanese.* Current Inquiry into Language, Linguistics, and Human Communication, 43. Carbondale, IL: Linguistic Research, 1982.

Linguistics—Grammar

1738. Imai, Takashi, and Mamoru Saito, eds. *Issues in Japanese Linguistics.* Studies in Generative Grammar, 29. Dordrecht, Netherlands; Providence, RI: Foris, 1987.

1739. Makino, Seiichi, and Michio Tsutsui. *A Dictionary of Basic Japanese Grammar / Nihongo Kihon Bunpo Jiten.* Tokyo: Japan Times, 1989.

1740. Rubin, Jay. *Gone Fishin': New Angles on Perennial Problems.* Power Japanese. Tokyo; New York: Kodansha International, 1992.

1741. Shibatani, Masayoshi. *Japanese Generative Grammar.* Syntax and Semantics, v.5. New York: Academic Press, 1976.

Linguistics—Neurolinguistics

1742. Paradis, Michel, Hiroko Hagiwara, and Nancy Hildebrandt. *Neurolinguistic Aspects of the Japanese Writing System.* Perspectives in Neurolinguistics, Neuropsychology, and Psycholinguistics. Orlando, FL: Academic Press, 1985.

Linguistics—Phonology

1743. Vance, Timothy J. *An Introduction to Japanese Phonology.* SUNY Series in Linguistics. Albany, NY: State University of New York Press, 1987.

Linguistics—Psycholinguistics—Bibliography

1744. Kess, Joseph F., and Tadao Miyamoto, comps. *Japanese Psycholinguistics: A Classified and Annotated Research Bibliography.* Amsterdam Studies in the Theory and History of Linguistic Science. Series V, Library and Information Sources in Linguistics, v. 24. Amsterdam; Philadelphia, PA: J. Benjamins, 1994.

Linguistics—Quantitative

1745. Mizutani, Shizuo, ed. *Japanese Quantitative Linguistics.* Quantitative Linguistics, v. 39. Bochum, Germany: N. Brockmeyer, 1989.

Linguistics—Semantics

1746. Backhouse, A. E. *The Lexical Field of Taste: A Semantic Study of Japanese Taste Terms.* Cambridge Studies in Linguistics, Supplement. Cambridge, UK; New York: Cambridge University Press, 1994.

1747. Suleski, Ronald. and Hiroko Masada. *Affective Expressions in Japanese: A Handbook of Value-Laden Words in Everyday Japanese.* Tokyo: Hokuseido Press, 1982.

Linguistics—Sociolinguistics

1748. Loveday, Leo. *Explorations in Japanese Sociolinguistics.* Pragmatics & Beyond, VII: 1. Amsterdam, Netherlands; Philadelphia, PA: J. Benjamins, 1986.

1749. Matsumoto, Michihiro. *The Unspoken Way: Haragei: Silence in Japanese Business and Society.* Tokyo; New York: Kodansha International, 1988.

1750. Naotsuka, Reiko, Nancy Sakamoto, et al. *Mutual Understanding of Different Cultures.* Osaka, Japan: Science Education Institute of Osaka Prefecture, 1981.

1751. Ozaki, Akito. *Requests for Clarification in Conversation between Japanese and Non-Japanese.* Pacific Linguistics, Series B, 0078-754X, 102. Canberra: Dept. of Linguistics, Research School of Pacific Studies, The Australian National University, 1989.

Linguistics—Syntax

1752. Miyagawa, Shigeru. *Structure and Case Marking in Japanese.* Syntax and Semantics, v. 22. San Diego, CA: Academic Press, 1989.

1753. Tateishi, Koichi. *The Syntax of "Subjects."* Stanford, CA: Center for the Study of Language and Information; Tokyo: Kurosio, 1994.

Linguistics—Tense

1754. Soga, Matsuo. *Tense and Aspect in Modern Colloquial Japanese.* Vancouver, B.C.: University of British Columbia Press, 1983.

Literature

1755. Colligan-Taylor, Karen. *The Emergence of Environmental Literature in Japan.* Environment, Problems, and Solutions. New York: Garland, 1990.

1756. Downer, Lesley. *On the Narrow Road to the Deep North: Journey into a Lost Japan.* London: Jonathan Cape, 1989.

1757. Gillespie, John K., ed. *Japan, A Literary Overview.* Review of National Literatures, v. 18. New York: Griffon House Publications for the Council on National Literatures, 1993.

1758. Guest, Harry. *Japan.* Traveler's Literary Companion. Lincolnwood, IL: Passport Books, 1995.

1759. Kato, Shuichi. *A History of Japanese Literature.* 3 vols. Translated by David Chibbett. London: Macmillan; Tokyo; New York: Kodansha International, 1979-1983.

1760. Keene, Donald. *Appreciations of Japanese Culture.* Tokyo; New York: Kodansha International, 1981.

1761. Keene, Donald. *Dawn to the West: Japanese Literature of the Modern Era.* 2 vols. New York: Holt, Rinehart, and Winston, 1984.

1762. Keene, Donald. *The Pleasures of Japanese Literature.* Companions to Asian Studies. New York: Columbia University Press, 1988.

1763. Keene, Donald. *World Within Walls: Japanese Literature of the Pre-Modern Era, 1600-1867.* New York: Holt, Rinehart, and Winston, 1984.

1764. Kobayashi, Hideo. *Literature of the Lost Home: Kobayashi Hideo – Literary Criticism, 1924-1939.* Edited and Translated by Paul Anderer. Stanford, CA: Stanford University Press, 1995.

1765. Konishi, Jin'ichi. *A History of Japanese Literature.* 3 vols. Edited by Earl Miner. Translated by Aileen Catten and Nicholas Teele. Princeton, NJ: Princeton University Press, 1984.

1766. Pollack, David. *Reading Against Culture: Ideology and Narrative in the Japanese Novel.* Ithaca, NY: Cornell University Press, 1992.

1767. Rimer, J. Thomas. *Pilgrimages: Aspects of Japanese Literature and Culture.* Honolulu, HI: University of Hawaii Press, 1988.

1768. Rimer, J. Thomas. *A Reader's Guide to Japanese Literature.* Tokyo; New York: Kodansha International, 1988.

1769. Tyler, Royall. *The Miracles of the Kasuga Deity.* Records of Civilization, Sources and Studies, no. 98. New York: Columbia University Press, 1990.

Literature—Authors

1770. Powell, Irena. *Writers and Society in Modern Japan.* Tokyo: New York: Kodansha International, 1983.

Literature—Authors—Dazai, Osamu, 1909-1948

1771. Dazai, Osamu. *Return to Tsugaru: Travels of a Purple Tramp.* Tokyo; New York: Kodansha International, 1985.

1772. Dazai, Osamu. *Self Portraits: Tales from the Life of Japan's Great Decadent Romantic.* Translated by Ralph F. McCarthy. Tokyo; New York: Kodansha International, 1991.

1773. Lyons, Phyllis I. *The Saga of Dazai Osamu: A Critical Study with Translations.* Stanford, CA: Stanford University Press, 1985.

Literature—Authors—Futabatei, Shimei, 1864-1909

1774. Ryan, Marleigh Grayer. *Japan's First Modern Novel: Ukigumo of Futabatei Shimei.* UNESCO Collection of Representative Works. Japanese Series. New York: Columbia University Press, 1967. Reprint: Michigan Classics in Japanese Studies, no. 1. Ann Arbor, MI: Center for Japanese Studies, University of Michigan Press, 1990.

Literature—Authors—Kaneko, Mitsuharu, 1895-1975

1775. Morita, James R. *Kaneko Mitsuharu.* Twayne's World Author Series, TWAS 555: Japan. Boston, MA: Twayne, 1980.

Literature—Authors—Masaoka, Shiki, 1867-1902

1776. Beichman, Janine. *Masaoka Shiki.* Twayne's World Authors Series, TWAS 661. Boston, MA: Twayne, 1982.

Literature—Authors—Matsuo, Bashō, 1644-1694

1777. Ueda, Makoto. *Matsuo Bashō.* Twayne's World Authors Series, TWAS 102. New York: Twayne, 1970. Reprint: *The Master Haiku Poet: Matsuo Bashō.* Tokyo; New York: Kodansha International, 1982.

Literature—Authors—Mishima, Yukio, 1925-1970

1778. Scott-Stokes, Henry. *The Life and Death of Yukio Mishima.* Rev. ed. New York: Noonday Press, 1995.

Literature—Authors—Mori, Ōgai, 1862-1922

1779. Marcus, Marvin. *Paragons of the Ordinary: The Biographical Literature of Mori Ōgai.* SHAPS Library of Asian Studies. Honolulu, HI: University of Hawaii Press, 1993.

Literature—Authors—Nagai, Kafū, 1879-1959

1780. Seidensticker, Edward. *Kafū the Scribbler: The Life and Writings of Nagai Kafū, 1879-1959.* Stanford, CA: Stanford University Press, 1965. Reprint: Michigan Classics in Japanese Studies, no. 3. Ann Arbor, MI: Center for Japanese Studies, University of Michigan, 1990.

Literature—Authors—Ōe, Kenzaburō, 1935-

1781. Ōe, Kenzaburō. *Japan, the Ambiguous, and Myself: The Nobel Prize Speech and Other Lectures.* New York: Kodansha International, 1995.

Literature—Authors—Ōtomo, Yakamochi, 716-785?

1782. Doe, Paula. *A Warbler's Song in the Dusk: The Life and Work of Otomo Yakamochi (718-785).* Berkeley, CA: University of California Press, 1982.

Literature—Authors—Shikitei, Sanba, 1776-1822

1783. Leutner, Robert W. *Shikitei Sanba and the Comic Tradition in Edo Fiction.* Cambridge, MA: Council on East Asian Studies, Harvard University, 1985.

Literature—Authors—Tanizaki, Jun'ichirō, 1886-1965

1784. Tanizaki, Jun'ichirō. *Childhood Years: A Memoir.* Translated by Paul McCarthy. Tokyo; New York: Kodansha International, 1988.

Literature—Authors—Tayama, Katai, 1871-1930

1785. Tayama, Katai. *Literary Life in Tōkyō, 1885-1915: Tayama Katai's Memoirs "Thirty Years in Tokyo."* Translated by Kenneth G. Henshall. Leiden, Netherlands; New York: Brill, 1987.

Literature—Authors—Ueda, Akinari, 1734-1809

1786. Young, Blake Morgan. *Ueda Akinari.* Vancouver, B.C.: University of British Columbia Press, 1982.

Literature—Authors—Yokomitsu, Riichi, 1898-1947

1787. Keene, Dennis. *Yokomitsu Riichi, Modernist.* Modern Asian Literature Series. New York: Columbia University Press, 1980.

Literature—Autobiographical

1788. Fowler, Edward. *The Rhetoric of Confession: Shishōsetsu in Early Twentieth-Century Japanese Fiction.* Berkeley, CA: University of California Press, 1988.

Literature—Bibliography

1789. Japan P.E.N. Club, comp. *Japanese Literature in Foreign Languages 1945-1990.* Tokyo: Japan Book Publishers Association, 1990.

1790. Makino, Yasuko, and Roberta K. Gumport. *Japan through Children's Literature: An Annotated Bibliography.* 2d ed. Westport, CT: Greenwood, 1985.

1791. Zenimoto, Kenji. *A General Catalogue of Hearn Collections in Japan and Overseas.* Matsue, Japan: Hearn Society, 1991-1992.

Literature—Buddhist

1792. Cassettari, Stephen. *Pebbles on the Road: A Collection of Zen Stories, and Paintings.* Pymble, Australia: Angus & Robertson, 1992.

1793. Dykstra, Yoshiko Kurata, trans. *Miraculous Tales of the Lotus Sutra: The Dainihon-koku Hokekyōkenki Priest Chingen.* Hirakata-City, Japan: International Research Institute, The Kansai University, 1984.

1794. Kamens, Edward. *The Buddhist Poetry of the Great Kamo Priestess: Daisaiin Senshi and Hosshin Wakashū.* Michigan Monograph Series in Japanese Studies, no. 5. Ann Arbor, MI: Center for Japanese Studies, University of Michigan, 1990.

1795. LaFleur, William R. *The Karma of Words: Buddhism and the Literary Arts in Medieval Japan.* Berkeley, CA: University of California Press, 1983.

1796. Mujū Ichien. *Sand and Pebbles (Shasekishū): The Tales of Mujū Ichien, a Voice for Pluralism in Kamakura Buddhism.* Translated and edited by Robert E. Morrell. SUNY Series in Buddhist Studies. Albany, NY: State University of New York Press, 1985.

1797. Nichisei. *Grass Hill: Poems and Prose by the Japanese Monk Gensei.* Translations from the Oriental Classics. New York: Columbia University Press, 1983.

1798. Pollack, David. *Zen Poems of the Five Mountains.* Studies in Religion / American Academy of Religion, no. 37. New York: Crossroads; Decatur, GA: Scholars Press, 1985.

1799. Sanford, James H., William R. LaFleur, and Masatoshi Nagatomi. *Flowing Traces: Buddhism in the Literary and Visual Arts of Japan.* Princeton, NJ: Princeton University Press, 1992.

1800. Stryk, Lucien. *The Awakened Self: Encounters with Zen.* Rev. ed. New York: Kodansha International, 1995.

1801. Ury, Marian, trans. *Poems of the Five Mountains: An Introduction to the Literature of the Zen Monasteries.* 2d rev. ed. Michigan Monograph Series in Japanese Studies, no. 10. Ann Arbor, MI: Center for Japanese Studies, University of Michigan, 1992.

Literature—Classical

1802. Chamberlain, Basil Hall, trans. *The Kojiki: Record of Ancient Matters.* Transactions of the Asiatic Society of Japan, vol. X, Supplement. Tokyo: Asiatic Society of Japan, 1882. Reprint: Rutland, VT: Tuttle, 1981.

1803. Childs, Margaret Helen. *Rethinking Sorrow: Revelatory Tales of Late Medieval Japan.* Michigan Monograph Series in Japanese Studies, no. 6. Ann Arbor, MI: Center for Japanese Studies, University of Michigan, 1991.

1804. Keene, Donald. *Seeds in the Heart: Japanese Literature from Earliest Times to the Late Sixteenth Century.* New York: Henry Holt, 1993.

1805. Marra, Michele. *The Aesthetics of Discontent: Politics and Reclusion in Medieval Japanese Literature.* Honolulu, HI: University of Hawaii Press, 1991.

1806. Marra, Michele. *Representations of Power: The Literary Politics of Medieval Japan.* Honolulu, HI: University of Hawaii Press, 1993.

1807. Matsuo, Bashō. *Narrow Road to the Interior.* Translated by Sam Hamill. Shambala Centaur Editions. Boston, MA: Shambhala, 1991.

1808. McCullough, Helen Craig, trans. *The Tale of the Heike.* Stanford, CA: Stanford University Press, 1988.

1809. McCullough, William H., and Helen Craig McCullough, trans. *A Tale of Flowering Fortunes: Annals of Japanese Aristocratic Life in the Heian Period.* 2 vols. Stanford, CA: Stanford University Press, 1980.

1810. Miner, Earl Roy, Hiroko Odagiri, and Robert E. Morrell. *The Princeton Companion to Classical Japanese Literature.* Princeton, NJ: Princeton University Press, 1984.

1811. Okada, H. Richard. *Figures of Resistance: Language, Poetry, and Narrating in the Tale of Genji and Other Mid-Heian Texts.* Postcontemporary Interventions. Durham, NC: Duke University Press, 1991.

1812. Plutschow, Herbert E. *Chaos and Cosmos: Ritual in Early and Medieval Japanese Literature.* Brill's Japanese Studies Library, v. 1. Leiden, Netherlands; New York: Brill, 1990.

1813. Rohlich, Thomas H., trans. *A Tale of Eleventh Century Japan: Hamamatsu Chūnagon Monogatari.* Princeton Library of Asian Translations. Princeton, NJ: Princeton University Press, 1983.

1814. Sei, Shonagon. *The Pillow Book of Sei Shonagon.* Translated and edited by Ivan Morris. Translations from the Oriental Classics. New York: Columbia University Press, 1991.

1815. Skord, Virginia S., trans. *Tales of Tears and Laughter: Short Fiction of Medieval Japan.* Honolulu, HI: University of Hawaii Press, 1991.

1816. Tahara, Mildred M., trans. *Tales of Yamato: A Tenth Century Poem-Tale.* Honolulu, HI: University Press of Hawaii, 1980.

1817. Varley, H. Paul. *Warriors of Japan as Portrayed in the War Tales.* Honolulu, HI: University of Hawaii Press, 1994.

1818. Watson, Burton, trans. *Japanese Literature in Chinese.* 2 vols. Translations from the Oriental Classics. New York: Columbia University Press, 1975-1976.

1819. Yoshida, Kenkō. *Essays in Idleness: The Tsurezuregusa of Kenkō.* Translated by Donald Keene. Records of Civilization: Sources and Studies, no 78. UNESCO Collection of Representative Works: Japanese Series. New York: Columbia University Press, 1967. Reprint: Rutland, VT: Tuttle, 1981.

Literature—Classical—Genji Monogatari

1820. Bowring, Richard John. *Murasaki Shikibu, The Tale of Genji.* Landmarks of World Literature. Cambridge, U.K.; New York: Cambridge University Press, 1988.

1821. Murasaki, Shikibu. *The Tale of Genji.* 2 vols. Translated by Edward Seidensticker. New York: Knopf, 1976.

1822. Murasaki, Shikibu. *The Tale of Genji: A Novel in Six Parts, by Lady Murasaki*. 2 vols. Translated by Arthur Waley. Boston, MA; New York: Houghton Mifflin, 1935.

1823. Pekarik, Andrew, ed. *Ukifune: Love in the Tale of Genji.* Companions to Asian Studies. New York: Columbia University Press, 1982.

1824. Shirane, Haruo. *The Bridge of Dreams: A Poetics of the Tale of Genji*. Stanford, CA: Stanford University Press, 1987.

Literature—Crime and Suspense

1825. Apostolou, John L., and Martin H. Greenberg, eds. *Murder in Japan: Japanese Stories of Crime and Detection.* New York: Dembner Books, 1987.

Literature—Folk

See also: Folktales

1826. Kelsey, W. Michael. *Konjaku Monogatari-shu*. Twayne's World Authors Series, TWAS 621. Boston, MA: Twayne, 1982.

1827. Ury, Marian. *Tales of Times Now Past: Sixty-Two Stories from a Medieval Japanese Collection*. Ann Arbor, MI: Center for Japanese Studies, University of Michigan, 1993.

Literature—Folk—Bibliography

1828. Algarin, Joanne P. *Japanese Folk Literature: A Core Collection and Reference Guide*. New York: Bowker, 1982.

Literature—Modern

1829. Honma, Kenshirō. *A History of Modern Japanese Literature*. Tokyo: Japan Science Press, 1980.

1830. Karatani, Kōjin. *Origins of Modern Japanese Literature*. Edited by Brett de Bary. Post-contemporary Interventions. Durham, NC: Duke University Press, 1993.

1831. Mitsios, Helen, ed. *New Japanese Voices: The Best Contemporary Fiction from Japan*. New York: Atlantic Monthly Press, 1991.

1832. Napier, Susan J. *The Fantastic in Modern Japanese Literature: The Subversion of Modernity.* The Nissan Institute / Routledge Japanese Studies Series. London: Routledge, 1996.

1833. Suzuki, Tomi. *Narrating the Self: Fictions of Japanese Modernity.* Stanford, CA: Stanford University Press, 1996.

1834. Treat, John Whittier. *Writing Ground Zero: Japanese Literature and the Atomic Bomb.* Chicago, IL: University of Chicago Press, 1995.

1835. Washburn, Dennis C. *The Dilemma of the Modern in Japanese Fiction.* Studies of the East Asian Institute. New Haven, CT; London: Yale University Press, 1995.

Literature—Poetry

1836. Akihito, Emperor of Japan, and Empress Michiko. *Tomoshibi / Light: Collected Poetry.* Edited by Marie Philomene and Masako Saito. New York: Weatherhill, 1991.

1837. Carter, Steven D., trans. *Waiting for the Wind: Thirty-Six Poets of Japan's Late Medieval Age.* Translations from the Oriental Classics. New York: Columbia University Press, 1989.

1838. Ebersole, Gary L. *Ritual Poetry, and the Politics of Death in Early Japan.* Princeton, NJ: Princeton University Press, 1989.

1839. Fitzsimmons, Thomas, and Gozo Yoshimasu, eds. *The New Poetry of Japan — The 70s and 80s.* Asian Poetry in Translation. Japan, # 15. Santa Fe, NM: KATYDID Books; Honolulu, HI, 1993.

1840. Kwon, Yung-Hee K. *Songs to Make the Dust Dance: The Ryōjin Hishō of Twelfth-Century Japan.* Berkeley, CA: University of California Press, 1994.

1841. Levy, Ian Hideo. *Hitomaro and the Birth of Japanese Lyricism.* Princeton, NJ: Princeton University Press, 1984.

1842. Miya, Shūji. *Testimony of Life: Shūji Miya's Tanka.* Nagoya, Japan: Poetry Nippon Press, 1990.

1843. Naumann, Nelly. *Kume-Lieder und Kume: Zu einem Problem der japanischen Frühgeschichte* [Kume Songs and Kume: On a Problem of Japanese Early History]. Abhandlungen für die Kunde des Morgenlandes, Bd. XLVI, 2. Marburg, Germany: Deutsche Morgenländische Gesellschaft; Wiesbaden, Germany: F. Steiner, 1981.

1844. Ramirez-Christensen, Esperanza U. *Heart's Flower: The Life and Poetry of Shinkei.* Stanford, CA: Stanford University Press, 1994.

1845. Smits, Ivo. *The Pursuit of Loneliness: Chinese and Japanese Nature Poetry in Medieval Japan, ca. 1050-1150.* Münchener ostasiatische Studien, Bd. 73. Stuttgart, Germany: F. Steiner, 1995.

1846. Watson, Burton, trans. *Kanshi: The Poetry of Ishikawa Jozan and other Edo-Period Poets.* San Francisco, CA: North Point Press, 1990.

1847. Wenck, Günther. *Wortgebrauch und Association in den erotischen Epigrammen des "Haifū Sue-Tsumu-Hana"* [Word Use and Association in the Erotic Epigrams of the "Haifū Sue-Tsumu-Hana"]. Wiesbaden, Germany: Harrasowitz, 1983.

Literature—Poetry—Haiku

1848. Matsuo, Bashō. *Back Roads to Far Towns: Basho's Travel Journal.* Translated by Cid Corman and Kamaike Susumu. Fredonia, NY: White Pine Press, 1986.

1849. Mayhew, Lenore, trans. *Monkey's Raincoat: Linked Poetry of the Basho School with Haiku Selections.* Rutland, VT: Tuttle, 1985.

1850. Sato, Hiroaki. *One Hundred Frogs: From Renga to Haiku to English.* New York: Weatherhill, 1983.

Literature—Poets

1851. Ueda, Makoto. *Modern Japanese Poets and the Nature of Literature.* Stanford, CA: Stanford University Press, 1983.

Literature—Poets—Saitō, Mokichi, 1882-1953

1852. Heinrich, Amy Vladeck. *Fragments of Rainbows: The Life and Poetry of Saitō Mokichi, 1882-1953.* Studies of the East Asian Institute. New York: Columbia University Press, 1983.

Literature—Popular

1853. Sakai, Cécile. *Histoire de la Littérature Populaire Japonaise: Faits et Perspectives (1900-1980)* [History of Japanese Popular Literature: Facts and Perspectives (1900-1980)]. Lettres Asiatiques. Japon. Paris: L'Harmattan, 1987.

Literature—Pre-Modern

1854. Kornicki, Peter F. *The Reform of Fiction in Meiji Japan.* Oxford Oriental Monograph, no. 3. London: Published by Ithaca Press for the Board of the Faculty of Oriental Studies, Oxford University, 1982.

1855. Rubin, Jay. *Injurious to Public Morals: Writers and the Meiji State.* Seattle, WA: University of Washington Press, 1984.

Literature—Short Stories

1856. Swann, Thomas E., and Kinya Tsuruta, eds. *Approaches to the Modern Japanese Short Story.* Tokyo: Waseda University Press, 1982.

Literature—Women

1857. Hosoda, Eishi. *The Thirty-Six Immortal Women Poets: A Poetry Album.* Translated by Andrew J. Pekarik. New York: Braziller, 1991.

1858. Mulhern, Chieko I., ed. *Japanese Women Writers: A Bio-Critical Sourcebook.* Westport, CT: Greenwood, 1994.

1859. Schierbeck, Sachiko Shibata. *Japanese Women Novelists in the 20th Century: 104 Biographies, 1900-1993.* English text revised by Marlene R. Edelstein. Copenhagen: Museum Tusculanum Press; University of Copenhagen, 1994.

1860. Schierbeck, Sachiko Shibata. *Postwar Japanese Women Writers: An Up-to-Date Bibliography with Biographical Sketches.* Edited by Soren Egerod. Occassional Papers; East Asian Institute, 0903-6822, 5. Copenhagen: East Asian Institute, University of Copenhagen, 1989.

1861. Tanaka, Yukiko, and Elizabeth Hanson, eds. *This Kind of Woman: Ten Stories by Japanese Women Writers, 1960-1976.* Translated by Mona Nagai, et al. Michigan Classics in Japanese Studies, no. 12. Ann Arbor, MI: Center for Japanese Studies, University of Michigan, 1994.

1862. Tanaka, Yukiko, ed. *To Live and to Write: Selections by Japanese Women Writers, 1913-1938.* Women in Translation. Seattle, WA: Seal Press, 1987.

1863. Tanaka, Yukiko, ed., trans. *Unmapped Territories: New Women's Fiction from Japan.* Seattle, WA: Women in Translation, 1991.

Local Government

1864. *Plain Talk About Tokyo: The Administration of the Tokyo Metropolitan Government.* TMG Municipal Library, no. 15. Tokyo: TMG, 1980.

1865. Reed, Steven R. *Japanese Prefectures and Policymaking.* Pitt Series in Policy and Institutional Studies. Pittsburgh, PA: University of Pittsburgh Press, 1986.

1866. Samuels, Richard J. *The Politics of Regional Policy in Japan: Localities Incorporated?* Princeton, NJ: Princeton University Press, 1983.

1867. Steiner, Kurt, Ellis S. Krauss, and Scott C. Flanagan, eds. *Political Opposition and Local Politics in Japan.* Princeton, NJ: Princeton University Press, 1980.

Local History *See*: History—Local

Madagascar—Relations with

1868. Ranaivosoa, Georges. *De Madagascar au Japon: Voyage au Coeur d'un Peuple* [From Madagascar to Japan: Voyage to the Heart of a People]. Antsakaviro, Antananarivo: Editions Madprint, 1983.

Manga *See*: Popular Culture

Maps

1869. Cortazzi, Hugh. *Isles of Gold: Antique Maps of Japan.* New York: Weatherhill, 1983.

1870. *Japan Atlas: A Pocket-Size Bilingual Atlas / Nihon Toshi Nikakokugo Atorasu: Pokettoban.* Tokyo: Kashiwashobo, 1992.

1871. Kokudo Chiriin / Geographical Survey Institute. *The National Atlas of Japan*. Rev. ed. Tokyo: Japan Map Center, 1990.

1872. Moriya, Yoshio, ed. *Teikoku's Complete Atlas of Japan*. 10th ed. Tokyo: Teikoku-Shoin, 1990.

1873. Umeda, Atsushi. *Tokyo, a Bilingual Atlas / Tōkyō Nika Kokugo Chizu*. Tokyo: Kodansha, 1987.

1874. Walter, Lutz, ed. *Japan: A Cartographic Vision: European Printed Maps from the Early 16th to the 19th Century*. Munich, Germany; New York: Prestel, 1994.

Marketing

1875. Czinkota, Michael R., and Jon Woronoff. *Japan's Market: The Distribution System*. New York: Praeger, 1986.

1876. Czinkota, Michael R., and Jon Woronoff. *Unlocking Japan's Markets: Seizing Marketing and Distribution Opportunities in Today's Japan*. Chicago, IL: Probus, 1991.

1877. Czinkota, Michael R., and Masaaki Kotabe, eds. *The Japanese Distribution System: Opportunities & Obstacles, Structures & Practices*. Chicago, IL: Probus, 1993.

1878. *Distribution Systems in Japan: An Original Survey*. 3d ed. Tokyo: Business Intercommunications, Inc., 1985.

1879. Herbig, Paul A. *Marketing Japanese Style*. Westport, CT: Quorum Books, 1995.

1880. Johansson, Johny K., and Ikujiro Nonaka. *Relentless: The Japanese Way of Marketing*. New York: HarperBusiness, 1996.

1881. Kikuchi, Takeshi, ed. *Japanese Distribution Channels*. New York: Haworth, 1994.

1882. Kotler, Philip, Liam Fahey, and Somkid Jatusripitak. *The New Competition*. Englewood Cliffs, NJ: Prentice-Hall, 1985.

1883. Muto, Kazuo. *Marketing Systems of Agricultural Products in Japan*. Tokyo: Japan FAO Association, 1987.

1884. *National Policies and Agricultural Trade: Country Study: Japan.* Paris: Organization for Economic Co-operation and Development, 1987.

1885. Skov, Lise, and Brian Moeran, eds. *Women, Media, and Consumption in Japan.* ConsumAsiaN Series. Honolulu, HI: University of Hawaii Press, 1995.

1886. Yip, George S., and Johny K. Johansson. *Global Market Strategies of U.S. and Japanese Businesses: Working Paper.* Report, no. 93-102. Cambridge, MA: Marketing Science Institute, 1993.

Marriage

1887. Edwards, Walter Drew. *Modern Japan through its Weddings: Gender, Person, and Society in Ritual Portrayal.* Stanford, CA: Stanford University Press, 1989.

1888. Hendry, Joy. *Marriage in Changing Japan: Community and Society.* London: Croom Helm, 1981.

Martial Arts *See*: Bushido

Marxism *See*: Socialism

Media

1889. Aalam, Marjane, and Philippe Regnier, eds. *The Japanese Press and Information System.* Geneva, Switzerland: Graduate Institute of International Studies, The Institute of Development Studies, 1989.

1890. Braw, Monica. *The Atomic Bomb Suppressed: American Censorship in Occupied Japan.* Asia and the Pacific. Armonk, NY: Sharpe, 1991.

1891. Fält, Olavi K. *Fascism, Militarism, or Japanism?: The Interpretation of the Crisis Years of 1930-1941 in the Japanese English-language Press.* Translated by Malcolm Hicks. Studia Historica Septentrionalia, 0356-8199, 8. Rovaniemi, Finland: Pohjois-Suomen Historiallinen Yhdistys: Societas Historica Finlandiae Septentrionalis, 1985.

1892. Feldman, Ofer. *Politics and the News Media in Japan.* Ann Arbor, MI: University of Michigan Press, 1993.

1893. Fujimoto, Nobuhiko. *The Magazine Industry in Japan: An Exploration of New Sales and Distribution Channels.* Urayasu City, Chiba-ken, Japan: Fujimoto, 1984.

1894. Gotō, Kazuhiko, et al. *A History of Japanese Television Drama: Modern Japan and the Japanese.* Tokyo: Japan Association of Broadcasting Art, 1991.

1895. *Japan's History as News: You are There.* Tokyo: Japan Times, 1987.

1896. *Japan's Mass Media.* 3rd rev. "About Japan" Series, 7. Tokyo: Foreign Press Center, Japan, 1994.

1897. Kasza, Gregory James. *The State and the Mass Media in Japan, 1918-1945.* Berkeley, CA: University of California Press, 1988.

1898. Kim, Young C. *Japanese Journalists and their World.* Charlottesville, VA: University Press of Virginia, 1981.

1899. Kuroyanagi, Tetsuko. *Totto-Chan, The Little Girl at the Window.* Translated by Dorothy Britton. Tokyo; New York: Kodansha International, 1982.

1900. Lee, Jung Bock. *The Political Character of the Japanese Press.* International Studies Series, no. 6. Seoul: Seoul National University Press, 1985.

1901. Löhr, Marc. *Entwicklung, Organisation und Arbeitsweise regionaler Tageszeitungen in Japan: Das Beispiel Shizuoka Shinbun* [Development, Organization and Work Method of Regional Daily Newspapers in Japan: The Shizuoka Shinbun Example]. Berliner Beiträge zur Social- und Wirtschaftswissenschaftlichen Japan-Forschung, Bd. 20. Bochum, Germany: Brockmeyer, 1991.

1902. Phar, Susan J., and Ellis S. Krauss. *Media and Politics in Japan.* Honolulu, HI: University of Hawaii Press, 1996.

1903. Seguy, Christiane. *Histoire de la Presse Japonaise: Le Développement de la Press à l'Époque Meiji et son Rôle dans la Modernisation du Japon* [History of the Japanese Press: The Development of the Press in the Meiji Period and its Role in the Modernization of Japan]. Bibliothèque Japonaise. Cergy, France: Publications Orientalistes de France, 1993.

1904. Westney, D. Eleanor. *Imitation and Innovation: The Transfer of Western Organizational Patterns to Meiji Japan.* Cambridge, MA: Harvard University, 1987.

Medicine

1905. Beukers, H., et al., eds. *Red-Hair Medicine: Dutch-Japanese Medical Relations.* Nieuwe Nederlandse bijdragen tot de geschiedenis der geneeskunde en der natuurwetenschappen, no. 36. Publications of the Netherlands Association for Japanese Studies, no. 5. Amsterdam; Atlanta, GA: Rodopi, 1991.

1906. Bowers, John Z. *When the Twain Meet: The Rise of Western Medicine in Japan.* Henry E. Sigerist supplements to the Bulletin of the History of Medicine, new ser., no. 5. Baltimore, MD: Johns Hopkins University Press, 1980.

1907. Hachiya, Michihiko. *Hiroshima Diary: The Journal of a Japanese Physician, August 6-September 30, 1945.* Translated and edited by Warner Wells. Chapel Hill, NC: University of North Carolina Press, 1995.

1908. Ishimure, Michiko. *Paradise in the Sea of Sorrow: Our Minamata Disease.* Kyoto, Japan: Yamaguchi Publishing House, 1990.

1909. Jannetta, Ann Bowman. *Epidemics and Mortality in Early Modern Japan.* Princeton, NJ: Princeton University Press, 1987.

1910. Japan Medical Review. *Directory of Japanese Healthcare Industry.* San Francisco, CA: Japan Publications, 1988.

1911. Johnston, William. *The Modern Epidemic: A History of Tuberculosis in Japan.* Harvard East Asian Monographs, 162. Cambridge, MA: Council on East Asian Studies, Harvard University, 1995.

1912. Lock, Margaret M. *East Asian Medicine in Urban Japan: Varieties of Medical Experience.* Comparative Studies of Health Systems and Medical Care, no. 4. Berkeley, CA: University of California Press, 1980.

1913. Maruyama, Meredith Enman, Louise Picon Shimizu, and Nancy Smith Tsurumaki. *Japan Health Handbook.* Tokyo; London: Kodansha International, 1995.

1914. Mori, W., and S. Homma, eds. *Medical Science and Health Care in the Coming Century: A Report from Japan*. Amsterdam; New York: Elsevier, 1987.

1915. Nagayo, Takeo. *History of Japanese Medicine in the Edo Era: Its Social and Cultural Backgrounds*. Nagoya, Japan: University of Nagoya Press, 1991.

1916. Norbeck, Edward, and Margaret Lock, eds. *Health, Illness and Medical Care in Japan: Cultural and Social Dimensions*. Honolulu, HI: University of Hawaii Press, 1987.

1917. Ohnuki-Tierney, Emiko. *Illness and Culture in Contemporary Japan: An Anthropological View*. Cambridge, U.K.; New York: Cambridge University Press, 1984.

1918. Ohnuki-Tierney, Emiko. *Illness and Healing Among the Sakhalin Ainu: A Symbolic Interpretation*. Cambridge, U.K.; New York: Cambridge University Press, 1981.

1919. Okimoto, Daniel I., and Aki Yoshikawa. *Japan's Health System: Efficiency and Effectiveness in Universal Care*. Washington, DC: Faulkner & Gray's Healthcare Information Center, 1993.

1920. Omura, Yoshiaki. *Acupuncture Medicine: Its Historical and Clinical Background*. Tokyo: Japan Publications, 1982.

1921. Powell, Margaret, and Masahira Anesaki. *Health Care in Japan*. London; New York: Routledge, 1990.

1922. Rabbitt Roff, Sue. *Hotspots: The Legacy of Hiroshima and Nagasaki*. London; New York: Cassell, 1995.

1923. Rosner, Erhard. *Medizingeschichte Japans* [Medical History of Japan]. Handbuch der Orientalistik. Funfte Abteilung, Japan, 3 Bd., 5. Abschnitt. Leiden, Netherlands; New York: Brill, 1989.

1924. Rotermund, Hartmut O. *Hosogami, ou, la Petite Verole Aisement: Materiaux pour L'Étude des Epidemies dans le Japon des XVIIIe, XIXe Siecles* [Hosogami, or, the Small Pox Ease: Material for the Study of Epidemics in Japan of the 18th and 19th Centuries]. Paris: Maisonneuve & Larose, 1991.

1925. Schull, William J. *Effects of Atomic Radiation: A Half-Century of Studies from Hiroshima and Nagasaki*. New York: Wiley, 1995.

1926. Sonoda, Kyoichi. *Health and Illness in Changing Japanese Society*. Tokyo: University of Tokyo Press, 1988.

Mergers

1927. Ishizumi, Kanji. *Acquiring Japanese Companies: Mergers and Acquisitions in the Japanese Market*. Rev. ed. Cambridge, MA: Blackwell, 1990.

1928. Kester, W. Carl. *Japanese Takeovers: The Global Contest for Corporate Control*. Boston, MA: Harvard Business School Press, 1991.

Middle East—Relations with

1929. Katakura, Kunio. *Japan and the Middle East*. Tokyo: The Middle East Institute of Japan, 1991.

1930. Kuroda, Yasumasa. *Japan in a New World Order: Contributing to the Arab-Israeli Peace Process*. Commack, NY: Nova Science, 1994.

1931. Morse, Ronald A. *Japan and the Middle East in Alliance Politics*. Conference Report. Woodrow Wilson International Center for Scholars. Washington, DC: Asia Program, International Securities Program, Wilson Center; Lanham, MD: University Press of America, 1986.

1932. Sugihara, Kaori, and J. A. Allan, eds. *Japan in the Contemporary Middle East*. Routledge / SOAS Contemporary Politics and Culture in the Middle East Series AACR2. London; New York: Routledge, 1993.

1933. Yoshitsu, Michael M. *Caught in the Middle East: Japan's Diplomacy in Transition*. Lexington, MA: Lexington Books, 1984.

Migration

1934. *Basic Plan for Immigration Control*. Tokyo: Japan Immigration Association, 1992.

1935. Moriyama, Alan Takeo. *Imingaisha: Japanese Emigration Companies and Hawaii, 1894-1908*. Honolulu, HI: University of Hawaii Press, 1985.

1936. White, James W. *Migration in Metropolitan Japan: Social Change and Political Behavior*. Japan Research Monograph, 2. Berkeley, CA: Institute of East Asian Studies, University of California, Berkeley, Center for Japanese Studies, 1982.

Military

1937. Matthews, Ron, and Keisuke Matsuyama. *Japan's Military Renaissance?* New York: St. Martin's Press, 1993.

1938. Polomka, Peter. *Japan as Peacekeeper: Samurai State, or New Civilian Power?* Canberra Papers on Strategy and Defence, no. 97. Canberra, Australia: Strategic and Defence Studies Centre, Research School of Pacific Studies, Australian National University, 1992.

Military Policy

1939. Brown, Eugene. *Japan's Search for Strategic Vision: The Contemporary Debate*. Carlisle Barracks, PA: Strategic Studies Institute, U.S. Army War College, 1993.

1940. Chinworth, Michael W. *Inside Japan's Defense: Technology, Economics, & Strategy*. Washington, DC: Brassey's, 1992.

1941. Fabig, K. *Japan, Wirtschaftsriese-Rustungszwerg: die japanische Rustungs- und Verteidigungspolitik seit 1945* [Japan, Economic Giant and Military Dwarf: The Japanese Arms and Defense Policy Since 1945]. Berliner Beitrage zur sozial- und wirtschaftswissenschaftlichen Japan-Forschung, Nr. 18. Bochum, Germany: N. Brockmeyer, 1984.

1942. Hamzah, B.A. *The Remilitarization of Japan: The Opportunities for and Challenges to Asean*. Seremban, Negeri Sembilan, Malaysia: Mawaddah Enterprise, 1991.

1943. Holland, Harrison M. *Managing Defense: Japan's Dilemma*. Lanham, MD: University Press of America, 1988.

1944. Kataoka, Tetsuya. *Waiting for a "Pearl Harbor": Japan Debates Defense*. Hoover Institution Publications, 232. Hoover International Studies. Stanford, CA: Hoover Institution Press, 1980.

1945. Keddell, Joseph P. *The Politics of Defense in Japan: Managing Internal and External Pressures*. Armonk, NY; London: Sharpe, 1993.

1946. McIntosh, Malcolm. *Japan Re-Armed*. London: Pinter, 1986.

Minorities—Ainu

1947. Kayano, Shigeru. *Our Land Was a Forest: An Ainu Memoir.* Translated by Kyoko Selden and Lili Selden. Boulder, CO: Westview, 1994.

1948. Kreiner, Josef, ed. *European Studies on Ainu Language and Culture.* Monographien aus dem Deutschen Institute für Japanstudien der Philipp-Franz-von-Siebold-Stiftung, Bd. 6. München, Germany: Iudicum, 1993.

1949. Munro, Neil Gordon. *Ainu Creed and Cult.* Edited by B.Z. Seligman. Kegan Paul Japan Library, no. 3. London; New York: Kegan Paul International, 1995.

1950. Olschleger, Hans-Dieter. *Umwelt und Wirtschaft der Ainu: Bemerkungen zur Ökologie einer Wildbeutergesellschaft* [Environment and Economy of the Ainu: Remarks on the Ecology of a Hunter Society]. Berlin, Germany: D. Reimer, 1989.

1951. Refsing, Kirsten. *The Ainu Language: The Morphology and Syntax of the Shizunai Dialect.* Aarhus, Denmark: Aarhus University Press, 1986.

1952. Shibatani, Masayoshi. *The Languages of Japan.* Cambridge Language Surveys. Cambridge, U.K.; New York: Cambridge University Press, 1990.

1953. Siddle, Richard. *Race, Resistance and the Ainu of Japan.* Sheffield Centre for Japanese Studies / Routledge Series. London; New York: Routledge, 1996.

1954. Sjoberg, Katarina. *The Return of the Ainu: Cultural Mobilization and the Practice of Ethnicity in Japan.* Studies in Anthropology; and History, v. 9. Chur, Switzerland; Langhorne, PA: Harwood Academic Publishers, 1993.

1955. Vovin, Alexander. *A Reconstruction of Proto-Ainu.* Brill's Japanese Studies Library 0925-6512, v. 4. Leiden, Netherlands; New York: Brill, 1993.

Minorities—Ainu—Bibliography

1956. Irimoto, Takashi. *Ainu Bibliography.* Sapporo, Japan: Hokkaido Daigaku, 1992.

Minorities—Buraku

1957. Grier, Louis N. *The River without Bridges: An Encounter with the Japanese Buraku: The Writings of Louis N. Grier, Jr.* Edited by Pat Tucker Spier. Shijonawate City, Osaka, Japan: Nihon Kirisuto Kyodan Buraku Liberation Center, 1986.

1958. Neary, Jan. *Political Protest and Social Control in Prewar Japan: The Origins of Buraku Liberation.* Studies on East Asia. Atlantic Highlands, NJ: Humanities Press International; Manchester, U.K.: Manchester University Press, 1989.

1959. Sabouret, Jean François. *L'Autre Japon: Les Burakumin* [The Other Japan: The Burakumin]. Textes à L'Appui. Paris: La Decouverte / Maspero, 1983.

1960. Suginohara, Juichi. *The Status Discrimination in Japan: Introduction to Buraku Problem.* Kobe City, Japan: Hyogo Institute of Buraku Problem, 1982.

Minorities—Koreans

1961. Hardacre, Helen. *The Religion of Japan's Korean Minority: The Preservation of Ethnic Identity.* Korea Research Monograph; 9. Berkeley, CA: Institute of East Asian Studies, University of California, Berkeley, Center for Korean Studies, 1984.

1962. Lee, Changsoom, and George De Vos. *Koreans in Japan: Ethnic Conflict and Accommodation.* Berkeley, CA: University of California Press, 1981.

1963. Weiner, Michael. *The Origins of the Korean Community in Japan, 1910-1923.* Studies on East Asia. Atlantic Highlands, NJ: Humanities Press International, 1989.

1964. Weiner, Michael. *Race and Migration in Imperial Japan.* Sheffield Centre for Japanese Studies / Routledge Series. London; New York: Routledge, 1994.

Minorities—Okinawans

1965. Lebra, William P. *Okinawan Religion: Belief, Ritual and Social Structure.* Honolulu, HI: University of Hawaii Press, 1966. Reprint: 1985.

Missions *See*: Religion—Christianity—Missions and Missionaries

Modern Art *See*: Art—Modern

Modern History *See*: History—Modern

Modern Literature *See*: Literature—Modern

Mombushō *See*: Educational Policy

Monarchy

See also: Royalty

1966. Banno, Junji, ed. *The Emperor System in Modern Japan.* Acta Asiatica, 59. Tokyo: Toho Gakkai, 1990.

1967. Fujitani, Takashi. *Splendid Monarchy: Power and Pageantry in Modern Japan.* Twentieth-Century Japan, 6. Berkeley, CA: University of California Press, 1996.

1968. Irokawa, Daikichi. *The Age of Hirohito: In Search of Modern Japan.* Translated by Mikiso Hane, and John K. Urda. New York: Free Press, 1995.

1969. Packard, Jerrold M. *Sons of Heaven: A Portrait of the Japanese Monarchy.* New York: Scribner, 1987.

1970. Takeda, Kiyoko. *The Dual-Image of the Japanese Emperor.* London: Macmillan Education, 1988.

Monastic Life *See*: Monks and Priests

Monetary Policy

1971. Das, Dilip K. *The Challenge of the Appreciating Yen and Japanese Corporate Response.* Pacific Economic Papers, no. 217. Canberra, Australia: Australia-Japan Research Centre, 1993.

1972. Das, Dilip K. *The Yen Appreciation and the International Economy.* London: Macmillan, 1993.

1973. Schmiegelow, Michele, ed. *Japan's Response to Crisis and Change in the World Economy.* Armonk, NY: Sharpe, 1986.

1974. Shinji, Takagi, ed. *Japanese Capital Markets: New Developments in Regulations and Institutions*. Cambridge, MA: Blackwell, 1993.

1975. Singleton, Kenneth J. *Japanese Monetary Policy*. National Bureau of Economic Research Project Report. Chicago, IL: University of Chicago Press, 1993.

1976. Thorn, Richard S. *The Rising Yen: The Impact of Japanese Financial Liberalization on World Capital Markets*. Singapore: ASEAN Economic Unit, Institute of Southeast Asian Studies, 1987.

Monkeys

1977. Fedigan, Linda Marie, and Pamela J. Asquith, eds. *The Monkeys of Arashiyama: 35 Years of Research in Japan and the West*. Albany, NY: State University of New York Press, 1991.

1978. Ohnuki-Tierney, Emiko. *The Monkey as Mirror: Symbolic Transformation in Japanese History and Ritual*. Princeton, NJ: Princeton University Press, 1987.

Monkeys—Bibliography

1979. Williams, Jean Balch. *Behavioral Observations of Feral and Free-ranging Japanese Monkeys (Macaca Fuscata): A Bibliography, 1983-1991*. Primate Information Center Topical Bibliographies, 91-003. Seattle, WA: Primate Information Center, Regional Primate Research Center, University of Washington, 1991.

Movie Directors

1980. Bock, Andie. *Japanese Film Directors*. Tokyo; New York: Kodansha International, 1985.

Movie Directors—Kurosawa, Akira, 1910-

1981. Desser, David. *The Samurai Films of Akira Kurosawa*. Studies in Cinema, no. 23. Ann Arbor, MI: UMI Research Press, 1983.

1982. Kurosawa, Akira. *Something Like an Autobiography*. Translated by Andie E. Bock. New York: Knopf, 1982.

Movie Directors—Mizoguchi, Kenji, 1898-1956

1983. Kirihara, Donald. *Patterns of Time: Mizoguchi and the 1930s.* Wisconsin Studies in Film. Madison, WI: University of Wisconsin Press, 1992.

1984. McDonald, Keiko I. *Mizoguchi.* Twayne's Filmmakers Series. Boston: Twayne, 1984.

Movie Directors—Ōshima, Nagisa, 1932-

1985. Oshima, Nagisa. *Cinema, Censorship and the State: The Writings of Nagisa Oshima, 1956-1978.* Cambridge, MA: MIT Press, 1992.

Movie Directors—Ozu, Yasujirō, 1903-1963

1986. Tomicek, Harry. *Ozu.* Edited by Peter Konlechner. Publikationen des Österreichischen Filmmuseums, Bd. 1. Vienna: Österreichisches Filmmuseum, 1988.

Movies

1987. Anderson, Joseph L., and Donald Richie. *The Japanese Film: Art and Industry.* Expanded ed. Princeton, NJ: Princeton University Press, 1982.

1988. Barrett, Gregory. *Archetypes in Japanese Films: The Sociopolitical and Religious Significance of the Principal Heroes and Heroines.* Selinsgrove, PA: Susquehanna University Press; London: Associated University Presses, 1989.

1989. Broderick, Mick, ed. *Hibakusha Cinema: Hiroshima, Nagasaki, and the Nuclear Image in Japanese Film.* Japanese Studies. London; New York: Kegan Paul International, 1996.

1990. Davis, Darrell William. *Picturing Japaneseness: Monumental Style, National Identity, Japanese Film.* Film and Culture. New York: Columbia University Press, 1996.

1991. Desser, David. *Eros Plus Massacre: An Introduction to the Japanese New Wave Cinema.* Bloomington, IN: Indiana University Press, 1988.

1992. Galbraith, Stuart. *Japanese Science Fiction, Fantasy, and Horror Films: A Critical Analysis of 103 Features Released in the United States, 1950-1992.* Jefferson, NC: McFarland, 1994.

1993. Hirano, Kyoko. *Mr. Smith Goes to Tokyo: The Japanese Cinema under the American Occupation, 1945-1952.* Washington, DC: Smithsonian Institute, 1992.

1994. McDonald, Keiko I. *Cinema East: A Critical Study of Major Japanese Film.* Rutherford, NJ: Fairleigh Dickinson University Press, 1983.

1995. McDonald, Keiko I. *Japanese Classical Theater in Films.* Rutherford, NJ: Fairleigh Dickinson University Press; London; Cranbury, NJ: Associated University Presses, 1994.

1996. Nolletti, Arthur, Jr., and David Desser, eds. *Reframing Japanese Cinema: Authorship, Genre, History.* Bloomington, IN: Indiana University Press, 1992.

1997. Richie, Donald. *Japanese Cinema: An Introduction.* Images of Asia. Hong Kong; New York: Oxford University Press, 1990.

1998. Richie, Donald. *The Japanese Movie.* Rev. ed. Tokyo; New York: Kodansha International, 1982.

1999. Sato, Tadao. *Currents in Japanese Cinema: Essays.* Translated by Gregory Barrett. Tokyo: Kodansha International, 1982.

2000. Tessier, Max, ed. *Cinéma et Littérature au Japon de L'Ère Meiji à nos Jours* [Cinema and Literature in Japan from the Meiji Era to our Days]. Cinema/ Singulier. Paris: Centre Georges Pompidou, 1986.

Movies—Filmography

2001. Buehrer, Beverly Bare. *Japanese Films: A Filmography and Commentary, 1921-1989.* Jefferson, NC: McFarland, 1990.

2002. Galbraith, Stuart. *The Japanese Filmography: A Complete Reference to 209 Filmmakers and the over 1250 Films Released in the United States, 1900 through 1994.* Jefferson, NC: McFarland, 1996.

2003. Grilli, Peter. *Japan in Film: A Comprehensive Annotated Catalogue of Documentary and Theatrical Films on Japan Available in the United States.* New York: Japan Society, 1984.

Murals *See*: Art—Painting—Mural

Music

2004. Ackermann, Peter. *Kumiuta, Traditional Songs for Certificates: A Study of their Texts and Implications.* Swiss Asian Studies. Monographs, vol. 10. Bern: New York: P. Lang, 1990.

2005. Ackermann, Peter. *Studien zur Koto-Musik von Edo* [Studies on Koto Music from Edo]. 2 vols. Studien zur traditionellen Musik Japans, Bd. 6. Kassel, Germany: Bärenreiter, 1986.

2006. Eppstein, Ury. *The Beginnings of Western Music in Meiji Era Japan.* Studies in the History and Interpretation of Music, v. 44. Lewiston, NY: Mellen Press, 1994.

2007. Gutzwiller, Andreas. *Die Shakuhachi der Kinko-Schule* [The Shakuhachi of the Kinko School]. Studien zur traditionellen Musik Japans, Bd. 5. Kassel, Germany: Bärenreiter, 1983.

2008. Hermann, Evelyn. *Shinichi Suzuki, the Man and his Philosophy.* Athens, OH: Ability Development Associates, 1981.

2009. Isaku, Patia R. *Mountain Storm, Pine Breeze: Folk Songs in Japan.* Tucson, AZ: University of Arizona Press, 1981.

2010. Kishibe, Shigeo. *The Traditional Music of Japan.* 2d ed. Tokyo: Japan Foundation, 1982.

2011. Kitahara, Ikuya, Misao Matsumoto, and Akira Matsuda. *The Encyclopedia of Musical Instruments: The Shakuhachi.* Tokyo: Ongakusha, 1990.

2012. Kubota, Hideki, and Hiroko Inoue. *Tune of the Yakumo-Goto: Myth and the Japanese Spirit.* Osaka, Japan: Yakumogoto Reminiscence Society, 1990.

2013. Malm, William P. *Six Hidden Views of Japanese Music.* Berkeley, CA: University of California Press, 1986.

2014. Markham, Elizabeth J. *Saibara: Japanese Court Songs of the Heian Period.* 2 vols. Cambridge, U.K.; New York: Cambridge University Press, 1983.

2015. Matsushita, Hitoshi. *A Checklist of Published Instrumental Music by Japanese Composers.* Tokyo: Academia Music, 1989.

2016. Müller, Gerhild. *Kagura: Die Lieder der Kagura-Zeremonie am Naishidokoro* [Kagura: The Songs of the Kagura Ceremony at the Naishidokoro]. Veröffentlichungen des Ostasiatischen Seminars der Johann-Wolfgang-Goethe-Universität, Frankfurt am Main, Reihe B, Bd. 2. Wiesbaden, Germany: Harrasowitz, 1971.

2017. Nakano, Ichiro. *101 Favorite Songs Taught in Japanese Schools.* Tokyo: Japan Times, 1983.

2018. Sawabe, Yukiko. *Neue Musik in Japan von 1950 bis 1960: Stilrichtungen und Komponisten* [New Music in Japan from 1950 to 1960: Style Directions and Composers]. Kölner Beiträge zur Musikforschung, Bd. 170. Regensburg, Germany: Gustav Bosse, 1992.

2019. Takahashi, Chikuzan. *The Autobiography of Takahashi Chikuzan: Adventures of a Tsugaru-Jamisen Musician.* Translated by Gerald Groemer. Detroit Monographs in Musicology / Studies in Music, no. 10. Warren, MI: Harmonic Park Press, 1991.

2020. Tamba, Akira. *The Musical Structure of No.* Translated by Patricia Matore. Tokyo: Tokai University Press, 1981.

2021. Tamba, Akira. *Musiques Traditionnelles du Japon: Des Origines au XVIe Siecle* [Traditional Music of Japan: From the Beginning until the 16th Century]. Arles, France: Actes Sud, 1995.

2022. Tamba, Akira. *La Théorie et L'Esthétique Musicale Japonaises: du 8e au 19e Siècle* [Japanese Musical Theory and Aesthetics: from the 8th to the 19th Century]. Bibliothèque Japonaise. Paris: Publications Orientalistes de France, 1988.

Music—Bibliography

2023. Tsuge, Gen'ichi. *Japanese Music: An Annotated Bibliography.* Garland Reference Library of the Humanities, vol. 472. New York: Garland, 1986.

Mythology

2024. Aston, W. G., trans. *Nihongi: Chronicles of Japan from the Earliest Times to A.D. 697.* 2 vols. Transactions and Proceedings of the Japan Society, London, Supplement I. London: Kegan, Paul, Trench, Trübner, 1896. Reprint: Rutland, VT: Tuttle, 1972.

2025. Phillipi, Donald. *Kojiki*. Tokyo: University of Tokyo Press, 1968. Reprint: Princeton, NJ: Princeton University Press, 1969.

2026. Piggott, Juliet. *Japanese Mythology*. Rev. ed. Library of the World's Myths and Legends. London; New York: Hamlyn, 1982.

Names - Dictionaries

2027. Koop, Albert James, and Hogitaro Inada. *Japanese Names and How to Read them: Manual for Art-Collectors and Students, being a Concise and Comprehensive Guide to the Reading and Interpretation of Japanese Proper Names both Geographical and Personal, as well as of Dates and other Formal Expressions*. Reading, U.K.: Eastern Press, 1923. Reprint: London: Routledge & Kegan Paul, 1985.

2028. O'Neill, Patrick Geoffrey. *Japanese Names: A Comprehensive Index by Characters and Readings*. New York: Weatherhill, 1972.

National Security

See also: 759

2029. Barnett, Robert W. *Beyond War: Japan's Concept of Comprehensive National Security*. Washington, DC: Pergamon-Brassey's, 1984.

2030. Kataoka, Tetsuya, and Ramon H. Myers. *Defending an Economic Superpower: Reassessing the U.S.-Japan Security Alliance*. Westview Special Studies on East Asia. Boulder, CO: Westview, 1989.

2031. Katzenstein, Peter J. *Cultural Norms and National Security: Police and Military in Postwar Japan*. Cornell Studies in Political Economy. Ithaca, NY: Cornell University Press, 1996.

2032. Katzenstein, Peter J., and Nobuo Okawara. *Japan's National Security: Structures, Norms and Policy Responses in a Changing World*. Cornell East Asia Series, 58. Ithaca, NY: East Asia Program, Cornell University, 1993.

2033. Katzenstein, Peter J., and Yutaka Tsujinaka. *Defending the Japanese State: Structures, Norms and the Political Responses to Terrorism and Violent Social Protest in the 1970s and 1980s*. Cornell East Asia Series, 53. Ithaca, NY: East Asia Program, Cornell University, 1991.

2034. Levin, Norman D. *The Wary Warriors: Future Directions in Japanese Security Policies*. Santa Monica, CA: Rand, 1993.

2035. Olsen, Edward A. *U.S.-Japan Strategic Reciprocity: A Neo-Nationalist View*. Stanford, CA: Hoover Institution Press, 1985.

2036. Samuels, Richard J. *"Rich Nation, Strong Army": National Security and the Technological Transformation of Japan*. Cornell Studies in Political Economy. Ithaca, NY: Cornell University Press, 1994.

Nationalism

2037. Ivy, Marilyn. *Discourses of the Vanishing: Modernity, Phantasm, Japan*. Chicago, IL: University of Chicago Press, 1995.

2038. Stronach, Bruce. *Beyond the Rising Sun: Nationalism in Contemporary Japan*. Westport, CT: Praeger, 1995.

2039. White, James W., Michio Umegaki, and Thomas R. H. Havens, eds. *The Ambivalence of Nationalism: Modern Japan between East and West*. Lanham, MD: University Press of America, 1990.

2040. Yoshino, Kosaku. *Cultural Nationalism in Contemporary Japan: A Sociological Enquiry*. London; New York: Routledge, 1992.

Natural Resources

2041. Akao, Nobutoshi, ed. *Japan's Economic Security: Resources as a Factor in Foreign Policy*. Aldershot, UK: Published for the Royal Institute of International Affairs by Gower, 1983.

Naval History *See*: History—Naval

Neighborhood

2042. Bestor, Theodore C. *Neighborhood Tokyo*. Studies of the East Asian Institute. Stanford, CA: Stanford University Press, 1989.

2043. Simko, Dusan. *Einwohner und Umweltbelastung in Tokyo: Fallstudie: die Nachbarschaft Ojima in Koto-ku* [Residential and Environmental Tax in Tokyo: Case Study: The Ojima Neighborhood in Koto-ku]. Stadtforschung Aktuell, Bd. 28. Basel, Switzerland; Boston, MA: Birkhauser, 1990.

Netherlands—Relations with

2044. Goodman, Grant Kohn. *The Dutch Impact on Japan (1640-1853)*. T'oung Pao, Monographie 5. Leiden, Netherlands: E. J. Brill, 1967. Reprint: *Japan: The Dutch Experience*. London; Dover, NH: Athlone Press, 1986.

2045. Opstall, Margot E. van, et. al. *Vier Eeuwen Nederland-Japan: Kunst, Wetenschap, Taal, Handel* [Four Centuries Netherlands-Japan: Art, Science, Language, Trade]. Lochem, Netherlands: Tijdstroom, 1983.

2046. Ozaki, Wasaburo, ed. *Bridge between Japan and the Netherlands*. 4 vols. Kadoma, Japan: Japan-Netherlands Society of the Kansai, 1979.

2047. Paul, H. *Nederlanders in Japan, 1600-1854: De VOC op Desjima*. [The Dutch in Japan, 1600-1854: The VOC at Deshima]. Weesp, Netherlands: Fibula-Van Dishoeck, 1984.

2048. Vermeulen, Ton. *The Deshima Dagregisters: Their Original Tables of Contents*. Intercontinenta, no. 6, etc. Leiden, Netherlands: Leiden Centre for the History of European Expansion, 1986.

Netsuke *See*: Art—Netsuke and Inro

New Religions *See*: Religion—New Movements

New Year

2049. Brandon, Reiko Mochinaga, and Barbara B. Stephan. *Spirit and Symbol: The Japanese New Year*. Honolulu, HI: Honolulu Academy of Arts in association with University of Hawaii Press, 1994.

New Zealand—Relations with

2050. Trotter, Ann. *New Zealand and Japan, 1945-1952: The Occupation and the Peace Treaty*. London; Atlantic Highlands, NJ: Athlone Press, 1990.

2051. Wevers, Maarten. *Japan, its Future, and New Zealand*. Private Bag, Wellington: Victoria University Press for the Institute of Policy Studies, 1988.

Newspapers *See*: Media

Nō *See*: Theater—Nō

Occupational Training *See*: Education—Vocational

Ocean Engineering

2052. Friedheim, Robert L., et al. *Japan and the New Ocean Regime.*
Westview Special Studies in Ocean Science and Policy. Boulder, CO:
Westview, 1984.

2053. Hanayama, Y. et al. *Who Speaks for Tokyo Bay?* Edited by Blair T.
Bower, and Katsuki Takao. Coastal Waters, 3. Rotterdam,
Netherlands; Brookfield, VT: A. A. Balkema, 1993.

2054. Jones, W. Glyn, comp. *The Japanese Offshore Industry:
Technology and Markets.* Letchworth, U.K.: Technical
Communications, 1988.

2055. Nagao, Yoshimi, ed. *Coastlines of Japan II.* Coastlines of the
World. New York: American Society of Civil Engineers, 1993.

Okinawans *See*: Minorities—Okinawans

Pacific Area—Relations with

2056. Cronin, Richard P. *Japan, the United States, and Prospects for the
Asia-Pacific Century: Three Scenarios for the Future.* New York: St.
Martin's Press; Singapore: Institute of Southeast Asian Studies, 1992.

2057. Plummer, Katherine. *The Shogun's Reluctant Ambassadors:
Japanese Sea Drifters in the North Pacific.* Portland, OR: Oregon
Historical Society, 1991.

Pacifism

2058. Getreuer, Peter. *Der verbale Pazifismus: die Verteidigung Japans
1972-1983 in demoskopischen Befunden* [Verbal Pacifism: Japanese
Defense 1972-1983 in Polling Results]. Beiträge zur Japanologie, Bd.
22. Vienna: Institut für Japanologie, Universität Wien, 1986.

Painting *See*: Art—Painting

Paper *See*: Art—Paper

Peasants

2059. Bix, Herbert P. *Peasant Protest in Japan, 1590-1884*. New Haven, CT: Yale University Press, 1986.

2060. Bowen, Roger W. *Rebellion and Democracy in Meiji Japan: A Study of Commoners in the Popular Rights Movement*. Berkeley, CA: University of California Press, 1980.

2061. Kelly, William W. *Deference and Defiance in Nineteenth-Century Japan*. Princeton, NJ: Princeton University Press, 1985.

2062. Vlastos, Stephen. *Peasant Protests and Uprisings in Tokugawa Japan*. Berkeley, CA: University of California Press, 1986.

2063. Walthall, Anne, ed., trans. *Peasant Uprisings in Japan: A Critical Anthology of Peasant Histories*. Chicago, IL: University of Chicago Press, 1991.

2064. Walthall, Anne. *Social Protest and Popular Culture in Eighteenth-Century Japan*. Monographs of the Association for Asian Studies, no. 43. Tucson, AZ: University of Arizona Press for the Association for Asian Studies, 1986.

2065. Watanabe, Shoichi. *The Peasant Soul of Japan*. Basingstoke, U.K.: Macmillan, 1989.

Personnel Management

2066. Amaya, Tadashi. *Recent Trends in Human Resource Development*. Japanese Industrial Relations Series, 17. Tokyo: Japan Institute of Labour, 1990.

2067. Ballon, Robert J. *Foreign Competition in Japan: Human Resources Strategies*. New York: Routledge, 1991.

2068. Hanami, Tadashi. *Managing Japanese Workers: Personnel Management: Law and Practice in Japan*. Tokyo: Japan Institute of Labour, 1991.

2069. Inohara, Hideo. *Human Resource Development in Japanese Companies*. Tokyo: Asian Productivity Organization; White Plains, NY: Quality Resources, 1990.

2070. *Japanese Corporate Decision Making.* JETRO Business Information Series. Tokyo: Japan External Trade Organization, 1992.

2071. Marsh, Robert Mortimer, and Hiroshi Mannari. *Organizational Change in Japanese Factories.* Monographs in Organizational Behavior and Industrial Relations, v. 9. Greenwich, CT: JAI Press, 1988.

2072. Nevins, Thomas J. *Labor Pains and the Gaijin Boss: Hiring, Managing, and Firing the Japanese.* Tokyo: Japanese Times, 1984.

2073. Nevins, Thomas J. *Taking Charge in Japan.* Tokyo: Japan Times, 1990.

Peru—Relations with

2074. Flor Belaunde, Pablo de la. *Japón en la Escena Internacional: Sus Relaciones con América Latina y el Perú [Japan in International Affairs: Relations with Latin America and Peru].* Serie Investigaciones, no. 9. Lima, Peru: Centro Peruano de Estudios Internacionales: Cotecna Inspection: Omic International, 1991.

Philippines—Relations with

2075. Constantino, Renato. *The Second Invasion: Japan in the Philippines.* Quezon City, Philippines: Karrel, 1989.

2076. Ohno, Takushi. *War Reparations and Peace Settlement: Philippines-Japan Relations 1945-1956.* Manila: Solidaridad, 1986.

Philosophy

See also: Confucianism

2077. Brull, Lydia. *Die japanische Philosophie: eine Einführung* [Japanese Philosophy: An Introduction]. Orientalistische Einführungen. Darmstadt, Germany: Wissenschaftliche Buchgesellschaft, 1989.

2078. Heine, Steven. *A Dream within a Dream: Studies in Japanese Thought.* Asian Thought and Culture, vol. 5. New York: P. Lang, 1991.

2079. Miyamoto, Musashi. *The Book of Five Rings.* Boston, MA: Shambhala, 1993.

2080. Moore, A., ed. *The Japanese Mind: Essentials of Japanese Philosophy and Culture*. Honolulu, HI: East-West Center Press: University of Hawaii Press, 1967. Reprint: Honolulu, HI: University of Hawaii Press, 1987.

2081. Nagatomo, Shigenori. *Attunement through the Body*. SUNY Series on the Body. Albany, NY: State University of New York Press, 1992.

2082. Okada, Mokichi. *Johrei: Divine Light of Salvation*. Kyoto, Japan: Society of Johrei, 1984.

2083. Sawada, Janine Anderson. *Confucian Values and Popular Zen: Sekimon Shingaku in Eighteenth Century Japan*. Honolulu, HI: University of Hawaii Press, 1993.

2084. Shaner, David Edward, Shigenori Nagatomo, and Yasao Yuasa. *Science and Comparative Philosophy: Introducing Yuasa Yasuo*. Leiden, Netherlands; New York: Brill, 1989.

2085. Yagyū, Munenori. *The Sword & the Mind*. Translated by Hiroaki Sato. Woodstock, NY: Overlook Press, 1986.

2086. Yasunaga, Toshinobu. *Ando Shoeki: Social and Ecological Philosopher of Eighteenth Century Japan*. New York: Weatherhill, 1992.

Photography

2087. Bennett, Terry. *Early Japanese Images*. Rutland, VT: Tuttle, 1996.

2088. Holborn, Mark. *Black Sun: The Eyes of Four: Roots and Innovation in Japanese Photography*. New York: Aperture, 1986.

2089. Japan Photographers Association. *A Century of Japanese Photography*. New York: Pantheon Books, 1980.

2090. *Photography and Beyond in Japan: Space, Time and Memory*. Tokyo: Hara Museum of Contemporary Art, 1995.

2091. Putzar, Edward. *Japanese Photography, 1945-1985*. Tucson, AZ: Pacific West, 1987.

2092. Winkel, Margarita. *Souvenirs from Japan: Japanese Photography at the Turn of the Century*. London: Bamboo, 1991.

Poetry *See*: Literature—Poetry

Poets *See*: Literature—Poets

Police

See also: 704

2093.   Ames, Walter L. *Police and Community in Japan.* Berkeley, CA: University of California Press, 1981.

2094.   Bayley, David H. *Forces of Order: Policing Modern Japan.* Berkeley, CA: University of California Press, 1991.

2095.   Tipton, Elise K. *The Japanese Police State: The Tokko in Interwar Japan.* Honolulu, HI: University of Hawaii Press, 1990.

Political History *See*: History—Political

Political Parties

2096.   Baerwald, Hans H. *Party Politics in Japan.* Boston, MA: Allen & Unwin, 1986.

2097.   Benjamin, Roger, and Kan Ori. *Tradition and Change in Postindustrial Japan: The Role of the Political Parties.* New York: Praeger, 1981.

2098.   Curtis, Gerald L. *The Japanese Way of Politics.* Studies of the East Asian Institute. New York: Columbia University Press, 1988.

2099.   Hrebenar, Ronald J. *The Japanese Party System.* 2d ed. Boulder, CO: Westview, 1992.

2100.   MacDougall, Terry Edward, ed. *Political Leadership in Contemporary Japan.* Michigan Papers in Japanese Studies, no. 1. Ann Arbor, MI: Center for Japanese Studies, University of Michigan, 1982.

2101.   Ramseyer, J. Mark, and Frances McCall Rosenbluth. *Japan's Political Marketplace.* Cambridge, MA: Harvard University Press, 1993.

Political Science

2102.   Williams, David. *Japan and the Enemies of Open Political Science.* London; New York: Routledge, 1996.

Politicians

2103. Kishima, Takako. *Political Life in Japan: Democracy in a Reversible World.* Princeton, NJ: Princeton University Press, 1991.

2104. Neary, Ian, ed. *Leaders and Leadership in Japan.* Richmond, U.K.: Japan Library, 1996.

2105. Oka, Yoshitake. *Five Political Leaders of Modern Japan: Ito Hirobumi, Okuma Shigenobu, Hara Takashi, Inukai Tsuyoshi, and Saionji Kimmochi.* Tokyo: University of Tokyo Press, 1986.

2106. Weinstein, Martin E. *The Human Face of Japan's Leadership: Twelve Portraits.* New York: Praeger, 1989.

Politics

2107. Bingman, Charles F. *Japanese Government Leadership and Management.* New York: St. Martin's Press, 1989.

2108. Calder, Kent E. *Crisis and Compensation: Public Policy and Political Stability in Japan, 1949-1986.* Princeton, NJ: Princeton University Press, 1988.

2109. Hastings, Sally A. *Neighborhood and Nation in Tokyo, 1905-1937.* Pitt Series in Policy and Institutional Studies. Pittsburgh, PA: University of Pittsburgh Press, 1995.

2110. Hayao, Kenji. *The Japanese Prime Minister and Public Policy.* Pitt Series in Policy and Institutional Studies. Pittsburgh, PA: University of Pittsburgh Press, 1993.

2111. Higuchi, Yoichi, and Christian Sautter, eds. *L'État et L'Individu au Japon* [State and Individual in Japan]. Études Japonaises, 1. Paris: Éditions de L'École des Hautes Études en Sciences Sociales, 1990.

2112. Jain, Purnendra. *Local Politics and Policymaking in Japan.* New Delhi: Commonwealth, 1989.

2113. Kataoka, Tetsuya. *The Price of a Constitution: The Origin of Japan's Postwar Politics.* New York: C. Russak, 1991.

2114. Kishimoto, Kōichi. *Politics in Modern Japan: Development and Organization.* 3d ed. Tokyo: Japan Echo, 1988.

2115. Kyogoku, Jun'ichi. *The Political Dynamics of Japan*. Tokyo: University of Tokyo Press, 1987.

2116. Masumi, Junnosuke. *Contemporary Politics in Japan*. Translated by Lonny E. Carlile. Berkeley, CA: University of California Press, 1995.

2117. Ozawa, Ichiro. *Blueprint for a New Japan: The Rethinking of a Nation*. Translated by Louisa Rubinfien. Edited by Eric Gower. Tokyo; New York: Kodansha International, 1994.

2118. Pempel, T. J. *Policy and Politics in Japan: Creative Conservatism*. Policy and Politics in Industrial States. Philadelphia, PA: Temple University Press, 1982.

2119. Richardson, Bradley M., and Scott C. Flanagan. *Politics in Japan*. Little, Brown Series in Comparative Politics. Country Study. Boston, MA: Little, Brown, 1984.

2120. Stockwin, J. A. A., et al. *Dynamic and Immobilist Politics in Japan*. Houndsmill, Basingstoke, U.K.: Macmillan, in association with St. Antony's College, Oxford, 1988.

2121. Tsuji, Kiyoaki, ed. *Public Administration in Japan*. Tokyo: University of Tokyo Press, 1984.

2122. Williams, David. *Japan: Beyond the End of History*. Nissan Institute / Routledge Japanese Studies Series. London; New York: Routledge, 1994.

2123. Wolferen, Karel van. *The Enigma of Japanese Power: People and Politics in a Stateless Nation*. With a new introduction and epilogue. New York: Vintage Books, 1990.

2124. Woronoff, Jon. *Politics, the Japanese Way*. Basingstoke, U.K.: Macmillan; New York: St. Martin's Press, 1986.

2125. Zhao, Quansheng. *Japanese Policymaking: The Politics Behind Politics: Informal Mechanisms and the Making of China Policy*. Westport, CT: Praeger, 1993.

Popular Culture

2126. Allison, Anne. *Permitted and Prohibited Desires: Mothers, Comics, and Censorship in Japan*. Boulder, CO: Westview, 1996.

2127. Buruma, Ian. *Japanese Mirror: Heroes and Villains of Japanese Culture.* London: J. Cape, 1984. Reprint: *Behind the Mask: On Sexual Demons, Sacred Mothers, Transvestites, Gangsters, and Other Japanese Cultural Heroes.* New York: New American Library, 1985.

2128. Martineau, Lisa. *Caught in a Mirror: Reflections of Japan.* London: Macmillan, 1993.

2129. McFarland, H. Neill. *Daruma: The Founder of Zen in Japanese Art and Popular Culture.* Tokyo; New York: Kodansha International, 1987.

2130. McKinstry, John, and Asako Nakajima. *Jinsei Annai, "Life's Guide": Glimpses of Japan Through a Popular Advice Column.* Armonk, NY: Sharpe, 1991.

2131. Moeran, Brian. *Language and Popular Culture in Japan.* Japanese Studies. Manchester, U.K.; New York: Manchester University Press, 1989.

2132. Powers, Richard Gid, and Hidetoshi Kato, eds. *Handbook of Japanese Popular Culture.* New York: Greenwood, 1989.

2133. Schodt, Frederik L. *Manga! Manga! The World of Japanese Comics.* Tokyo; New York: Kodansha International, 1983.

2134. Tsurumi, Shunsuke. *A Cultural History of Postwar Japan, 1945-1980.* Japanese Studies. London; New York: KPI, 1987.

2135. *Visions of Japan.* 3 vols. Tokyo: A de S, 1992.

Popular Literature *See*: Literature—Popular

Population

2136. *Demographic Transition in Japan and Rural Development.* Population and Development Series, no. 1. Tokyo: Asian Population and Development Association, 1985.

2137. Farris, William Wayne. *Population, Disease, and Land in Early Japan, 645-900.* Harvard-Yenching Institute Monograph Series, 24. Cambridge, MA: Council on East Asian Studies, Harvard University, 1985.

2138. Kuroda, Toshio, et al. *Urbanization and Development in Japan.* "Population and Development" Series, no. 3. Tokyo: Population and Development Association, 1986.

2139. *Population and the Family in Japan.* "Population and Development" series, no. 9. Tokyo: Asian Population and Development Association, 1989.

Postmodernism

2140. Miyoshi, Masao, and H. D. Harootunian. *Postmodernism and Japan.* Post-Contemporary Interventions. Durham, NC: Duke University Press, 1989.

Pre-Modern Literature *See*: Literature—Pre-modern

Preschool *See*: Education—Preschool

Press *See*: Media

Prints *See*: Art—Prints

Private Schools *See*: Education—Private Schools

Product Liability

2141. Goto, Takanori. *Japan's Dark Side to Progress: The Struggle for Justice for Pharmaceutical Victims of Japan's Postwar Economic Boom.* Chiba, Japan: Manbonsha, 1991.

Production Management

2142. Abe, Etsuo, and Robert Fitzgerald, eds. *The Origins of Japanese Industrial Power: Strategy, Institutions and the Development of Organisational Capability.* Ilford, U.K.; Portland, OR: F. Cass, 1995.

2143. Asaka, Tetsuichi, and Ozeki Kazuo, eds. *Handbook of Quality Tools, the Japanese Approach.* Cambridge, MA: Productivity Press, 1990.

2144. Cooper, Robin. *When Lean Enterprises Collide: Competing through Confrontation.* Boston, MA: Harvard Business School Press, 1995.

2145. Ogawa, Eiji. *Modern Production Management: A Japanese Experience*. Tokyo: Asian Productivity Organization, 1984.

2146. Schonberger, Richard J. *Japanese Manufacturing Techniques: Nine Hidden Lessons in Simplicity*. New York: Free Press, 1982.

2147. Shingo, Shigeo. *A Revolution in Manufacturing: The SMED System*. Stamford, CT: Productivity Press, 1985.

2148. Shinohara, Isao. *NPS, New Production System: JIT Crossing Industry Bounderies*. Cambridge, MA: Productivity Press, 1988.

Protectionism

2149. Maswood, Syed Javed. *Japan and Protection: The Growth of Protectionist Sentiment and the Japanese Response*. Routledge Japanese Studies Series. London; New York: Routledge, 1989.

2150. Naka, Norio. *Predicting Outcomes in United States-Japan Trade Negotiations: The Political Process of the Structural Impediments Initiative*. Westport, CT: Quorum Books, 1996.

Proverbs *See*: Language—Proverbs

Psychology and Psychiatry

2151. Doi, Takeo. *The Anatomy of Self: The Individual Versus Society*. Translated by Mark A. Harbison. Tokyo; New York: Kodansha International, 1986.

2152. Johnson, Frank A. *Dependency and Japanese Socialization: Psychoanalytic and Anthropological Investigations into Amae*. New York: New York University Press, 1993.

2153. Mita, Munesuke. *Social Psychology of Modern Japan*. Japanese Studies. London; New York: Kegan Paul International, 1992.

2154. Perlman, Michael. *Hiroshima Forever: The Ecology of Mourning*. Barrytown, NY: Barrytown Ltd. for Station Hill Arts, 1995.

2155. Reynolds, David K. *Naikan Psychotherapy: Meditation for Self-Development*. Chicago, IL: University of Chicago Press, 1983.

2156. Reynolds, David K. *The Quiet Therapies: Japanese Pathways to Personal Growth*. Honolulu, HI: University Press of Hawaii, 1980.

2157. Rosenberger, Nancy R., ed. *Japanese Sense of Self.* Publications of the Society for Psychological Anthropology. Cambridge, U.K.; New York: Cambridge University Press, 1992.

Publishers and Publishing

2158. Bauermeister, Junko. *Entwicklung des modernen japanischen Verlagswesens: Fallstudie Iwanami shoten* [Development of the Modern Japanese Publishing Trade: Case Study Iwanami Shoten]. Berliner Beiträge zur sozial- und wirtschaftswissenschaftlichen Japan-Forschung; Bd. 6. Bochum, Germany: Studienverlag Brockmeyer, 1980.

2159. Forrer, Matthi. *Eirakuya Toshiro, Publisher at Nagoya: A Contribution to the History of Publishing in 19th Century Japan.* Japonica Neerlandica, v. 1. Amsterdam: J. C. Gieben, 1985.

2160. Kuroki, Tsutomu. *An Introduction to Japanese Government Publications.* Guides to Official Publications, v. 10. Oxford, U.K.; Elmsford, NY: Pergamon, 1981.

2161. May, Ekkehard. *Die Kommerzialisierung der japanischen Literatur in der späten Edo-Zeit (1750-1868): Rahmenbedingungen und Entwicklungstendenzen der erzählenden Prosa im Zeitalter ihrer ersten Vermarktung* [The Commercialization of Japanese Literature in the Late Edo Period (1750-1868): Scale Determination and Development Trends of Narrative Prose at the time of their First Marketing]. Wiesbaden, Germany: Harrassowitz, 1983.

Quality Circles

2162. Ishikawa, Kaoru. *What is Total Quality Control? The Japanese Way.* Translated by David J. Lu. Englewood Cliffs, NJ: Prentice-Hall, 1985.

2163. Mizuno, Shigeru. *Company-Wide Total Quality Control.* Tokyo: Asian Productivity Organization, 1988.

2164. *Quality Control Circles at Work: Cases from Japan's Manufacturing and Service Sectors.* Tokyo: Asian Productivity Organization, 1984.

Railroads

2165. Ericson, Steven J. *The Sound of the Whistle: Railroads and the State in Meiji Japan.* Harvard East Asian Monographs, 168; Subseries on the history of Japanese Business and Industry. Cambridge, MA: Council on East Asian Studies, 1996.

2166. Mizutani, Fumitoshi. *Japanese Urban Railways: A Private-Public Comparison.* Aldershot, U.K.: Avebury, 1994.

2167. Noguchi, Paul H. *Delayed Departures, Overdue Arrivals: Industrial Familialism and the Japanese National Railways.* Honolulu, HI: University of Hawaii Press, 1990.

Rakugo *See:* Theater—Rakugo

Red Army *See:* Socialism

Red Cross

2168. Checkland, Olive. *Humanitarianism and the Emperor's Japan, 1877-1977.* New York: St. Martin's Press, 1994.

Religion

2169. Bremen, Jan van, and D. P. Martinez, eds. *Ceremony and Ritual in Japan: Religious Practices in an Industrialized Society.* Nissan Institute / Routledge Japanese Studies Series. London; New York: Routledge, 1995.

2170. Davis, Winston Bradley. *Japanese Religion and Society: Paradigms of Structure and Change.* Albany, NY: State University of New York Press, 1992.

2171. Earhart, H. Byron. *Japanese Religion, Unity and Diversity.* 3d ed. Religious Life of Man series. Belmont, CA: Wadsworth, 1982.

2172. Earhart, H. Byron. *Religions of Japan: Many Traditions within one Sacred Way.* Religious Traditions of the World. San Francisco, CA: Harper & Row, 1984.

2173. Ellwood, Robert S., and Richard Pilgrim. *Japanese Religion: A Cultural Perspective.* Prentice-Hall Series in World Religions. Englewood Cliffs, NJ: Prentice-Hall, 1985.

2174. Frank, Bernard. *L'Intérêt pour les Religions Japonaises dans la France du XIXe Siècle et les Collections d'Emile Guimet* [Interest in Japanese Religion in France of the 19th Century and the Emile Guimet Collections]. Essais et Conférences. Paris: Presses Universitaires de France, 1986.

2175. Kitagawa, Joseph Mitsuo. *On Understanding Japanese Religion.* Princeton, NJ: Princeton University Press, 1987.

2176. Kornicki, P. F., and I. J. McMullen, eds. *Religion in Japan: Arrows to Heaven and Earth.* University of Cambridge Oriental Publications, 50. Cambridge, U.K.; New York: Cambridge University Press, 1996.

2177. Murakami, Shigeyoshi. *Japanese Religion in the Modern Century.* Translated by H. Byron Earhart. Tokyo: University of Tokyo Press, 1980.

2178. Nishitani, Keiji. *Religion and Nothingness.* Translated by Jan van Bragt. Nanzan Studies in Religion and Culture, 2. Berkeley, CA: University of California Press, 1982.

2179. Reader, Ian. *Religion in Contemporary Japan.* Honolulu, HI: University of Hawaii Press, 1991.

Religion—Bibliography

2180. Earhart, H. Byron. *The New Religions of Japan: A Bibliography of Western-language Materials.* 2d ed. Michigan Papers in Japanese Studies no. 9. Ann Arbor, MI: Center for Japanese Studies, University of Michigan, 1983.

2181. Schwade, Arcadio. *Shintō-bibliography in Western Languages: Bibliography on Shintō and Religious Sects, Intellectual Schools and Movements Influenced by Shintōism.* Leiden, Netherlands: Brill, 1986.

Religion—Buddhism

2182. Goodwin, Janet R. *Alms and Vagabonds: Buddhist Temples and Popular Patronage in Medieval Japan.* Honolulu, HI: University of Hawaii Press, 1994.

2183. Grapard, Allan G. *The Protocol of the Gods: A Study of the Kasuga Cult in Japanese History.* Berkeley, CA: University of California Press, 1992.

2184. Inagaki, Hisao, and P. G. O'Neill. *A Dictionary of Japanese Buddhist Terms: Based on References in Japanese Literature.* 4th ed., with supplement. Kyoto, Japan: Nagata Bunshodo, 1992.

2185. Inagaki, Hisao. *A Glossary of Zen Terms.* Kyoto, Japan: Nagata Bunshodo, 1991.

2186. Kamens, Edward. *The Three Jewels: A Study and Translation of Minamoto Tamenori's Sanbōe.* Michigan Monograph Series in Japanese Studies, no. 2. Ann Arbor, MI: Center for Japanese Studies, University of Michigan, 1988.

2187. Ketelaar, James Edward. *Of Heretics and Martyrs in Meiji Japan: Buddhism and its Persecution.* Princeton, NJ: Princeton University Press, 1990.

2188. Leggett, Trevor. *The Warrior Kōans: Early Zen in Japan.* London; Boston, MA: Arkana, 1985.

2189. McMullin, Neil. *Buddhism and the State in Sixteenth-Century Japan.* Princeton, NJ: Princeton University Press, 1984.

2190. Morrell, Robert E. *Early Kamakura Buddhism: A Minority Report.* Nanzan Studies in Religion and Culture. Berkeley, CA: Asian Humanities Press, 1987.

2191. Okawa, Ryūhō. *The Laws of the Sun: The Revelation of Buddha that Enlightens the New Age.* Tokyo: Institute for Research in Human Happiness, 1990.

2192. Shaner, David Edward. *The Bodymind Experience in Japanese Buddhism: A Phenomenological Perspective of Kūkai and Dōgen.* SUNY Series in Buddhist Studies. Albany, NY: State University of New York Press, 1985.

2193. Thakur, Upendra. *India and Japan: A Study in Interaction during 5th century - 14th century A.D.* New Delhi: Abhinav Publications, 1992.

2194. Thelle, Notto R. *Buddhism and Christianity in Japan: From Conflict to Dialogue, 1854-1899*. Honolulu, HI: University of Hawaii Press, 1987.

2195. Tyler, Susan C. *The Cult of Kasuga seen through its Art*. Michigan Monograph Series in Japanese Studies, no. 8. Ann Arbor, MI: Center for Japanese Studies, University of Michigan, 1992.

Religion—Buddhism—Zen

2196. Heine, Steven. *Dōgen and the Kōan Tradition: A Tale of Two Shōbōgenzō Texts*. SUNY Series in Philosophy and Psychotherapy. Albany, NY: State University of New York Press, 1993.

2197. Heisig, James W., and John C. Maraldo, eds. *Rude Awakenings: Zen, the Kyoto School, and the Question of Nationalism*. Nanzan Studies in Religion and Culture. Honolulu, HI: University of Hawaii Press, 1995.

2198. Hyers, M. Conrad. *Once-Born, Twice-Born Zen: The Soto and Rinzai Schools of Japanese Zen*. Wolfeboro, NH: Longwood Academic, 1989.

2199. Leggett, Trevor, comp. *Three Ages of Zen: Samurai, Feudal and Modern*. Rutland, VT: Tuttle, 1993.

2200. Loori, John Daido. *Two Arrows Meeting in Mid-air: The Zen Koan*. Edited by Bonnie Myotai Treace, and Konrad Ryushin Marchaj. Tuttle Library of Enlightenment. Boston, MA: Tuttle, 1994.

2201. Muller, Claudius, ed. *Zen und die Kultur Japans: Klosteralltag in Kyoto: mit 100 Fotografien aus dem Kloster Tenryuji von Hiroshi Moritani* [Zen and Japanese Culture: Everyday Life in a Monastery in Kyoto: With 100 Photographs from the Tenryuji Monastery by Hiroshi Moritani]. Berlin, Germany: D. Reimer, 1993.

2202. Odin, Steve. *The Social Self in Zen and American Pragmatism*. SUNY Series in Constructive Postmodern Thought. Albany, NY: State University of New York Press, 1996.

2203. Roth, Martin, and John Stevens. *Zen Guide: Where to Meditate in Japan*. New York: Weatherhill, 1985.

2204. Shigematsu, Sōiku, trans. *A Zen Forest: Sayings of the Masters*. New York: Weatherhill, 1992.

2205. Shigematsu, Sōiku, comp. *A Zen Harvest: Japanese Folk Zen Sayings: Haiku, Dodoitsu, and Waka.* San Francisco, CA: North Point Press, 1988.

2206. Suzuki, Daisetz Teitaro. *Living by Zen: A Synthesis of the Historical and Practical Aspects of Zen Buddhism.* London: Rider, 1991.

2207. Suzuki, Daisetz Teitaro. *The Training of the Zen Buddhist Monk.* Kyoto, Japan: Eastern Buddhist Society, 1934. Reprint: Yorktown, NY: Globe Press Books, 1991.

2208. Suzuki, Daisetz Teitaro. *Zen and Japanese Culture.* Princeton, NJ: Princeton University Press, 1959. Reprint: Bollingen Series, 64. Mythos. Princeton, NJ: Princeton University Press, 1993.

2209. Suzuki, Daisetz Teitaro. *The Zen Koan as a Means of Attaining Enlightenment.* London, Rider, 1950. Reprint: Boston, MA: Tuttle, 1994.

2210. Tanahashi, Kazuaki. *Penetrating Laughter, Hakuin's Zen & Art.* Woodstock, NY: Overlook Press, 1984.

Religion—Buddhist Sects—Hua-yen

2211. Cleary, Thomas F. *Entry into the Inconceivable: An Introduction to Hua-yen Buddhism.* Honolulu, HI: University of Hawaii Press, 1983.

2212. Tanabe, George Joji. *Myōe the Dreamkeeper: Fantasy and Knowledge in Early Kamakura Buddhism.* Harvard East Asian Monographs, 156. Cambridge, MA: Council on East Asian Studies, Harvard University, 1992.

Religion—Buddhist Sects—Ji

2213. Ippen. *No Abode: The Record of Ippen.* Translated by Dennis Hirota. Kyoto, Japan: Ryukoko University, 1986.

Religion—Buddhist Sects—Rinzai

2214. Collcutt, Martin. *Five Mountains: The Rinzai Zen Monastic Institution in Medieval Japan.* Harvard East Asian Monographs, 85. Cambridge, MA: Council on East Asian Studies, Harvard University, 1981.

Religion—Buddhist Sects—Shin

2215. Dobbins, James C. *Jōdō Shinshū: Shin Buddhism in Medieval Japan.* Religion in Asia and Africa Series. Bloomington, IN: Indiana University Press, 1989.

2216. Ōtani, Chōjun. *Les Problèmes de la Foi et de la Pratique chez Rennyo à Travers ses lettres, Ofumi* [Problems of Faith and Practice of Rennyo through his Letters, Ofumi]. Bibliothèque de L'Institut des Hautes Études Japonaises. Paris: Maisonneuve & Larose, 1991.

Religion—Buddhist Sects—Shingon

2217. Miyata, Taisen. *A Study of the Ritual Mudrās in the Shingon Tradition: A Phenomenological Study on the Eighteen Ways of Esoteric Recitation (Jūhachi-dō Nenju kubi shidai,Chūn-ryū) in the Koyasan Tradition.* Sacramento, CA: s.n., 1984.

2218. Snodgrass, Adrian. *The Matrix and Diamond World Mandalas in Shingon Buddhism.* 2 vols. Satapitaka Series, v. 354-355. New Delhi, India: Aditya Prakashan, 1988.

2219. Yamamoto, Chikyō. *History of Mantrayana in Japan.* Satapitaka Series, v. 346. New Delhi: Sharada Rani, 1987.

Religion—Buddhist Sects—Sōtō

2220. Cleary, Thomas, trans. *Record of Things Heard from the Treasury of the Eye of the True Teaching: The Shōbōgenzō Zuimonki: Talks of Zen Master Dōgen, as recorded by Zen Master Ejo.* Boulder, CO: Prajna Press, 1980.

2221. Cleary, Thomas, trans. *Shōbōgenzō, Zen Essays, by Dōgen.* Honolulu, HI: University of Hawaii Press, 1986.

2222. Cleary, Thomas, ed., trans. *Timeless Spring: A Soto Zen Anthology.* Tokyo; New York: Weatherhill, 1980.

Religion—Buddhist Sects—Tendai

2223. Groner, Paul. *Saichō: The Establishment of the Japanese Tendai School.* Berkeley Buddhist Studies Series, 7. Berkeley, CA: Center for South and Southeast Asian Studies, University of California, Berkeley, Institute of Buddhist Studies, 1984.

2224. Gyōnen. *The Essentials of the Eight Traditions: By Gyōnen.* Translated by Leo M. Pruden. With: Saichō. *The Candle of the Latter Dharma: by Saichō.* Translated by Robert Rhodes. BDK English Tripitaka, 107-I, III. Berkeley, CA: Numata Center for Buddhist Translation and Research, 1994.

2225. Saso, Michael R. *Tantric Art and Meditation: The Tendai Tradition.* Honolulu, HI: Tendai Educational Foundation, 1990.

2226. Stevens, John. *The Marathon Monks of Mount Hiei.* Boston, MA: Shambhala, 1988.

Religion—Christianity

2227. Breen, John, and Mark Williams, eds. *Japan and Christianity: Impacts and Responses.* New York: St. Martin's Press, 1995.

2228. Cary, Otis. *A History of Christianity in Japan.* 2 vols. Richmond, U.K.: Curzon Press, 1993.

2229. Chung, Jun Ki. *Social Criticism of Uchimura Kanzō and Kim Kyo-shin.* Seoul, Korea: UBF Press, 1988.

2230. Elison, George. *Deus Destroyed: The Image of Christianity in Early Modern Japan.* Cambridge, MA: Harvard University Press, 1973. Reprint: Harvard East Asian Monographs, 141. Cambridge, MA: Council on East Asian Studies, Harvard University, 1988.

2231. Fischer, Edward. *Japan Journey: The Columban Fathers in Nippon.* New York: Crossroad, 1984.

2232. Francis, Carolyn Bowen, and John Masaaki Nakajima. *Christians in Japan.* New York: Friendship Press, 1991.

2233. Fujita, Neil S. *Japan's Encounter with Christianity: The Catholic Mission in Pre-Modern Japan.* New York: Paulist Press, 1991.

2234. Hammer, Raymond J. *Japan's Religious Ferment: Christian Presence amid Faiths Old and New.* Christian Presence Series. New York: Oxford University Press, 1962. Reprint: Westport, CT: Greenwood, 1985.

2235. Lande, Aasulv. *Meiji Protestantism in History and Historiography: A Comparative Study of Japanese and Western Interpretations of Early Protestantism in Japan.* Studien zur interkulturellen Geschichte des Christentums, Bd. 58. Frankfurt am Main, Germany: New York: P. Lang, 1989.

2236. Phillips, James M. *From the Rising of the Sun: Christians and Society in Contemporary Japan.* American Society of Missiology Series, no. 3. Maryknoll, NY: Orbis Books, 1981.

2237. Picken, Stuart D. B. *Christianity and Japan: Meeting, Conflict, Hope.* Tokyo; New York: Kodansha International, 1983.

2238. Reid, David. *New Wine: The Cultural Shaping of Japanese Christianity.* Nanzan Studies in Asian Religions, 2. Berkeley, CA: Asian Humanities Press, 1991.

2239. Snider, K. Lavern. *Ten More Growing Churches in Japan Today.* Osaka, Japan: Japan Free Methodist Mission, 1985.

2240. Whelan, Christal, trans. *The Beginning of Heaven and Earth: The Sacred Book of Japan's Hidden Christians.* Honolulu, HI: University of Hawaii Press, 1996.

2241. Yoshinobu, Kumuzawa, and David L. Swain, eds. *Christianity in Japan, 1971-1990.* Tokyo: Kyo Bun Kwan (The Christian Literature Society of Japan), 1991.

Religion—Christianity—Missions and Missionaries

2242. Boxer, C. R. *Portuguese Merchants and Missionaries in Feudal Japan, 1543-1640.* Variorum Reprint, CS232. London: Variorum Reprints, 1986.

2243. Francis, Mabel, and Gerald B. Smith. *One Shall Chase a Thousand: The Story of Mabel Francis.* The Jaffrey Collection of Missionary Portraits, v. 9. Camp Hill, PA: Christian Publications, 1993.

2244. *Iezusukai Nihon Shokanshu / Jesuit Letters Concerning Japan.* Historical Documents in Foreign Languages Relating to Japan. Original Texts, Selection 3, v. 1, etc. Tokyo: Tokyo Daigaku Shiryo Hensanjo, 1990-

2245. Ion, A. Hamish. *The Cross and the Rising Sun: The Canadian Protestant Missionary Movement in the Japanese Empire, 1872-1931.* 2 vols. Waterloo, Ont.: Wilfrid Laurier University Press, 1990-1993.

2246. Kilson, Marion. *Mary Jane Forbes Greene (1845-1910), Mother of Japan Mission: An Anthropological Portrait.* Studies in Women and Religion, v. 30. Lewiston, NY: Mellen Press, 1991.

2247. Laker, Mary Eugenia. *Notre Dame Goes to Japan.* St. Louis, MO: School Sisters of Notre Dame, St. Louis Province, 1988.

2248. Minton, Wilson P. *A Tour of Japan in 1920: An American Missionary's Diary with 129 Photographs.* Edited by David W. Carstetter. Jefferson, NC: McFarland, 1992.

2249. Moran, Joseph Francis. *The Japanese and the Jesuits: Allesandro Valignano in Sixteenth-Century Japan.* London; New York: Routledge, 1993.

2250. Moran, J. F. *The Language Barrier and the Early Jesuits in Japan.* Stirling Occasional Papers on Japan, no. 4. Stirling, U.K.: The Scottish Centre for Japanese Studies, University of Stirling, 1992.

2251. Notehelfer, F. G. *American Samurai: Captain L. L. Janes and Japan.* Princeton, NJ: Princeton University Press, 1985.

2252. Powles, Cyril Hamilton. *Victorian Missionaries in Meiji Japan: The Shiba Sect, 1873-1900.* Publications Series, v. 4, no. 1. Toronto, Ont.: University of Toronto-York University Joint Centre of Modern East Asia, 1987.

2253. Prang, Margaret. *A Heart at Leisure from Itself: Caroline Macdonald of Japan.* Vancouver. BC: UBC Press, 1995.

2254. Ross, Andrew C. *A Vision Betrayed: The Jesuits in Japan and China 1542-1742.* Edinburgh, U.K.: Edinburgh University Press; Maryknoll, NY: Orbis Books, 1994.

2255. Stebbins, Richard Poate, ed. *The Japan Experience: The Missionary Letters of Belle Marsh Poate and Thomas Pratt Poate, 1876-1892.* American University Studies Series IX, History, vol. 110. New York: P. Lang, 1992.

2256. Taylor, Sandra C. *Advocate of Understanding: Sydney Gulick and the Search for Peace with Japan.* Kent, OH: Kent State University Press, 1984.

Religion—Folk

2257. Hori, Ichiro. *Folk Religion in Japan: Continuity and Change.* Edited by Joseph M. Kitagawa, and Alan C. Miller. Haskell Lectures on History of Religion. New Series, no. 1. Chicago, IL: University of Chicago Press, 1968. Reprint: 1983.

Religion—Islam

2258. Morimoto, Abu Bakr. *Islam in Japan: Its Past, Present and Future.* Translated by Iskander Chowdhury. Tokyo: Islamic Center Japan, 1980.

Religion—Monks and Priests

2259. Kashiwahara, Yūsen, and Kōyū Sonoda, eds. *Shapers of Japanese Buddhism.* Translated by Gaynor Sekimori. Tokyo: Kosei, 1994.

2260. Stevens, John. *Three Zen Masters: Ikkyū, Hakuin, and Ryōkan.* Kodansha Biographies. Tokyo; New York: Kodansha International, 1993.

2261. Takuan, Sōhō. *The Unfettered Mind: Letters of the Zen Master to the Sword Master.* Translated by William Scott Wilson. Tokyo; New York: Kodansha International, 1986.

Religion—Monks and Priests—Bankei, 1622-1693

2262. Bankei. *The Unborn: The Life and Teaching of the Zen Master Bankei, 1622-1693.* Translated by Norman Waddell. San Francisco, CA: North Point Press, 1984.

Religion—Monks and Priests—Dōgen, 1200-1253

2263. Kim, Hee-Jin. *Dōgen Kigen, Mystical Realist.* Monographs of the Association for Asian Studies, no. 29. Tucson, AZ: University of Arizona Press for the Association for Asian Studies, 1975. Reprint: 1987.

2264. Kodera, Takashi James. *Dōgen's Formative Years in China: An Historical Study and Annotated Translation of the Hōkyō-ki.* London: Routledge & Kegan Paul, 1980.

Religion—Monks and Priests—Hōnen, 1133-1212

2265. Shunjō. *Honen the Buddhist Saint: His Life and Teaching.* Compiled by Imperial Order. Translated by Harper H. Coates, and Ryugaku Ishizuka. Kyoto, Japan: Chion'in, 1925. Reprint: *Honen the Buddhist Saint.* Oriental Religions, 21. New York: Garland, 1981.

Religion—Monks and Priests—Ikkyū, 1394-1481

2266. Covell, Jon Carter, and Sobin Yamada. *Unraveling Zen's Red Thread: Ikkyu's Controversial Way.* Elizabeth, NJ: Hollym International, 1980.

2267. Sanford, James H. *Zen-man Ikkyū.* Studies in World Religions, no. 2. Chico, CA: Scholars Press, 1981.

Religion—Monks and Priests—Myocho, 1282-1337

2268. Kraft, Kenneth. *Eloquent Zen: Daitō and Early Japanese Zen.* Honolulu, HI: University of Hawaii Press, 1992.

Religion—Monks and Priests—Myōe, 1173-1232

2269. Kawai, Hayao. *The Buddhist Priest Myōe: A Life of Dreams.* Venice, Italy: Lapis Press, 1992.

Religion—Monks and Priests—Nichiren, 1222-1282

2270. Dollarhide, Kenneth, trans. *Nichiren's Senji-shō: An Essay on the Selection of the Proper Time.* Studies in Asian Thought and Religion, v. 1. New York: Mellen, 1982.

2271. Rodd, Laurel Rasplica, trans. *Nichiren, Selected Writings*. Asian Studies at Hawaii, no. 26. Honolulu, HI: University Press of Hawaii, 1980.

2272. Watson, Burton, et al., trans. *Letters of Nichiren*. Edited by Philip B. Yampolsky. Translations from the Asian Classics. The Columbia Asian Studies Series. New York: Columbia University Press, 1996.

2273. Watson, Burton, et al., trans. *Selected Writings of Nichiren*. Edited by Philip B. Yampolsky. Translations from the Oriental Classics. New York: Columbia University Press, 1990.

Religion—Monks and Priests—Rennyo, 1415-1499

2274. Rogers, Minor, and Ann Rogers. *Rennyo: The Second Founder of Shin Buddhism: With a Translation of his Letters*. Nanzan Studies in Asian Religions, 3. Berkeley, CA: Asian Humanities Press, c1991.

Religion—Monks and Priests—Satomi, Myōdō, 1896-1978

2275. Satomi, Myōdō. *Passionate Journey: The Spiritual Autobiography of Satomi Myōdō*. Translated and edited by Sallie B. King. Albany, NY: State University of New York Press, 1993.

Religion—Monks and Priests—Shinran, 1173-1263

2276. Takahatake, Takamichi. *Young Man Shinran: A Reappraisal of Shinran's Life*. SR Supplements, v. 18. Waterloo, Ont.: Wilfrid Laurier University Press for the Canadian Corporation for Studies in Religion, 1987.

Religion—Monks and Priests—Suzuki, Daisetz Teitaro, 1870-1966

2277. Abe, Mazao, ed. *A Zen Life: D. T. Suzuki Remembered*. New York: Weatherhill, 1986.

2278. King, Winston Lee. *Death was His Kōan: The Samurai-Zen of Suzuki Shōsan*. Nanzan Studies in Religion and Culture. Berkeley, CA: Asian Humanities Press, 1986.

Religion—New Movements—Aum Shinrikyō

2279. Kaplan, David E., and Andrew Marshall. *The Cult at the End of the World: The Terrifying Story of the Aum Doomsday Cult: From the Subways of Tokyo to the Nuclear Arsenals of Russia.* New York: Crown, 1996.

Religion—New Movements—Gedatsukai

2280. Earhart, H. Byron. *Gedatsukai and Religion in Contemporary Japan: Returning to the Center.* Religion in Asia and Africa Series. Bloomington IN: Indiana University Press, 1989.

2281. Kiyota, Minoru. *Gedatsukai, its Theory and Practice: A Study of a Shinto-Buddhist Syncretic School in Contemporary Japan.* Buddhist Culture Series. Los Angeles, CA: Buddhist Books International, 1982.

Religion—New Movements—Kurozumikyō

2282. Hardacre, Helen. *Kurozumikyō and the New Religions of Japan.* Princeton, NJ: Princeton University Press, 1986.

2283. Kurozumi, Tadaaki. *The Opening Way: Kurozumi Munetada, Founder of Kurozumikyō.* Translated by Julie Iezzi and Harold Wright. Edited by Willis Stoesz. Lanham, MD: University Press of America, 1994.

Religion—New Movements—Ōmoto

2284. Berthon, Jean-Pierre. *Omoto: Espérance Millénariste d'une Nouvelle Religion Japonaise* [Omoto: Millenary Hopes of a New Japanese Religion]. Cahiers d'Etudes et de documents sur les religions du Japon, 6. Paris: Editions Atelier Alpha Bleue, 1985.

2285. Ōishi, Sakae. *Nao Deguchi: A Biography of the Foundress of Oomoto.* Translated by Charles Rowe and Yasuko Matsudaira. Kameoka, Japan: Oomoto Foundation, 1982.

Religion—New Movements—Reiyūkai

2286. Hardacre, Helen. *Lay Buddhism in Contemporary Japan: Reiyūkai Kyōdan.* Princeton, NJ: Princeton University Press, 1984.

Religion—New Movements—Risshō Kōseikai

2287. Guthrie, Stewart. *A Japanese New Religion: Risshō Kōsei-kai in a Mountain Hamlet.* Michigan Monograph Series in Japanese Studies, no. 1. Ann Arbor, MI: Center for Japanese Studies, University of Michigan, 1988.

Religion—New Movements—Sōka Gakkai

2288. Metraux, Daniel Alfred. *The History and Theology of Sōka Gakkai: A Japanese New Religion.* Studies in Asian Thought and Religion, v. 9. Lewiston, NY: Mellen, 1988.

Religion—New Movements—Tenrikyō

2289. Ellwood, Robert S., Jr. *Tenrikyo, a Pilgrimage Faith: The Structure and Meaning of Modern Japanese Religion.* Tenri, Japan: Oyasato Research Institute, Tenri University, 1982.

2290. Kano, Matao. *The Mysteries of Destiny.* Translated by Yama Trans. Matao Kano's Destiny Series, v. 1. Torrance, CA: Yama Trans, 1981.

2291. Lanbe, Johannes. *Oyagami: die heutige Gottesvorstellung der Tenrikyō* [Oyagami: The Current Divine Image of the Tenrikyō]. Studien zur Japanologie, Bd. 14. Wiesbaden, Germany: Harrasowitz, 1978.

2292. *The Life of Oyasama, Foundress of Tenrikyo.* 2d ed. Tenri, Japan: Tenrikyo Church Headquarters, 1982.

2293. Straelen, H. J. J. M. van. *The Religion of Divine Wisdom: Japan's Most Powerful Religious Movement.* Asian Folklore and Social Life Monographs, v. 108. Tokyo: Chinese Association for Folklore, 1954. Reprint: Taipei: Orient Cultural Service, 1983.

Religion—Pilgrims and Pilgrimages

2294. Edwards, Ron. *The Gentle Rain on Shikoku.* Kuranda, Australia: Rams Skull Press, 1990.

2295. Edwards, Ron. *Walking on Yellow Radish.* Kuranda, Australia: Rams Skull Press, 1990.

2296. Statler, Oliver. *Japanese Pilgrimage.* New York: Morrow, 1983.

Religion—Shamanism

2297. Blacker, Carmen. *The Catalpa Bow: A Study of Shamanistic Practices in Japan.* 2d ed. London; Boston, MA: G. Allen & Unwin, 1986.

2298. Miller, Roy Andrew, and Nelly Naumann. *Altjapanisch FaFuri: zu Priestertum und Schamanismus im vorbuddhistischen Japan* [Ancient Japanese FaFuri: On Priesthood and Shamanism in Pre-Buddhist Japan]. Mitteilungen der Deutschen Gesellschaft für Natur- und Völkerkunde Ostasiens, Bd. 116. Hamburg, Germany: Gesellschaft für Natur- und Völkerkunde Ostasiens, 1991.

Religion—Shintō

2299. Ashkenazi, Michael. *Matsuri: Festivals of a Japanese Town.* Honolulu, HI: University of Hawaii Press, 1993.

2300. Egenter, Nold. *Göttersitze aus Schilf und Bambus: jährlich gebaute Kultfackeln als Male, Zeichen und Symbole: Eine bauethnologische Untersuchung der Ujigami-Rituale des Volks-Shintō um die Stadt Ōmihachiman, Japan* [Sacred Symbols of Reed and Bamboo: Annually Built Cult Torches as Spatial Signs and Symbols: A Study of the Building Traditions of the Ujigami Shintō Rituals as Practiced Around the Town of Ōmihachiman in Japan]. Swiss Asian Studies, Monographs, v. 4. Bern; Las Vegas, NV: P. Lang, 1982.

2301. Holtom, Daniel Clarence. *The Political Philosophy of Modern Shintō: A Study of the State Religion of Japan.* Chicago, IL, 1922. Reprint: New York: AMS Press, 1984.

2302. Lowell, Percival. *Occult Japan; or the Way of the Gods; an Esoteric Study of Japanese Personality and Possession.* Boston, MA: Houghton, Mifflin, 1894. Reprinted as: *Occult Japan: Shinto, Shamanism, and the Way of the Gods.* Rochester, VT: Inner Traditions International, 1990.

2303. Muraoka, Tsunetsugu. *Studies in Shinto Thought.* Translated by Delmer M. Brown and James T. Araki. Tokyo: Japanese National Commission for Unesco, 1964. Reprint: Classics of Modern Japanese Thought and Culture. New York: Greenwood, 1988.

2304. Nelson, John K. *A Year in the Life of a Shinto Shrine.* Seattle, WA: University of Washington Press, 1996.

2305. Picken, Stuart D. B. *Shinto, Japan's Spiritual Roots.* Tokyo; New York: Kodansha International, 1980.

2306. Ross, Floyd Hiatt. *Shinto, the Way of Japan.* Boston, MA: Beacon Press, 1965. Reprint: Westport, CT: Greenwood, 1983.

Religion—Women

2307. Nefsky, Marilyn F. *Stone Houses and Iron Bridges: Tradition and the Place of Women in Contemporary Japan.* Toronto Studies in Religion, vol. 12. New York: P. Lang, 1991.

2308. Ooms, Emily Groszos. *Women and Millenarian Protest in Meiji Japan: Deguchi Nao and Ōmotokyō.* Cornell East Asia Series, 61. Ithaca, NY: East Asia Program, Cornell University, 1993.

Religious Freedom

2309. O'Brien, David M., and Yasuo Ohkoshi. *To Dream of Dreams: Religious Freedom and Constitutional Politics in Postwar Japan.* Honolulu, HI: University of Hawaii Press, 1996.

Religious Rites and Ceremonies

2310. Davis, Winston Bradley. *Dojo: Magic and Exorcism in Modern Japan.* Stanford, CA: Stanford University Press, 1980.

2311. Fauré, Bernard. *Visions of Power: Imagining Medieval Japanese Buddhism.* Translated by Phyllis Brooks. Princeton, NJ: Princeton University Press, 1996.

2312. Kaiser, Thomas, ed. *Bärenfest: vom Dialog mit der Wildnis; die Ainu Hokkaidos, Japan* [Bear Festival: About a Dialogue with Wilderness: The Ainu of Hokkaido, Japan]. Zurich, Switzerland: Völkerkundemuseum der Universität Zürich, 1991.

2313. Mace, François. *La Mort et les Funerailles dans le Japon Ancien* [Death and Burials in Ancient Japan]. Bibliothèque Japonaise. Paris: Publications Orientalistes de France, 1986.

2314. Payne, Richard Karl. *The Tantric Ritual of Japan: Feeding the Gods, the Shingon Fire Ritual.* Satapitaka series, v. 365. New Delhi: International Academy of Indian Culture and Aditya Prakashan, 1991.

Retail Trade

2315. Larke, Roy. *Japanese Retailing*. London; New York: Routledge, 1994.

Robotics

See also: Automation

2316. Sadamoto, Kuni, ed. *Robots in the Japanese Economy: Facts about Robots and their Significance*. Tokyo: Survey Japan, 1981.

2317. Schodt, Frederik L. *Inside the Robot Kingdom: Japan, Mechatronics, and the Coming Robotopia*. Tokyo; New York: Kodansha International, 1988.

Romanticism

2318. Doak, Kevin Michael. *Dreams of Difference: The Japanese Romantic School and the Crisis of Modernity*. Berkeley, CA: University of California Press, 1994.

Royalty

See also: Monarchy

2319. Behr, Edward. *Hirohito: Behind the Myth*. New York: Villard Books, 1989.

2320. Honjō, Shigeru. *Emperor Hirohito and his Chief Aide-de-Camp: The Honjō Diary, 1933-36*. Translated by Mikiso Hane. Tokyo: University of Tokyo Press, 1982.

2321. Hoyt, Edwin Palmer. *Hirohito: The Emperor and the Man*. New York: Praeger, 1992.

2322. Large, Stephen S. *Emperor Hirohito and Showa Japan: A Political Biography*. London; New York: Routledge, 1992.

2323. Manning, Paul. *Hirohito: The War Years*. New York: Dodd, Mead, 1986.

2324. Setsuko, Princess Chichibu. *The Silver Drum: A Japanese Imperial Memoir*. Translated by Dorothy Britton. Folkestone, U.K.: Global Books, 1996.

2325. Vining, Elizabeth Gray. *Windows for the Crown Prince.* Philadelphia, PA: Lippincott, 1952.

Rural Development

2326. Moore, Richard H. *Japanese Agriculture: Patterns of Rural Development.* Boulder, CO: Westview, 1990.

2327. Ogura, Takekazu B., ed. *Lights and Shadows of Rural Development in Japan.* Report of Study Group on International Issues (SGII), no. 10. Tokyo: Food and Agriculture Policy Research Center (FAPRC), 1991.

2328. Singh, Rana P.B., and Shōgo Yuihama. *Changing Japanese Rural Habitat: Perspective and Prospect of Agricultural Dimension.* International Centre for Rural Habitat Studies Publications, no. 5. Varanasi, India: International Geographical Union, Working Group, Transformation of Rural Habitat in Developing Countries and International Centre for Rural Habitat Studies, 1981.

Rural History *See*: History—Rural

Russia / USSR—Relations with

2329. *A Border Yet Unresolved: Japan's Northern Territories.* Tokyo: Northern Territories Issue Association, 1981.

2330. Adami, Norbert R. *Eine schwierige Nachbarschaft: die Geschichte der russisch-japanischen Beziehungen* [A Difficult Neighborliness: The History of the Russian-Japanese Relations]. Munich, Germany: Iudicium, 1990.

2331. Glaubitz, Joachim. *Between Tokyo and Moscow: The History of an Uneasy Relationship, 1972 to the 1990s.* London: C. Hurst, 1995.

2332. Glaubitz, Joachim. *Fremde Nachbarn: Tokyo und Moskau: ihre Beziehungen vom Beginn der 70er Jahre bis zum Ende der Sowjetunion* [Strange Neighbors: Tokyo and Moscow: Their Relations from the Beginning of the Seventies until the end of the Soviet Union]. Internationale Politik und Sicherheit, Bd. 19. Baden-Baden, Germany: Nomos, 1992.

2333. Goodby, James E., Vladimir I. Ivanov, and Nobuo Shimotamai, eds. *"Northern Territories" and Beyond: Russian, Japanese, and American Perspectives.* Westport, CT: Praeger, 1995.

2334. Hasegawa, Tsuyoshi, Jonathan Haslam, and Andrew Kuchins, eds. *Russia and Japan: An Unresolved Dilemma between Distant Neighbors.* Research Series, no. 87. Berkeley, CA: International and Area Studies, University of California at Berkeley, 1993.

2335. Jain, Rajendra Kumar. *The USSR and Japan, 1945-1980.* Atlantic Highlands, NJ: Humanities Press, 1981.

2336. *Japan's Triangular Diplomacy.* Conflict Studies, no. 129. London: Institute for the Study of Conflict, 1981.

2337. Mayer, Hans Jürgen. *Die japanisch-sowjetischen Beziehungen, 1956-1973/74: Bestimmungsfaktoren und Interaktionen Analyse einer latenten Konfrontation* [The Japanese-Soviet Relations, 1956-1973/74: Regulatory Factors and Interactions, Analysis of a Latent Confrontation]. Mitteilungen des Instituts für Asienkunde Hamburg, Nr. 142. Hamburg, Germany: Institut für Asienkunde, 1985.

2338. Nimmo, William F. *Japan and Russia: A Reevaluation in the Post-Soviet Era.* Contributions in Asian Studies, no. 3. Westport, CT: Greenwood, 1994.

2339. Rees, David. *The Soviet Seizure of the Kuriles.* New York: Praeger, 1985.

2340. Rimer, J. Thomas, ed. *A Hidden Fire: Russian and Japanese Cultural Encounters, 1868-1926.* Stanford, CA: Stanford University Press; Washington, DC: Woodrow Wilson Center Press, 1995.

2341. Robertson, Myles L. C. *Soviet Policy Towards Japan: An Analysis of Trends in the 1970s and 1980s.* Cambridge Studies in International Relations, 1. Cambridge, U.K.; New York: Cambridge University Press, 1988.

2342. Rozman, Gilbert. *Japan's Response to the Gorbachev Era, 1985-1991: A Rising Superpower Views a Declining One.* Princeton, NJ: Princeton University Press, 1992.

Ryūkyūans *See:* Minorities—Okinawans

Sake *See:* 1061; 1063

Samurai

2343. Daidōji, Shigesuke. *The Warrior's Primer of Daidoji Yuzan.* Translated by William Scott Wilson. Burbank, CA: Ohara, 1984.

2344. Ikegami, Eiko. *The Taming of the Samurai: Honorific Individualism and the Making of Modern Japan.* Cambridge, MA: Harvard University Press, 1995.

2345. Katchmer, George A. *Professional Budo: Ethics, Chivalry and the Samurai Code.* Jamaica Plain, MA: YMAA Publication Center, 1995.

2346. King, Winston L. *Zen and the Way of the Sword: Arming the Samurai Psyche.* New York: Oxford University Press, 1993.

2347. Matsumae, Shigeyoshi, ed. *Toward an Understanding of Budo Thought.* Tokyo: Tokai University Press, 1987.

2348. Matsuno, Tsuneyoshi. *Wives of the Samurai: Their Eventful Lives During the Period of Civil Wars.* New York: Vantage Press, 1989.

2349. Newman, John. *Bushido: The Way of the Warrior: A New Perspective on the Japanese Military Tradition.* New York: Gallery Books, 1989.

2350. Sato, Hiroaki. *Legends of the Samurai.* Woodstock, NY: Overlook Press, 1995.

2351. Stevens, John. *Three Budo Masters: Jigoro Kano (judo), Gichin Fumakoshi (karate), Morihei Ueshiba (aikido).* Tokyo; London: Kodansha International, 1995.

2352. Turnbull, Stephen R. *The Book of the Samurai: The Warrior Class of Japan.* London: Arms & Armour, 1982.

2353. Turnbull, Stephen R. *The Lone Samurai and the Martial Arts.* London: Arms & Armour, 1990.

2354. Turnbull, Stephen R. *The Samurai: A Military History.* London: Osprey, 1977. Reprint: London: Philip, 1987.

2355. Turnbull, Stephen R. *Samurai Warlords: The Book of the Daimyo.* London: Blandford, 1989.

2356. Wilson, William Scott, trans. *Ideals of the Samurai: Writings of Japanese Warriors.* Edited by Gregory N. Lee. Burbank, CA: Ohara, 1982.

Schools *See*: Education

Science

2357. Anderson, Alun M. *Science and Technology in Japan.* Longman Guide to the World Science and Technology, 4. Harlow, Essex, U.K.: Longman, 1984.

2358. Bartholomew, James R. *The Formation of Science in Japan: Building a Research Tradition.* New Haven, CT: Yale University Press, 1989.

2359. Dearing, James W. *Growing a Japanese Science City: Communication in Scientific Research.* Nissan Institute / Routledge Japanese Studies Series. London; New York: Routledge, 1995.

2360. Irvine, John. *Evaluating Applied Research: Lessons from Japan.* London; New York: Pinter, 1988.

2361. *Japan Science & Technology Outlook: Based on Kagakugijutsu Hakusho, a White Paper of the Science and Technology Agency.* Tokyo: Fuji Corporation, 1983.

2362. Nakayama, Shigeru. *Science, Technology, and Society in Postwar Japan.* Japanese Studies Series. London; New York: Kegan Paul International, 1991.

2363. *Researchers, National Laboratories in Japan.* Saitama Prefecture, Japan: Research Development Corporation of Japan, 1993.

2364. Science and Technology Agency, Prime Minister's Office, Japan. *White Paper on Science and Technology: The Relationship between Young People and Science and Technology.* Tokyo: Science and Technology Agency, Prime Minister's Office, 1993.

2365. Sugimoto, Masayoshi, and David L. Swain. *Science and Culture in Traditional Japan.* Cambridge, MA: Massachusetts Institute of Technology Press, 1978. Reprint: Rutland, VT: Tuttle, 1989.

2366. Watanabe, Masao. *The Japanese and Western Science.* Translated by Otto Theodore Benfey, Philadelphia, PA: University of Pennsylvania Press, 1990.

2367. Yoshikawa, Hideo, and Joanne Kauffman. *Science has no National Borders: Harry C. Kelly and the Reconstruction of Science and Technology in Postwar Japan.* Cambridge, MA: MIT Press, 1994.

Science—Dictionaries

2368. Tung, Louise Watanabe. *Japanese/English English/Japanese Glossary of Scientific Terms.* New York: Wiley, 1993.

Sculpture: *See*: Art—Sculpture

Secondary Education *See*: Education—Secondary

Sexuality

2369. Bornoff, Nicholas. *Pink Samurai: Love, Marriage & Sex in Contemporary Japan.* New York: Pocket Books, 1991.

2370. Hoshii, Iwao. *Sex in Ethics and Law.* Hoshii, Iwao, 1905- World of Sex, v. 4. Perspectives on Japan and the West. Woodchurch, U.K.: Norbury, 1987.

2371. Leupp, Gary P. *Male Colors: The Construction of Homosexuality in Tokugawa Japan (1603-1868).* Berkeley, CA: University of California Press, 1995.

2372. Watanabe, Tsuneo, and Jun'ichi Iwata. *Love of the Samurai: A Thousand Years of Japanese Homosexuality.* London: Gay Men's Press, 1989.

Shamanism *See*: Religion—Shamanism

Shintō *See*: Religion—Shintō

Shipping

2373. Tomohei, Shida, and Peter N. Davies. *The Japanese Shipping and Shipbuilding Industries: A History of their Modern Growth.* London: Athlone Press, 1990.

Shrines *See*: Architecture—Temples and Shrines

Singapore—Relations with

2374. Wee, Mon-Cheng. *The Chrysanthemum and the Orchid: Observations of a Diplomat.* Singapore: Maruzen Asia, 1982.

Small Businesses

2375. *Japan's Small Businesses Today: A Closer Look at 100 Industrial Segments.* Tokyo: Keiei Joho Shuppan, 1988.

2376. Yamazaki, Mitsuru. *Japan's Community-Based Industries: A Case Study of Small Industry.* Tokyo: Asian Productivity Organization, 1980.

Social Class

2377. Ishida, Hiroshi. *Class Structure and Status Hierarchies in Contemporary Japan.* Nissan Occasional Paper Series, no. 7. Oxford, U.K.: Nissan Institute of Japanese Studies, 1988.

2378. Kerbo, Harold R., and John A. McKinstry. *Who Rules Japan?: The Inner Circles of Economic and Political Power.* Westport, CT: Praeger, 1995.

2379. Kosaka, Kenji, ed. *Social Stratification in Contemporary Japan.* Japanese Studies. London; New York: Kegan Paul International, 1994.

2380. Lebra, Takie Sugiyama. *Above the Clouds: Status Culture of the Modern Japanese Nobility.* Berkeley, CA: University of California Press, 1993.

2381. Lebra, Takie Sugiyama, ed. *Japanese Social Organization.* Honolulu, HI: University of Hawaii Press, 1992.

2382. Smith, Herman W. *The Myth of Japanese Homogeneity: Social Ecological Diversity in Education and Socialization.* Commack, NY: Nova Science, 1995.

2383. Steven, Rob. *Classes in Contemporary Japan.* Cambridge, U.K.; New York: Cambridge University Press, 1983.

2384. Turner, Christena L. *Japanese Workers in Protest: An Ethnography of Consciousness and Experience.* Berkeley, CA: University of California Press, 1995.

Social Mobility

2385. Ishida, Hiroshi. *Social Mobility in Contemporary Japan: Educational Credentials, Class and the Labour Market in a Cross-National Perspective.* Stanford, CA: Stanford University, 1992.

2386. Kimmonth, Earl H. *The Self-Made Man in Meiji Japanese Thought: From Samurai to Salary Man.* Berkeley, CA: University of California Press, 1981.

Social Protest

2387. Apter, David E., and Nagayo Sawa. *Against the State: Politics and Social Protest in Japan.* Cambridge, MA: Harvard University Press, 1984.

2388. Sugimoto, Yoshio. *Popular Disturbance in Postwar Japan.* Asian Studies Monograph Series. Hong Kong: Asian Research Service, 1981.

2389. White, James W. *Ikki: Social Conflict and Political Protest in Early Modern Japan.* Ithaca, NY: Cornell University Press, 1995.

Social Relations

2390. Fukutake, Tadashi. *The Japanese Social Structure: Its Evolution in the Modern Century.* Translated by Ronald P. Dore. Tokyo: University of Tokyo Press, 1982.

2391. Goodman, Roger, and Kirsten Refsing, eds. *Ideology and Practice in Modern Japan.* Nissan Institute / Routledge Japanese Studies Series. London; New York: Routledge, 1992.

2392. Phar, Susan J. *Losing Face: Status Politics in Japan.* Berkeley, CA: University of California Press, 1990.

Social Security

2393. Anderson, Stephen J. *Welfare Policy and Politics in Japan: Beyond the Developmental State.* New York: Paragon House, 1993.

2394. Hiraishi, Nagahisa. *Social Security*. Japanese Industrial Relations Series, 5. Tokyo: Japan Institute of Labour, 1980.

2395. Social Insurance Agency, Japanese Government. *Outline of Social Insurance in Japan, 1983*. Japan: Japan International Social Security Association, 1983.

2396. Yamasaki, Yasuhiko, and Tetsuya Hosaka. *Social Security in Japan*. 1st revision. "About Japan" Series, 17. Tokyo: Foreign Press Center, Japan, 1995.

Social Values

2397. Kumagai, Fumie, and Donna J. Keyser. *Unmasking Japan Today: The Impact of Traditional Values on Modern Japanese Society*. Westport, CT: Praeger, 1996.

2398. Sai, Yasutaka. *The Eight Core Values of the Japanese Businessman: Toward an Understanding of Japanese Management*. Binghamton, NY: International Business Press, 1995.

2399. Taylor, Jared. *Shadows of the Rising Sun: A Critical View of the "Japanese Miracle."* New York: Morrow, 1983.

Socialism

2400. Crump, John. *The Origins of Socialist Thought in Japan*. London: Croom Helm; New York: St. Martin's Press, 1983.

2401. Farrell, William Regis. *Blood and Rage: The Story of the Japanese Red Army*. Issues in Low-intensity Conflict Series. Lexington, MA: Lexington Books, 1990.

2402. Hoston, Germaine A. *Marxism and the Crisis of Development in Prewar Japan*. Princeton, NJ: Princeton University Press, 1986.

2403. Kassian, Peter. *Takabatake Motoyuki: das Leben, Wirken und Denken eines staatssozialistischen Intellektuellen der Taishō-Zeit* [Takabatake Motoyuki: The Life Work and Thought of a National Socialist Intellectual of the Taishō Period]. Bonner Zeitschrift für Japanologie, Bd. 5. Bonn, Germany: Förderverein "Bonner Zeitschrift für Japanologie," 1984.

2404. Kenrick, Douglas M. *The Success of Competitive Communism in Japan*. Houndmills, U.K.: Macmillan, 1988.

2405. Large, Stephen S. *Organized Workers and Socialist Politics in Interwar Japan*. London; New York: Cambridge University Press, 1981.

2406. *Le Marxisme au Japon*. Actuel Marx, no. 2. Paris: L'Harmattana, 1987.

2407. Miyamoto, Kenji. *Selected Works*. Tokyo: Japan Press Service, 1985.

2408. Silverberg, Miriam Rom. *Changing Song: The Marxist Manifestos of Nakano Shigeharu*. Princeton, NJ: Princeton University Press, 1990.

Society

2409. Burks, Ardath W. *Japan: A Postindustrial Power*. 3d ed. rev. Westview Profiles. Nations of Contemporary Asia. Boulder, CO: Westview, 1991.

2410. Clammer, John R. *Difference and Modernity: Social Theory and Contemporary Japanese Society*. Japanese Studies. London; New York: Kegan Paul International, 1995.

2411. Cortazzi, Hugh. *Modern Japan: A Survey*. Basingstoke, U.K.: Macmillan, 1993.

2412. Fukutake, Tadashi. *Japanese Society Today*. 2d ed. Tokyo: University of Tokyo Press, 1981.

2413. Hendry, Joy. *Understanding Japanese Society*. 2d ed. Nissan Institute / Routledge Japanese Studies Series. London; New York: Routledge, 1995.

2414. Masatsugu, Mitsuyuki. *The Modern Samurai Society: Duty and Dependence in Contemporary Japan*. New York: American Management Associations, AMACOM, 1982.

2415. Mouer, Ross E., and Yoshio Sugimoto. *Images of Japanese Society: A Study in the Social Construction of Reality*. Japanese Studies Series. London; New York: KPI, 1986.

2416. Reischauer, Edwin O. *The Japanese Today: Change and Continuity*. Cambridge, MA: Belknap Press of Harvard University Press, 1977. Reprint: Cambridge, MA: Belknap Press of Harvard University Press, 1995.

2417. Smith, Robert John. *Japanese Society: Tradition, Self, and the Social Order*. Lewis Henry Morgan Lectures; 1980. Cambridge, U.K.; New York: Cambridge University Press, 1983.

2418. Tasker, Peter. *Inside Japan: Wealth, Work and Power in the New Japanese Empire*. London: Sidgwick & Jackson, 1987.

2419. Woronoff, Jon. *The Japanese Social Crisis*. Houndmills, U.K.: Macmillan; New York: St. Martin's Press, 1996.

Sociology

2420. Kawamura, Nozomu. *Sociology and Society of Japan*. Japanese Studies. London; New York: Kegan Paul International, 1994.

2421. Misumi, Juji. *The Behavioral Science of Leadership: An Inter-Disciplinary Japanese Research Program*. Ann Arbor, MI: University of Michigan Press, 1985.

2422. Möhwald, Ulrich. *The Emergence of Sociological Empirical Research in Japan during the 1930s: An Overview*. Social and Economic Research on Modern Japan. Berliner Beiträge zur sozial- und wirtschafts-wissenschaftlichen Japan-Forschung. Occasional Papers, no. 60. Berlin, Germany: U. Schiller, 1986.

2423. Plath, David W. *Long Engagements, Maturity in Modern Japan*. Stanford, CA: Stanford University Press, 1980.

2424. Plath, David W., ed. *Work and Lifecourse in Japan*. Albany, NY: State University of New York Press, 1983.

South and Southeast Asia—Relations with

2425. *ASEAN-Japan Relationship Towards the 21st Century*. Singapore: Japanese University Graduates Association of Singapore, 1987.

2426. Jomo, ed. *The Sun Also Sets*. Petaling Jaya, Selangor, Malaysia: INSAN, 1983.

2427. Lim, Hua Sing. *Japan's Role in ASEAN: Issues and Prospects*. Singapore: Times Academic Press, 1994.

2428. Sudo, Sueo. *The Fukuda Doctrine and ASEAN: New Dimensions in Japanese Foreign Policy*. Singapore: Institute of Southeast Asian Studies, 1992.

2429. Sudo, Sueo. *Southeast Asia in Japanese Security Policy.* Pacific Strategic Papers, 3. Singapore: Institute of Southeast Asian Studies, 1992.

2430. Swan, William L. *Japanese Economic Activity in Siam: From the 1890s to the Outbreak of the Pacific War.* Gaya: Centre for South East Asian Studies, 1986.

South and Southeast Asia—Relations with—Bibliography

2431. Iwasaki, Ikuo. *Japan and Southeast Asia: A Bibliography of Historical, Economic and Political Relations.* Tokyo: Library, Institute of Developing Economies, 1983.

Soviet Union *See*: Russia / USSR

Space *See*: Architecture—Space

Spain—Relations with

2432. Gil, Juan. *Hidalgos y Samurais: España y Japón en los Siglos XVI y XVII* [Knights and Samurai: Spain and Japan in the 16th and 17th Centuries]. Madrid: Alanza Editorial, 1991.

Sports—Aikido

2433. Bagot, Brian N. *Aikido: Traditional Art & Modern Sport.* Marlborough, U.K.: Crowood, 1990.

2434. Gleason, William. *The Spiritual Foundations of Aikido.* Rochester, VT: Destiny Books, 1994.

2435. Homma, Gaku. *Aikido Sketch Diary: Dojo 365 Days.* Translated by Yutaka Kikuchi. Berkeley, CA: Frog, 1994.

2436. Obata, Toshihiro. *Samurai Aikijutsu: Techniques of the Samurai Swordsmen.* Thousand Oaks, CA: Dragon Books, 1988.

2437. Saotome, Mitsugi. *Aikido and the Harmony of Nature.* Boston, MA: Shambhala, 1993.

2438. Ueshiba, Morihei. *The Essence of Aikido: Spiritual Teachings of Morihei Ueshiba.* Compiled by John Stevens. Tokyo; New York: Kodansha International, 1993.

Sports—Baseball

2439. Whiting, Robert. *The Chrysanthemum and the Bat: Baseball Samurai Style*. New York: Dodd, Mead, 1977. Reprint: New York: Avon Books, 1983.

2440. Whiting, Robert. *You Gotta Have Wa*. New York: Macmillan; London: Collier Macmillan, 1989.

Sports—Iaido

2441. Craig, Darrell. *Iai-Jitsu: Center of the Circle*. Tokyo: Lotus Press, 1981. Reprint: Rutland, VT: Tuttle, 1988.

2442. Finn, Michael. *Iaido, the Way of the Sword*. Boulder, CO: Palladin Press, 1985.

2443. Warner, Gordon, and Donn F. Draeger. *Japanese Swordsmanship: Technique and Practice*. Reprint: New York: Weatherhill, 1990.

Sports—Jiu-jitsu

2444. Craig, Darrell. *Japan's Ultimate Martial Art: Jujitsu Before 1882*. Boston, MA: Tuttle, 1995.

Sports—Kendō

2445. Budden, Paul. *Looking at a Far Mountain: A Study of Kendo Kata*. London: Ward Lick, 1992.

2446. Kiyota, Minoru. *Kendō: Its Philosophy, History, and Means to Personal Growth*. London; New York: Kegan Paul International, 1995.

2447. Obata, Toshishiro. *Crimson Steel: The Sword Technique of the Samurai*. Thousand Oaks, CA: Dragon Books, 1987.

2448. Parulski, George R., Jr. *Sword of the Samurai: The Classical Art of Japanese Swordsmanship*. Boulder, CO: Paladin Press, 1985.

2449. Sasamori, Junzo, and Gordon Warner. *This is Kendo: The Art of Japanese Fencing*. Reprint: Rutland, VT: Tuttle, 1989.

Sports—Ninjutsu

2450. Campbell, Sid. *Exotic Weapons of the Ninja*. Boulder, CO: Paladin Press, 1994.

2451. Draeger, Donn F. *Ninjutsu: The Art of Invisibility: Japan's Feudal-Age Espionage and Assassination Methods*. New ed. Phoenix, AZ: Phoenix Books, 1986.

2452. Hatsumi, Masaaki. *Essence of Ninjutsu: The Nine Traditions*. Chicago, IL: Contemporary Books, 1988.

2453. Lewis, Peter. *Art of the Ninja*. London: Ward Lock, 1988.

2454. Shinichi, Kano. *Ninja, Men of Iga*. Thousand Oaks, CA: Dragon, 1989.

2455. Turnbull, Stephen R. *Ninja: The True Story of Japan's Secret Warrior Cult*. Poole, U.K.: Firebird Books, 1992.

Sports—Sumo

2456. Cuyler, P. L. *Sumo: From Rite to Sport*. Rev. ed. New York: Weatherhill, 1985.

2457. Patmore, Angela. *The Giants of Sumo*. London: Macdonald, 1990.

2458. Sackett, Joel, and Wes Benson. *Rikishi: The Men of Sumo*. New York: Weatherhill, 1986.

2459. Sharnoff, Lora. *Grand Sumo: The Living Sport and Tradition*. Rev. ed. New York: Weatherhill, 1993.

Statistics

2460. *Hundred-Year Statistics of Wholesale Price Indexes in Japan*. Tokyo: Research and Statistics Department, Bank of Japan, 1987.

2461. *Japan Business Atlas*. Tokyo: Business International of Delaware, Japan Branch, 1987.

2462. Matsuoka, Mikihiro, and Brian Rose. *The DIR Guide to Japanese Economic Statistics*. Oxford, U.K.: New York: Oxford University Press, 1994.

2463. Mizoguchi, Toshiyuki. *Reforms of Statistical System under Socio-Economic Changes: Overview of Statistical Data in Japan.* Economic Research Series (Hitotsubashi Daigaku. Keizai Kenkyujo), no. 32. Tokyo: Maruzen, 1995.

2464. *Statistical Services in Japan.* Tokyo: International Statistical Affairs Division, Statistical Standards Depart., Statistics Bureau, Management and Coordination Agency, 1995.

2465. Taguchi, Gen'ichi. *Taguchi Methods: Design of Experiments.* Edited and translated by Yuin Wu. Quality Engineering Series, v. 4. Dearborn, MI: ASI Press; Tokyo: Japanese Standards Association, 1993.

Subcontracting

2466. Nishiguchi, Toshihiro. *Strategic Industrial Sourcing: The Japanese Advantage.* New York: Oxford University Press, 1994.

2467. Thoburn, John J., and Makoto Takashima. *Industrial Subcontracting in the UK and Japan.* Avebury Business School Library. Aldershot, U.K.; Brookfield, VT: Ashgate, 1992.

Suburbs

2468. Ben-Ari, Eyal. *Changing Japanese Suburbia: A Study of Two Present-Day Localities.* Japanese Studies. London; New York: Kegan Paul International, 1991.

Suicide

2469. Iga, Mamoru. *The Thorn in the Chrysanthemum: Suicide and Economic Success in Modern Japan.* Berkeley, CA: University of California Press, 1986.

2470. Pinguet, Maurice. *La Mort Volontaire au Japon* [Voluntary Death in Japan]. Bibliothèque des Histoires. Paris: Gallimard, 1984.

Sumi-e *See*: Art—Painting—Ink

Swords *See*: Arms and Armor

Tattoos

2471. Fellman, Sandi. *The Japanese Tattoo*. New York: Abbeville Press, 1986.

2472. Gulik, Willem R. van. *Irezumi: The Pattern of Dermatography in Japan*. Mededeling van het Rijksmuseum voor Volkenkunde Leiden, no. 22. Leiden, Netherlands: Brill, 1982.

2473. Martischnig, Michael. *Tatowierung ostasiatischer Art: zu sozialgeschichte und handwerklicher Ausführung von gewerblichem Hautstich in Vergangenheit und Gegenwart in Japan* [Tattooing East Asian Style: Toward a Social History and Technical Explanation of Commercial Skin Engraving in Past and Present Japan]. Sitzungsberichte (Österreichische Akademie der Wissenschaften. Philosophisch-Historische Klasse), 495 Bd. Mitteilungen des Instituts für Gegenwartsvolkskunde, Nr. 19. Vienna: Verlag der Österreichischen Akademie der Wissenschaften, 1987.

2474. Richie, Donald, and Ian Buruma. *The Japanese Tattoo*. New York: Weatherhill, 1980.

Taxation

2475. Ishi, Hiromitsu. *The Japanese Tax System*. 2d ed. Oxford, U.K.; New York: Clarendon, 1993.

2476. Kuboi, Takashi. *Business Practices and Taxation in Japan*. 5th ed. Tokyo: Japan Times, 1993.

Tea Ceremony

2477. Anderson, Jennifer Lea. *An Introduction to Japanese Tea Ritual*. Albany, NY: State University of New York Press, 1991.

2478. Hirota, Dennis, comp. and ed. *Wind in the Pines:; Classic Writings on the Way of Tea as a Buddhist Path*. Fremont, CA: Asian Humanities Press, 1995.

2479. *Japan, the Art of the Tea Ceremony*. Washington, DC: National Gallery of Art, 1988.

2500. Raz, Jacob. *Audience and Actors: A Study of Their Interaction in the Japanese Traditional Theatre.* Leiden, Netherlands: Brill, 1983.

2501. Shields, Nancy K. *Fake Fish: The Theater of Kobo Abe.* New York: Weatherhill, 1996.

2502. Suzuki, Tadashi. *The Way of Acting: The Theatre Writings of Tadashi Suzuki.* New York: Theatre Communications Group, 1986.

2503. Tschudin, Jean Jacques. *La Ligue du Théatre Prolitarien Japonais* [The Confederation of Japanese Proletarian Theater]. Lettres Asiatiques. Japon. Paris: L'Harmattan, 1989.

2504. Yamazaki, Masakazu. *Mask and Sword: Two Plays for the Contemporary Japanese Theater.* Translated by J. Thomas Rimer. Modern Asian Literature Series. New York: Columbia University Press, 1980.

Theater—Bunraku

2505. Adachi, Barbara C. *Backstage at Bunraku: A Behind-the-Scenes Look at Japan's Traditional Puppet Theatre.* New York: Weatherhill, 1985.

2506. Gerstle, Andrew, Kiyoshi Inobe, and William P. Malm. *Theater as Music: The Bunraku Play "Mt. Imo and Mt. Se": An Exemplary Tale of Womanly Virtue.* Michigan Monograph Series in Japanese Studies, 4. Ann Arbor, MI: Center for Japanese Studies, University of Michigan, 1990.

Theater—Joruri

2507. Gerstle, C. Andrew. *Circles of Fantasy: Convention in the Plays of Chikamatsu.* Harvard East Asian Monograph, 116. Cambridge, MA: Council on East Asian Studies, Harvard University, 1986.

Theater—Kabuki

2508. Brandon, James R., ed. *Chushingura: Studies in Kabuki and the Puppet Theater.* Honolulu, HI: University of Hawaii Press, 1982.

2509. Gunji, Masakatsu, and Chiaki Yoshida. *The Kabuki Guide.* Translated by Christopher Holmes. Tokyo; New York: Kodansha International, 1987.

2510. Leims, Thomas. *Die Entstehung des Kabuki: Transkulturation Europa-Japan im 16. Und 17. Jahrhundert* [The Origin of Kabuki: Transculturation Europe-Japan in the 16th and 17th Century]. Brill's Japanese Studies Library, v. 2. Leiden, Netherlands; New York: Brill, 1990.

2511. Nakamura, Matazo. *Kabuki, Backstage, Onstage: An Actor's Life.* Tokyo; New York: Kodansha International, 1990.

2512. Powell, Brian. *Kabuki in Modern Japan: Mayama Seika and His Plays.* Houndmills, U.K.: Macmillan in association with St. Anthony's College, Oxford, 1990.

Theater—Kyogen

2513. Kenney, Don, comp. *The Kyogen Book: An Anthology of Japanese Classical Comedies.* Tokyo: Japan Times, 1989.

Theater—Nō

2514. Bethe, Monica, and Karen Brazell. *Dance in the Nō Theater.* 3 vols. Cornell University East Asia Papers, no. 29. Ithaca, NY: China-Japan Program, Cornell University, 1982.

2515. Goff, Janet Emily. *Noh Drama and the Tale of Genji: The Art of Allusion in Fifteen Classical Plays.* Princeton Library of Asian Translations. Princeton, NJ: Princeton University Press, 1991.

2516. Hare, Thomas Blenman. *Zeami's Style: The Noh Plays of Zeami Motokiyo.* Stanford, CA: Stanford University Press, 1986.

2517. Keene, Donald. *No and Bunraku: Two Forms of Japanese Theatre.* Photographs by Kaneko Keizo. New York: Columbia University Press, 1990.

2518. Konparu, Kunio. *The Noh Theater: Principles and Perspectives.* New York: Weatherhill / Tankosha, 1983.

2519. Martzel, Gérard. *Le Dieu Masqué: Fêtes et Théâtre au Japon* [The Masked God: Festivals and Theater in Japan]. Bibliothèque Japonaise. Paris: Publications Orientalistes de France, 1982.

2520. Martzel, Gérard. *La Fête D'Ogi et le Nō de Kurokawa* [The Ogi Festival and Kurokawa's Noh]. Bibliothèque Japonaise. Paris: Publications Orientalistes de France, 1982.

2521. Mitchell, John Dietrich, and Miyoko Watanabe. *Staging Japanese Theater: Noh & Kabuki: Ikkaku Sennin (The Holy Hermit Unicorn) and Narukami (The Thunder God)*. Theatre Production Book. Key West, FL: Institute for Advanced Studies in the Theatre Arts Press in association with Florida Keys Educational Foundation, Inc., Florida Keys Community College, 1994.

2522. Poorter, Erika de. *Zeami's Talks on Sarugaku: An Annotated Translation of the Sarugaku Dangi: With an Introduction on Zeami Motokiyo*. Japonica Neerlandica, v. 2. Amsterdam: J. C. Gieben, 1986.

2523. Sekine, Masaru. *Ze-Ami and his Theories of Noh Drama*. Gerrards Cross, U.K.: C. Smythe, 1985.

2524. Waley, Arthur. *The Nō Plays of Japan*. London: G. Allen & Unwin, 1921. Reprint: London: Unwin Paperbacks, 1988.

Theater—Rakugo

2525. Morioka, Heinz, and Miyoko Sasaki. *Rakugo, the Popular Narrative Art of Japan*. Harvard East Asian Monographs, 138. Cambridge, MA: Council on East Asian Studies, Harvard University, 1990.

2526. Sakai, Anne. *La Parole Comme Art: Le Rakugo Japonais* [Speech as Art: Japanese Rakugo]. Lettres Asiatiques. Japon. Paris: L'Harmattan, 1992.

Theater Costumes *See*: Art—Costumes—Theater

Tibet—Relations with

2527. Berry, Scott. *Monks, Spies, and a Soldier of Fortune: The Japanese in Tibet*. New York: St. Martin's Press, 1995.

Tōkyō *See*: History—Local—Tōkyō

Trade

2528. Bhagwati, Jagdish N., and Robert E. Hudec, eds. *Fair Trade and Harmonization: Prerequisites for Free Trade?* 2 vols. Cambridge, MA: MIT Press, 1996.

Trade—Bibliography

2529. Neri, Rita E. *U.S./Japan Foreign Trade: An Annotated Bibliography of Socioeconomic Perspectives*. Garland Reference Library of Social Science, v. 403. New York: Garland, 1988.

Trade Unions *See*: Labor—Trade Unions

Trading Companies

2530. Eli, Max. *Japan Incorporated: Global Strategies of Japanese Trading Corporations*. London; New York: McGraw-Hill, 1990.

2531. Parker, Paul. *Information Specialization and Trade: Trading Companies and the Coal Trade of Europe and Japan*. Pacific Economic Papers, no. 207. Canberra: Australia-Japan Research Centre, 1992.

2532. Yonekawa, Shin'ichi. *General Trading Companies: A Comparative and Historical Study*. Tokyo: United Nations University Press, 1990.

2533. Yoshihara, Kunio. *Sogo Shosha: The Vanguard of the Japanese Economy*. Tokyo; New York: Oxford University Press, 1982.

2534. Yoshino, M. Y., and Thomas B. Lifson. *The Invisible Link: Japan's Sogo Shosha and the Organization of Trade*. Cambridge, MA: MIT Press, 1986.

Travel

2535. Vaporis, Constantine Nomikos. *Breaking Barriers: Travel and the State in Early Modern Japan*. Harvard East Asia Monographs, 163. Cambridge, MA: Council on East Asian Studies, Harvard University, 1994.

Travel Guides

2536. Durston, Diane, and Lucy Birmingham. *Old Kyoto: A Guide to Traditional Ships, Restaurants, and Inns*. Tokyo; New York; Kodansha International, 1986.

2537. Kanno, Eiji, and Constance O'Keefe. *Japan Solo*. Traveler's Bookshelf. New York: Warner Books, 1988.

2538. Kirchman, Hans. *Baedeker's Tokyo.* New York: Prentice-Hall, 1987.

2539. Strauss, Robert, Christ Taylor, and Tony Wheeler. *Japan.* 4th ed. Lonely Planet Travel Survival Kit. Hawthorn, Australia; Berkeley, CA: Lonely Planet, 1991.

Travel Writing

2540. Beato, Felice, Raimund von Stillfried, and Pierre Loti. *Once Upon a Time: Visions of Old Japan.* Translated by Linda Coverdale. New York: Friendly Press 1986.

2541. Bird, Isabella L. *Unbeaten Tracks in Japan: An Account of Travels in the Interior including Visits to the Aborigines of Yezo and the Shrine of Nikkō and Isē.* 2 vols. London: J. Murray, 1880. Reprint: *Unbeaten Tracks in Japan.* Virago / Beacon Travelers. Boston, MA: Beacon Press, 1987.

2542. Booth, Alan. *The Roads to Sata: A 2000-Mile Walk through Japan.* New York: Weatherhill, 1985.

2543. Brown, J. D. *The Sudden Disappearance of Japan: Journeys through a Hidden Land.* Santa Barbara, CA: Capra Press, 1994.

2544. Davidson, Cathy N. *36 Views of Mount Fuji: On Finding Myself in Japan.* New York: Dutton, 1993.

2545. Fogel, Joshua A. *The Literature of Travel in the Japanese Rediscovery of China, 1862-1945.* Stanford, CA: Stanford University Press, 1996.

2546. Gayn, Mark. *Japan Diary.* Rutland, VT: Tuttle, 1981.

2547. Meyer, Carolyn. *A Voice from Japan: An Outsider Looks in.* San Diego, CA: Harcourt Brace Jovanovich, 1988.

2548. Price, David, and Jean-François Guerry. *Travels in Japan.* London: Olive Press, 1986.

2549. Sato, Hiroaki, trans. *Bashō's Narrow Road; Spring and Autumn Passages: Two Works.* Berkeley, CA: Stone Bridge Press, 1996.

2550. Waycott, Angus. *Paper Doors: Japan from Scratch.* London: Andre Deutsch, 1994.

Trees

2551.　Valavanis, William N. *The Japanese Five Needle Pine: Nature, Gardens, Bonsai, Taxonomy.* Edited by Edwin C. Symmes, Jr., and Dorothy O'Quinn. Encyclopedia of Classical Bonsai Art, v. 2. Atlanta, GA: Symmes Systems, 1976.

2552.　Vertrees, J. D. *Japanese Maples: Momiji and Kaede.* 2d ed. Portland, OR: Timber Press, 1987.

Ukiyo-e *See*: Art—Prints

Unions *See*: Labor—Trade Unions

United Kingdom—Relations with

2553.　Buckley, Roger. *Occupation Diplomacy: Britain, the United States, and Japan, 1945-1952.* International Studies. Cambridge, U.K.; New York: Cambridge University Press, 1982.

2554.　Cortazzi, Hugh, and Gordon Daniels, eds. *Britain and Japan 1859-1991: Themes and Personalities.* London; New York: Routledge, 1991.

2555.　Newall, Paul. *Japan and the City of London.* London; Atlantic Highlands, NJ: Athlone Press, 1996.

2556.　Nish, Ian. *The Anglo-Japanese Alliance: The Diplomacy of Two Island Empires, 1894-1907.* 2d ed. University of London Historical Studies, 18. London; Dover, NH: Athlone Press, 1985.

2557.　Nish, Ian. *Britain & Japan: Biographical Portraits.* Folkestone, UK: Japan Library, 1994.

2558.　Tames, Richard. *Encounters with Japan.* New York: St. Martin's Press, 1991.

United States—Diplomatic Relations with

2559.　Anhalt, Gert. *Okinawa zwischen Washington und Tokyo: Betrachtungen zur politischen und sozialen Entwicklung, 1945-1972* [Okinawa between Washington and Tokyo: Reflections on Political and Social Development, 1945-1972]. Marburger Japan-Reihe, Bd. 5. Marburg, Germany: Förderverein Marburger Japan-Reihe, 1991.

2560. Armacost, Michael H. *Friends or Rivals?: The Insider's Account of U.S.-Japan Relations.* New York: Columbia University Press, 1996.

2561. Ben-Zvi, Abraham. *The Illusion of Deterrence: The Roosevelt Presidency and the Origins of the Pacific War.* Studies in International Politics. Boulder, CO: Westview, 1987.

2562. Boyle, John Hunter. *Modern Japan: The American Nexus.* Fort Worth, TX: Harcourt Brace Jovanovich, 1993.

2563. Buckley, Roger. *U.S.-Japan Alliance Diplomacy, 1945-1990.* Cambridge Studies in International Relations, 21. Cambridge, U.K.; New York: Cambridge University Press, 1992.

2564. Emmerson, John K., and Harrison M. Holland. *The Eagle and the Rising Sun: America and Japan in the Twentieth Century.* Reading, MA: Addison-Wesley, 1988.

2565. Frost, Ellen L. *For Richer, For Poorer: The New U.S.-Japan Relationship.* New York: Council on Foreign Relations, 1987.

2566. Green, Michael J. *Arming Japan: Defense Production, Alliance Politics, and the Postwar Search for Autonomy.* New York: Columbia University Press, 1995.

2567. Gudykunst, William B., and Tsukasa Nishida. *Bridging Japanese / North American Differences.* Communicating Effectively in Multicultural Contexts, 1. Thousand Oaks, CA: Sage, 1994.

2568. Hilgenberg, James. *From Enemy to Ally: Japan, the American Business Press, & the Early Cold War.* Lanham, MD: University Press of America, 1993.

2569. Holland, Harrison M. *Japan Challenges America: Managing an Alliance in Crisis.* Boulder, CO: Westview, 1992.

2570. Ibe, Hideo. *Japan Thrice-Opened: An Analysis of Relations between Japan and the United States.* Translated by Lynne E. Riggs and Manabu Takechi. New York: Praeger, 1992.

2571. Kitamura, Hiroshi, Ryohei Murata, and Hisahiko Okazaki. *Between Friends: Japanese Diplomats Look at Japan-U.S. Relations.* Translated by Daniel R. Zoll. New York: Weatherhill, 1985.

2572. Krooth, Richard, and Hiroshi Fukurai. *Common Destiny: Japan and the United States in the Global Age*. Jefferson, NC: McFarland, 1990.

2573. Lauren, Paul Gordon, and Raymond Finlay, eds. *Destinies Shared: U.S.-Japanese Relations*. Westview Special Studies on East Asia. Boulder, CO: Westview, 1989.

2574. Makin, John H., and Donald C. Hellman, eds. *Sharing World Leadership?: A New Era for America & Japan*. AEI Studies, 488. Washington, DC: American Enterprise Institute for Public Policy Research, 1989.

2575. Morse, Ronald A., ed. *U.S.-Japan Relations: An Agenda for the Future*. Lanham, MD: University Press of America; Honolulu: Pacific Forum, 1989.

2576. Nakamura, Masanori. *The Japanese Monarchy: Ambassador Joseph Grew and the Making of the "Symbol Emperor System," 1931-1991*. Asia and the Pacific. Armonk, NY: Sharpe, 1992.

2577. Nester, William R. *Power Across the Pacific: A Diplomatic History of American Relations with Japan*. New York: New York University Press, 1996.

2578. Satō, Ryuzō. *The Chrysanthemum and the Eagle: The Future of U.S.-Japan Relations*. New York: New York University Press, 1994.

2579. Schodt, Frederik L. *America and the Four Japans: Friend, Foe, Model, Mirror*. Berkeley, CA: Stone Bridge Press, 1994.

2580. Shiels, Frederick L. *Tokyo and Washington: Dilemmas of a Mature Alliance*. Lexington, MA: Lexington Books, 1980.

2581. Sneider, Richard L. *U.S.-Japanese Security Relations: A Historical Perspective*. Occasional Papers of the East Asian Institute. New York: East Asian Institute, Toyota Research Program, Columbia University, 1982.

2582. Statler, Oliver. *Shimoda Story*. New York: Random House, 1969. Reprint: Honolulu, HI: University of Hawaii Press, 1986.

2583. Watts, William. *The United States and Japan: A Troubled Partnership*. Cambridge, MA: Ballinger, 1984.

2584. Welfield, John. *An Empire in Eclipse: Japan in the Postwar American Alliance System: A Study in the Interaction of Domestic Politics and Foreign Policy.* London; Atlantic Highlands, NJ: Athlone Press, 1988.

2585. Wiley, Peter Booth, and Ichiro Korogi. *Yankees in the Land of the Gods: Commodore Perry and the Opening of Japan.* New York: Viking, 1990.

United States—Economic Relations with

2586. Abe, Kiyoshi, William Gunther, and Harold See, eds. *Economic, Industrial, and Managerial Coordination between Japan and the USA.* New York: St. Martin's Press, 1992.

2587. Abegglen, James C. *The Strategy of Japanese Business.* Cambridge, MA: Ballinger, 1984.

2588. Adams, F. Gerard. *Economic Activity, Trade, and Industry in the U.S.-Japan-World Economy: A Macro Model Study of Economic Interactions.* Westport, CT: Praeger, 1993.

2589. Atlantic Council of the United States. *The United States and Japan: Cooperative Leadership for Peace and Global Prosperity.* Lanham, MD: University Press of America, 1990.

2590. Bergsten, C. Fred, and Marcus Noland. *Reconcilable Differences: United States-Japan Economic Conflict.* Washington, DC: Institute for International Economics, 1993.

2591. Burstein, Daniel. *Turning the Tables: A Machiavellian Strategy for Dealing with Japan.* New York: Simon & Schuster, 1993.

2592. Cohen, Stephen D. *Uneasy Partnership: Competition and Conflict in U.S.-Japanese Trade Relations.* Cambridge, MA: Ballinger, 1985.

2593. Conteh-Morgan, Earl. *Japan and the United States: Global Dimensions of Economic Power.* American University Studies. Series X, Political Science, v. 36. New York: P. Lang, 1992.

2594. *The Japan-U.S. Relationship: Bilateral and Global Contexts.* Iranyzatok a Vilaggazdasagban, sz. 67. Budapest: Hungarian Scientific Council for World Economy, 1991.

2595. Lorell, Mark A. *Troubled Partnership: A History of U.S.-Japan Collaboration on the FS-X Fighter.* RAND Studies Published with Transaction. New Brunswick, NJ: Transaction, 1996.

2596. Mason, T. David, and Abdul M. Turay, eds. *US-Japan Trade Friction: Its Impact on Security Cooperation in the Pacific Basin.* Basingstoke, U.K.: Macmillan, 1991.

2597. McKinney, Jerome B. *Risking a Nation: U.S. Japanese Trade Failure and the Need for Political, Social, and Economic Reformation.* Lanham, MD: University Press of America, 1995.

2598. Moran, Robert T. *Getting Your Yen'$ Worth: How to Negotiate with Japan, Inc.* Houston, TX: Gulf Publishing, 1985.

2599. Nester, William R. *Japanese Industrial Targeting: The Neomercantilist Path to Economic Superpower.* London: Macmillan, 1991.

2600. Ohmae, Ken'ichi. *Beyond National Borders: Reflections on Japan and the World.* Homewood, IL: Dow Jones-Irwin, 1987.

2601. Okawara, Yoshio. *To Avoid Isolation: An Ambassador's View of U.S./Japanese Relations.* Columbia, SC: University of South Carolina Press, 1990.

2602. Renwick, Neil. *Japan's Alliance Politics and Defence Production.* New York: St. Martin's Press, 1995.

2603. Sato, Ryuzo, and Paul Wachtel, eds. *Trade Friction and Economic Policy: Problems and Prospects for Japan and the United States.* Cambridge, U.K.: New York: Cambridge University Press, 1987.

2604. Sato, Ryuzo, and John A. Rizzo, eds. *Unkept Promises, Unclear Consequences: U.S. Economic Policy and the Japanese Response.* Cambridge, U.K.; New York: Cambridge University Press, 1988.

2605. Stallings, Barbara, and Gabriel Szekely, eds. *Japan, the United States, and Latin America: Toward a Trilateral Relationship in the Western Hemisphere?* St. Anthony's / Macmillan Series. Houndmills, UK: Macmillan in association with St. Anthony's College, Oxford, 1993.

2606. Tweeten, Luther, ed. *Japanese and American Agriculture: Tradition and Progress in Conflict.* Boulder, CO: Westview, 1993.

Urban Development

2607. Fujita, Kumiko, and Richard Child Hill, eds. *Japanese Cities in the World Economy. Conflicts in Urban and Regional Development.* Philadelphia, PA: Temple University Press, 1993.

2608. Hanayama, Yuzuru. *Land Markets and Land Policy in a Metropolitan Area: A Case Study of Tokyo.* Boston, MA: Oelgeschlager, Gunn & Hain in association with Lincoln Institute of Land Policy, 1986.

2609. Hebbert, Michael, and Norihiro Nakai. *How Tokyo Grows: Land Development and Planning on the Metropolitan Fringe.* ST / ICERD Occasional Paper, no. 11. London: Suntory-Toyota International Centre for Economics and Related Disciplines: London School of Economics and Political Science, 1988.

2610. *A Hundred Years of Tokyo City Planning.* TMG Municipal Library, no. 28. Tokyo: Tokyo Metropolitan Government, 1994.

2611. Minerbi, Luciano, et al., eds. *Land Readjustment: The Japanese System; A Reconnaissance and a Digest.* Boston, MA: Oelgeschlager, Gunn & Hain, in association with the Lincoln Institute of Land Policy, 1986.

2612. Nexus World Project. *Nexus World.* Fukuoka, Japan: Fukuoka Jisho, 1991.

2613. Shapira, Philip, Ian Masser, and David W. Edgington, eds. *Planning for Cities and Regions in Japan.* Liverpool, U.K.: Liverpool University Press, 1994.

2614. *The Tokyo Metropolitan Housing Master Plan: Achieving the Goal of More Comfortable Housing.* TMG Municipal Library, no. 26. Tokyo; Tokyo Metropolitan Government, 1992.

2615. Yamato, Minoru, ed. *Breaking New Ground: Projects of the Housing and Urban Development Corporation.* Process, Architecture, no. 114. Tokyo: Process Architecture Co., Ltd, 1993.

USA *See*: United States

USSR *See*: Russia / USSR

Villages

2616. Dore, Ronald Philip. *Shinohata, a Portrait of a Japanese Village*. Berkeley, CA; Los Angeles, CA: University of California Press, 1994.

2617. Ooms, Herman. *Tokugawa Village Practice: Class, Status, Power, Law*. Berkeley, CA: University of California Press, 1996.

2618. Saga, Jun'ichi. *Memories of Silk and Straw: A Self-Portrait of Small-Town Japan*. Translated by Garry O. Evans. Tokyo; New York: Kodansha International, 1987.

2619. Seshaiah, S. *Land Reform and Social Change in a Japanese Village*. Bangalore, India: Shiney, 1980.

Vocational Training *See*: Education—Vocational

Whaling

2620. Government of Japan. *Papers on Japanese Small-Type Coastal Whaling: 1986-1995*. Tokyo; Institute of Cetacean Research, 1996.

2621. Kalland, Arne, and Brian Moeran. *Endangered Culture: Japanese Whaling in Culture Perspective*. NIAS preprints, 0904-827X, no. 2. Copenhagen: Nordic Institute of Asian Studies, 1990.

2622. Kalland, Arne, and Brian Moeran. *Japanese Whaling: End of an Era?* Scandinavian Institute of Asian Studies monograph series, no. 61. London: Curzon Press, 1992.

2623. Takahashi, Jun'ichi. *Women's Tales of Whaling: Onnatachi no Hogei Monogatari*. Tokyo: Japan Whaling Association, 1988.

Women

2624. Bernstein, Gail Lee. *Haruko's World: A Japanese Farm Woman and her Community*. Stanford, CA: Stanford University Press, 1983.

2625. Bingham, Marjorie Wall, and Susan Hill Gross. *Women in Japan: From Ancient Times to the Present*. Women in World Area Studies. St. Louis Park, MN: Glenhurst, 1987.

2626. Bumiller, Elisabeth. *The Secrets of Mariko: A Year in the Life of a Japanese Woman and her Family*. New York: Times Books, 1995.

2627. Freed, Anne O., Yukiko Kurokawa, and Hiroshi Kawai. *The Changing Worlds of Older Women in Japan*. Manchester, CT: Knowledge, Ideas & Trends, 1993.

2628. Fukuzawa, Yukichi. *Fukuzawa Yukichi on Japanese Women: Selected Works*. Tokyo: University of Tokyo Press, 1988.

2629. Hane, Mikiso, trans., ed. *Reflections on the Way to the Gallows: Rebel Women in Prewar Japan*. Berkeley, CA: University of California Press with Pantheon Press, 1988.

2630. Imamura, Anne E. *Urban Japanese Housewives: At Home and in the Community*. Studies of the East Asian Institute. Honolulu: University of Hawaii Press, 1987.

2631. Iwao, Sumiko. *The Japanese Woman: Traditional Image and Changing Reality*. New York: Free Press, 1993.

2632. *Japanese Women Today*. Tokyo: Prime Minister's Office, 1990.

2633. Johnson, Carmen. *Wave-Rings in the Water: My Years with the Women of Postwar Japan*. Alexandria, VA: Charles River Press, 1996.

2634. Kanematsu, Elizabeth. *Women in Society: Japan*. New York: M. Cavendish, 1993.

2635. Knapp, Bettina Liebowitz. *Images of Japanese Women: A Westerner's View*. Troy, NY: Whitston, 1992.

2636. Lebra, Takie Sugiyama. *Japanese Women: Constraint and Fulfillment*. Honolulu, HI: University of Hawaii Press, 1984.

2637. Mulhern, Chieko Irie, ed. *Heroic With Grace: Legendary Women of Japan*. Armonk, NY: Sharpe, 1991.

2638. National Women's Education Centre, comp. *Women in a Changing Society: The Japanese Scene*. UNESCO Supported Series on Women's Studies in Asia and the Pacific. Bangkok: UNESCO, 1990.

2639. Phar, Susan J. *Political Women in Japan: The Search for a Place in Political Life*. Berkeley, CA; London: University of California Press, 1981.

2640. Robins-Mowry, Dorothy. *The Hidden Sun: Women of Modern Japan*. Boulder, CO: Westview, 1983.

2641. Saso, Mary. *Women in the Japanese Workplace.* London: H. Shipman, 1990.

2642. Smith, Robert John, and Ella Lury Wiswell. *The Women of Suye Mura.* Chicago, IL: University of Chicago Press, 1982.

2643. Tanaka, Yukiko. *Contemporary Portraits of Japanese Women.* Westport, CT: Praeger, 1995.

2644. Trager, James. *Letters from Sachiko: A Japanese Woman's View of Life in the Land of the Economic Miracle.* New York: Atheneum, 1982.

2645. Yamakawa, Kikue. *Women of the Mito Domain: Recollections of Samurai Family Life.* Translated by Kate Wildman Nakai. Tokyo: University of Tokyo Press, 1992.

Women—Bibliography

2646. Huber, Kristina Ruth. *Women in Japanese Society: An Annotated Bibliography of Selected English Language Materials.* Bibliographies and Indexes in Women's Studies, no. 16. New York: Greenwood, 1992.

2647. Koh, Hesung Chun, comp., ed. *Korean and Japanese Women: An Analytic Bibliographical Guide.* Westport, CT: Published under auspices of the Human Relations Area Files by Greenwood, 1982.

2648. Mamola, Claire Zebrosky. *Japanese Women Writers in English Translation: An Annotated Bibliography.* Garland Reference Library of the Humanities, vol. 877. New York: Garland, 1989.

Women—Employment

2649. Brinton, Mary C. *Women and the Economic Miracle: Gender and Work in Postwar Japan.* California Series on Social Choice and Political Economy, 21. Berkeley, CA: University of California Press, 1992.

2650. Cook, Alice Hanson. *Working Women in Japan: Discrimination, Resistance, and Reform.* Cornell International Industrial and Labor Relations Reports, no. 10. Ithaca, NY: New York State School of Industry and Labor Relations, 1980.

2651. Hunter, Janet, ed. *Japanese Women Working*. London; New York: Routledge, 1993.

2652. Imamura, Anne E., ed. *Re-Imagining Japanese Women*. Berkeley, CA: University of California Press, 1996.

2653. Kondo, Dorinne K. *Crafting Selves: Power, Gender, and Discourses of Identity in a Japanese Workplace*. Chicago, IL: University of Chicago Press, 1990.

2654. Lam, Alice C. L. *Women and Japanese Management: Discrimination and Reform*. London; New York: Routledge, 1992.

2655. Lo, Jeannie. *Office Ladies, Factory Women: Life and Work at a Japanese Company*. Armonk, NY: Sharpe, 1990.

2656. Nakamura, Masanori, ed. *Technology Change and Female Labour in Japan*. Technology Transfer, Transformation and Development. Tokyo; New York: United Nations University Press, 1994.

2657. Roberts, Glenda Susan. *Staying on the Line: Blue-Collar Women in Contemporary Japan*. Honolulu, HI: University of Hawaii Press, 1994.

2658. Tsurumi, E. Patricia. *Factory Girls: Women in the Thread Mills of Meiji Japan*. Princeton, NJ: Princeton University Press, 1990.

Women—Feminism

2659. Bernstein, Gail Lee, ed. *Recreating Japanese Women, 1600-1945*. Berkeley, CA: University of California Press, 1991.

2660. Buckley, Sandra, ed. *Broken Silence: Voices of Japanese Feminism*. Berkeley, CA: University of California Press, 1996.

2661. Condon, Jane. *A Half Step Behind: Japanese Women of the 80s*. New York: Dodd, Mead, 1985.

2662. Fujimura-Fanselow, Kumiko, and Atsuko Kameda, eds. *Japanese Women: New Feminist Perspectives on the Past*. New York: The Feminist Press at the City University of New York, 1995.

2663. Sievers, Sharon L. *Flowers in Salt: The Beginnings of Feminist Consciousness in Modern Japan*. Stanford, CA: Stanford University Press, 1983.

2664. Sugahara, Mariko. *Japanese Women Yesterday and Today.* "About Japan" series, 5. Tokyo: Foreign Press Center, 1986.

2665. *Voices from the Japanese Women's Movement.* Edited by AMPO, Japan Asia Quarterly Review. Japan in the Modern World. Armonk, NY: Sharpe, 1996.

Women in Religion *See*: Religion—Women

Women's Language *See*: Language—Women

Women's Literature *See*: Literature—Women

Writing

2666. Anderson, Olov Bertil. *Bushu, a Key to the Radicals of Japanese Script.* London: Curzon Press, 1981.

2667. Dolby, William. *The Japanese Scripts.* Edinburgh, U.K.: W. Dolby, 1988.

2668. Kitagawa, Mary M., and Chisato Kitagawa. *Making Connections with Writing: An Expressive Writing Model in Japanese Schools.* Portsmouth, NH: Heinemann, 1987.

2669. Seeley, Christopher. *A History of Writing in Japan.* Brill's Japanese Studies Library, v. 3. Leiden, Netherlands; New York: Brill, 1991.

2670. Stalph, Jürgen. *Grundlagen einer Grammatik der sinojapanischen Schrift* [A Basic Grammar of Sino-Japanese Script]. Veröffentlichungen des Ostasien-Instituts der Ruhr-Universität Bochum, Bd. 39. Wiesbaden, Germany: Harrassowitz, 1989.

2671. Unger, J. Marshall. *Script Reform in Occupation Japan.* New York: Oxford University Press, 1996.

Yakuza

2672. Kaplan, David E., and Alec Dubro. *Yakuza: The Explosive Account of Japan's Criminal Underworld.* Reading, MA: Addison-Wesley, 1986.

2673.   Saga, Jun'ichi. *The Gambler's Tale: A Life in Japan's Underworld.* Tokyo; New York: Kodansha International, 1991. Reprinted as: *Confessions of a Yakuza: A Life in Japan's Underworld.* Translated by John Bester. Tokyo; London: Kodansha International, 1995.

2674.   Seymour, Christopher. *Yakuza Diary: Doing Time in the Japanese Underworld.* New York: Atlantic Monthly Press, 1996.

Youth

See also: Juvenile Delinquency

2675.   Greenfield, Karl Taro. *Speed Tribes: Days   and Nights with Japan's Next Generation.* New York: HarperCollins, 1994.

2676.   Wardell, Steven. *Rising Sons and Daughters: Life among Japan's New Young.* Cambridge, MA: Plympton Press International, 1995.

Zen *See*: Religion—Buddhism—Zen

AUTHOR INDEX

Numbers refer to entry numbers, not page numbers.

ABOUT THE AUTHOR

Ria Koopmans-de Bruijn received her graduate degree Doctorandus (Drs) in Japanese Studies from Leiden University, The Netherlands, in 1986, and her MLS from CUNY, Queens College in 1994. She has been the East Asian Studies Librarian at the C. V. Starr East Asian Library of Columbia University in the City of New York since 1993, worked as a volunteer Japanese language cataloger in the Oriental Division of the New York Public Library, and as an independent scholar has published and presented papers on historical Japanese-Dutch relationships, and on Japanese serpent symbolism. She is a member in a number of professional organizations, among them the Association for Asian Studies (AAS), European Association of Japanese Studies (EAJS), American Library Association (ALA), and Council on East Asian Libraries (CEAL). Her area of specialization is Japanese folklore and cultural history, and she has a particular interest in multidisciplinary approaches to the study of Japanese culture.